Language and Learning

**SUNY Series,
The Social Context of Education**

Christine E. Sleeter, Editor

Edited by
Beverly McLeod

Language and Learning

Educating Linguistically Diverse Students

STATE UNIVERSITY OF NEW YORK PRESS

This work is part of the Studies of Education Reform program, supported by the U.S. Department of Education, Office of Educational Research and Improvement, Office of Research, under contract No. RR 91–172003. The program supports studies and disseminates practical information about implementing and sustaining successful innovations in American education. The opinions in this document do not necessarily reflect the position or policy of the U.S. Department of Education, and no official endorsement should be inferred.

Studies of Education Reform, Office of Research, Office of Educational Research and Improvement, U.S. Department of Education

Production by Ruth Fisher
Marketing by Nancy Farrell

Published by
State University of New York Press, Albany

Library of Congress Cataloging-in-Publication Data

Language and learning : educating linguistically diverse students /
    edited by Beverly McLeod.
        p.   cm. — (SUNY series, the social context of education)
    Includes bibliographical references and index.
    ISBN 0–7914–1891–X (CH). — ISBN 0–7914–1892–8 (PB)
    1. Language and education—United States.   2. Children of
    immigrants—Education—United States.   3. Linguistic minorities—
    Education—United States.   I. McLeod, Beverly, 1947– .
    II. Series: SUNY series, social context of education.
    P40.8.L3663   1994
    371.97—dc20   93–11659
                                                                        CIP

10 9 8 7 6 5 4 3 2 1

CONTENTS

v

LIST OF TABLES AND FIGURES

Tables

Figures

Published in cooperation with:

THE NATIONAL CENTER FOR
RESEARCH ON CULTURAL DIVERSITY
AND SECOND LANGUAGE LEARNING

FOREWORD

In the Spring of 1990, the Office of Educational Research and Improvement (OERI) of the U.S. Department of Education convened a working meeting in Washington, D.C., bringing together a select group of educators—policymakers, practitioners, teacher union officials, heads of major education associations, and State and Federal Officials. The participants focused their attention on the status of education reform efforts around the country and made specific recommendations to the OERI for engaging in a systematic examination of education reform. Twelve major reform topics were identified, leading the OERI to sponsor a competition for awarding individual contracts to establish evaluation studies under each topic. The primary objective of each three and one-half year project was to systematically evaluate the education reform efforts initiated by states, local school districts, and individual schools. Each project focused on a different aspect of education reform, including teaching, curriculum, school organization, connections with entities outside the school, and special student populations, such as preschool children, students at risk, and linguistically and culturally diverse students.

The book that follows is a compilation of comissioned papers written by eminent scholars and presented at a conference on student diversity sponsored, in 1992, by The National Center for Research on Cultural Diversity and Second Language Learning, University of California at Santa Cruz, which had been selected as one of the twelve contractors to specifically examine education reform issues related to Student Diversity. As project officer during the first two years of the contract, I was privileged to work closely with such nationally recognized scholars as Barry McLaughlin, an authority on second language learning; Roland Tharp, an expert on the cultural aspects of teaching and learning; and Eugene Garcia, an authority on bilingual education and the education of Hispanic students. Beverly McLeod, a researcher in cross-cultural psychology, did an excellent job in coordinating the entire project and editing the papers generated by the center's Conference on Student Diversity.

How to effectively educate a student population which is rapidly becoming more linguistically and culturally diverse is one of the biggest challenges facing our country's educators. Today, more than 30 percent of our children and youth are from minority groups. Forecasters predict that if current trends in immigration and birthrates persist, the Hispanic population will increase almost 21 percent, the Asian segment 22 percent, African Americans almost 12 percent and non-Hispanic Whites about 2 percent by the turn of the century. The Center for Demographic Policy predicts that the number of U.S. citizens who are Hispanic or non-White will more than double by the year 2030.

The nation's schools, staffed largely by White, middle-aged, middle-class, female teachers, are under considerable pressure to reform their educational programs, especially teaching and instruction. Currently, the primary emphasis of most instructional strategies for dealing with students from non-English language backgrounds is rapid acquisition of English, the development of "basic" skills, and transmission of knowledge. We are learning, however, that an overemphasis on basic skills, while subjecting children to rote learning, repetitive exercises, and superficial levels of student/teacher interaction, is ineffective and contributes to student boredom, apathy, and lack of motivation, while decreasing opportunities for student engagement on higher order cognitive tasks. In recent years, a number of cognitive scientists have recommended alternative approaches to educating these students—one that sparks their curiosity, encourages them to solve real problems, prepares them to take personal responsibility for learning, and engages them in the critical moral and social issues that confront society.

Some current research indicates that features of effective instruction for children from non-English language backgrounds include activity settings, language development, use of varied sensory modalities, increased cooperative and group activities, and a respectful and accommodating sensitivity to students' prior knowledge, life experiences, cultural norms, and values. In addition, the one critical element in assisting learners to develop thinking skills—the ability to form, express, and exchange ideas in speech and writing—is the opportunity to engage in serious dialogue with the teacher about what the student is learning at the moment. The level of questioning and the sharing of ideas and knowledge that occur in "instructional conversation" have been found to promote a much higher level of student engagement in academic tasks than having children quietly sitting at their desks filling in worksheets.

The Student Diversity Study focused on key areas that often make the difference in academic success. We learned, among other things, that in order to succeed academically, students must develop a high level of competence in reading and writing, usually by the late elementary grades. Students who lack this competence will have difficulty for the rest of their school career. In middle school, students begin to encounter complex material, particularly in mathematics and science; their mastery of each course determines whether they advance to higher levels and fulfill requirements for high school graduation or college admission. For students whose native language is not the same as the language of the school, becoming literate in a second language and learning complex material in that language present almost overwhelming challenges.

This book defines the issues involved in designing educational programs for students in these circumstances and raises many questions for educators at all levels to consider. Other pertinent reform issues which were explored during the course of the study and presented in this book are the political and pedagogical tension between native language development and English language instruction, the rhetoric surrounding education reform vs. its effect on different student populations, the rationale and consequences of programs with a compensatory vs. accelerated objective, the evidence for cultural specificity in learning styles vs. the necessity of discovering universal teaching strategies, and the significance of defining knowledge as inculcation vs. knowledge as reflective experience.

In my current position as Acting Director of the U.S. Department of Education's Office of Bilingual Education and Minority Languages Affairs (OBEMLA), I have been intimately involved with many of the same questions, problems, and concerns reflected in this book. I believe that *Language and Learning* sheds light on the complex challenge faced by the education practitioners in developing high quality education for the linguistically and culturally diverse population in our schools today. I believe, also, that it has important contributions towards informing policy-making and educational administration.

René C. Gonzalez, Ph.D.
Acting Director
Office of Bilingual Education and
   Minority Languages Affairs
U.S. Department of Education

INTRODUCTION

American schools face an unprecedented challenge in the 21st century—educating the world's most linguistically diverse student body. Although most American schoolchildren speak English as a native language, increasing numbers of students come from other language backgrounds. Children from immigrant families or from American ethnic groups that communicate primarily in another language or dialect may not have the opportunity to become fluent in standard English at home.

Other types of diversity coincide with diversity in language. Individuals and groups vary in cultural practices and attitudes, educational preparation, circumstances of immigration, and economic status. Educators can no longer assume a common language, culture, life situation, or understanding among students, or between student and teacher.

Efforts to reform and improve education during the past decade have seldom addressed this diversity. This book considers the promise and perils of the education reform movement for students from non-English language backgrounds and the implications of increased linguistic diversity for American education. The students who are the subject of this book include those whose native or home language is other than English. The major concern of the book is the large proportion of such students with poor academic achievement.

The first section focuses specifically on reform, discussing the relationship between reform proposals and the educational needs of these students, and exploring the power of language in education and reform. The second section addresses cultural diversity in curriculum, pedagogy, and staffing in relation to the education of students from English-language and other-language backgrounds. The third section summarizes research on teaching language arts, and the last section discusses research on teaching mathematics and science to students from non-English language backgrounds.

In order to create a context for the chapters that follow, the remainder of this introduction will present the dimensions of linguistic and cultural diversity faced by educators.

Diversity—Present and Future

According to the 1990 U.S. Census and the Council of Chief State School Officers (CCSSO, 1990):

- Nearly one-third of all children under 18 are from ethnic or racial minority groups.

- As many as 7.6 million students belong to culturally distinct groups that may speak a dialectical variant of standard English.

- An additional 5.8 million students come from homes in which the primary language is not English.

- For the majority of the latter group, English is not their first language.

- Many of these children enter school with limited English proficiency (LEP).

Estimates of the number of school-age youth with limited English proficiency range from 5 to 7.5 million (*Numbers and Needs*, 1993, March), constituting as many as one out of six of the nation's 5–17 year olds. Recent immigration has contributed greatly to linguistic diversity among schoolchildren; six percent of U.S. students are immigrants, most with a native language other than English (McCarty First & Willshire Carrera, 1988). But three-quarters of students under the age of 15 with limited English proficiency were born in the United States (CCSSO, 1990).

While the proportion of immigrant and other LEP students may be relatively small, the numbers can be large, especially since these students are not distributed evenly across the country. Nine states have at least 25,000 LEP students (CCSSO, 1990; Olsen, 1990). New York and Texas each have more than half a million such students, and California has close to a million (*Numbers and Needs*, 1992). In California the minorities have become the majority; more than half of public school students are Hispanic or non-White. One in four K–3 students in California cannot speak English fluently (Guido, 1992).

Linguistic diversity among students in U.S. schools is predicted to persist and increase, according to the U.S. Census (*Numbers and Needs*, 1991; Educational Research Service [ERS], 1990; Pallas, Nutriello, & McDill, 1989) and a report on Hispanics and education (Chavez, 1991).

- During the 1980s, the number of LEP students grew two-and-one-half times faster than regular school enrollment.

- The Hispanic population in the United States grew by 53 percent in the 1980s, and the number of Asian Americans doubled.

- Between 1990 and 2010, the school-age population of Whites will decline by 9 percent; Blacks will increase by 5 percent, Hispanics by 42 percent, and other ethnic groups by 39 percent.

- In 1982, three out of four children were non-Hispanic White; in 2020 only one out of two will be. In 1982, one out of ten children were Hispanic; in 2020 one in four will be.

- Spanish is the native language of 65 percent to 70 percent of all LEP students, while 10 percent to 15 percent speak Asian languages.

Diversity within Diversity

Large states and school districts not only must accommodate large numbers of students from non-English language backgrounds, but also must cope with the linguistic diversity of their student bodies, which can represent dozens of native languages in a single school, or more than 100 in a district. It is not only large states or districts that need be concerned about the education of linguistic minority students. Clusters of students from non-English language backgrounds attend schools throughout the country (National Forum, 1990).

Schools are also facing another "diversity within diversity"; students from non-English language backgrounds vary widely in their prior academic preparation and age. Students may enter American schools for the first time at any grade level; they may move frequently, have many absences, or spend periods of time away from school. Some immigrant students have had excellent schooling in their home country before coming to the United States, others have had their schooling interrupted, and still others have never attended school. This great variety in student circumstances makes it impossible for a single program to meet all needs.

These demographic realities mean that the problems discussed in this book are not isolated to inner city schools or ethnic minority and immigrant communities. The majority of teachers and students across the country will spend some of their time in classrooms that include students from culturally diverse and non-English language backgrounds.

Our Immigrant Heritage

Educating an ethnically and linguistically diverse student population is not a new challenge for American schools. Throughout the history of the United States, large numbers of children from immigrant families have attended public schools.

But immigrants have tended to come in waves. The 1950s and 1960s were low immigration periods, while the number of immigrants arriving in the past two decades has exceeded the record highs of the early 1900s (ERS, 1990).

From 1900 to 1910, nearly 9 million immigrants entered the United States, increasing the population by 10 percent. In the 1980s, more than 7 million immigrants came to the United States, accounting for only a 4 percent increase in the now-much-larger population (*Numbers and Needs*, 1993, May). In the early decades of this century, as many as one in seven people in the United States were foreign born. The current rate of one in thirteen seems high only in comparison to the low immigration decades of the 1950s and 1960s, when one in twenty American residents were foreign born (ERS, 1990).

Not only has the flow of immigrants increased dramatically, but the pattern of immigration has shifted. Before the immigration laws changed in 1965 to allocate an equal quota to each country in the world, three-quarters of immigrants to the United States came from Europe. They spoke languages and brought cultures with which Americans, and U.S. school systems, had some familiarity. Now, nearly three-quarters of legal immigrants come from Asia and Latin America. Half of Asian and Pacific Islander Americans are recent immigrants (Nieto, 1992). In addition to large numbers of Spanish speakers, schools encounter students whose native language is Korean, Tagalog, Hindi, Farsi, Hmong, or Mandarin.

Now three-quarters of Americans claim European descent; by 2050 only half will (Wolff, Rutten, & Bayers, 1992). But American society is not alone in facing the challenge of ethnic and linguistic diversity. Australia, Canada, France, and Belgium all have higher percentages of foreign-born residents than the United States (Wolff et al., 1992).

Many people are under the impression that children from non-English-speaking families in past generations were easily assimilated by American schools and that they learned English without special programs. But the truth is that immigrant students have always lagged behind native-born English speakers in school achievement, and have always had high dropout rates (Wong Fillmore & Valadez, 1986). What has changed is the economic structure of the United States; the manufacturing jobs that supported workers whose academic English proficiency was insufficient to earn them a high school diploma no longer exist. New economic realities mean that the academic failure of large groups of students is now a societal problem, rather than merely a personal concern.

Diversity and Academic Achievement

For many students from non-English language backgrounds, American education is not a successful experience. A disproportionate number do not reach acceptable achievement levels in English literacy, mathematics, and science. No matter what criterion is used (grades, test scores, dropout rates, college acceptance rates), linguistic minority students do not perform as well in school as their majority group contemporaries.

- Hispanic high school students score three years behind their non-Hispanic White counterparts in writing and four years behind in science and mathematics (De La Rosa & Maw, 1990).

- In some ethnic minority groups, a large percentage of the students leave school without a high school diploma (McCarty First & Willshire Carrera, 1988). The high dropout rate for African American students is exceeded by the rates for students from non-English language backgrounds (National Association of State Boards of Education [NASBE], no date; National Center for Education Statistics, 1992):

Non-Hispanic Whites	10%
African Americans	24%
Hispanics	31%
Hispanic immigrants	43%
Native Americans	48%
Asian immigrants	60%
Foreign-born students	70%

Education Reform and Student Diversity

At this time of unparalleled diversity in the student population, it is ironic that calls for reform during the past decade have focused on excellence but neglected equity. Advocates for students from non-English language backgrounds are concerned that higher graduation requirements and more standardized testing will exacerbate the already wide disparity between these students and native English speakers.

But some reformers argue that excellence and equity must be viewed as mutually dependent goals rather than as opposing objectives. T. F. Green, for example, argues that "the pursuit of excellence is more likely to produce gains in equity than policies in pursuit of equality are likely to produce gains in excellence" (quoted in O'Day & Smith, forthcoming).

Reform advocates such as O'Day and Smith see the solution in "content-based systemic reform" that combines state or national curriculum standards with local responsibility and control. Assessment initiatives such as The New Standards Project also combine internationally comparable standards of achievement with locally designed evaluations. Such a dual focus would ensure that all students are offered a high quality education and held to high standards while giving teachers and principals the flexibility to address the particular needs and backgrounds of their students.

Perhaps the most radical notion of the new reformers, one that contradicts longstanding beliefs about the intellectual capacity of different groups, is that an academically challenging curriculum should be offered to all students. Variations in student performance would result from differences in *individual* aptitude, effort, and interest, rather than occurring along ethnic, linguistic, or socioeconomic lines. Perhaps the most important change required is a change in perspective—viewing the students who are the focus of this book as individuals rather than as members of a group with a "problem."

Students as Whole People

Medical practitioners have often been accused of treating patients impersonally by referring to them as "the appendicitis in room 309" or "last week's cardiac case." Members of stigmatized groups have campaigned for designations that highlight their humanity rather than their condition, preferring to be called "people with AIDS" rather than "AIDS victims," or "a person with mental retardation" instead of "a mentally retarded person." Some people prefer to be described as "physically challenged" or "differently abled" instead of "handicapped" or "disabled" because the latter terms focus on their limitations rather than their capabilities.

Educational labels also frequently depersonalize students by categorizing them into groups and by emphasizing what they cannot do. For this reason, some people dislike the term limited English proficient (LEP), because it seems to define students by their lack of English skills. Similarly, some people object to terms such as "language minority" or "linguistic minority." The authors of a report by the National Association of State Boards of Education (NASBE, no date) on the impact of diversity on education decided not to use the word "minority" to describe any group. Even though such terms may be numerically correct in particular contexts, they are often misleading and may connote inferior status.

People sometimes assume that those with one stigmatizing characteristic have multiple problems. Wheelchair users and people with blindness often report being addressed by others in a loud voice, as if the speaker thinks they also have deficient hearing. Similarly, it is often assumed that children who cannot speak English also lack the intellectual capacity for high level academic work. A report on California schools observes that "it is as if there were a tacit understanding that poor and minority children have innate deficits which schools can cope with but not overcome" (BW Assoc., 1988, p. 140). Students whose lack of English fluency becomes their defining characteristic risk acquiring other negative labels that color their treatment.

It is difficult to find a satisfactory term, one without pejorative overtones, to describe the students who are the concern of this book. When juxtaposed with students from monolingual English language families, they may be called students from other language backgrounds or non-English language backgrounds. But even the words "other" and "non" carry undesirable connotations.

The designations "culturally and linguistically diverse" or "diverse" have often been used as code words and misapplied to a group of culturally homogeneous students or even to an individual student. An individual cannot be considered culturally diverse unless he or she is of mixed heritage. Furthermore, a group of Mandarin-speaking immigrant students or Mexican American students whose families speak Spanish are culturally "different" from native English-speaking students, rather than "diverse." A classroom including these three types of students can properly be described as culturally and linguistically diverse.

This book focuses on students whose families' primary language is not English, many of whom are immigrants, who are now contributing to the linguistic and cultural diversity of American classrooms. The purpose of this book is to discuss the challenges faced by these students, and by the schools responsible for educating all students. The message of this book is that every student should be viewed as an individual; while these students may need language instruction in order to take full advantage of the educational environment, other students may require prescription glasses, or help with homework, or a caring adult committed to their success.

A century ago, it was taken for granted that the immigrant generation would be lost educationally, that only their children or grandchildren would be able to enter the educational mainstream and aspire to a college degree. But today's ethic of equal opportunity means that schools should offer all children a reasonable chance to reach their potential, regardless of their educational preparation, socioeconomic status, or language background. The goal of this book is to offer a variety of perspectives on meeting this challenge, and to shift the concern about language and learning from the periphery of the educational enterprise to its heart.

REFERENCES

BW Associates. (1988). *Restructuring California education: A design for public education in the twenty-first century*. Recommendations to the California Business Roundtable. Berkeley, CA: Author.

Chavez, C. A. (1991, May). *"State of the play" in educational research on Latino/Hispanic youth*. Unpublished manuscript.

Council of Chief State School Officers (CCSSO) (1990). *School success for limited English proficient students: The challenge and state response*. Washington, DC: Author.

De La Rosa, D., & Maw, C. (1990). *Hispanic education: A statistical portrait 1990*. Washington, DC: Policy Analysis Center, Office of Research, Advocacy, and Legislation, National Council of La Raza.

Educational Research Service (ERS) (1990). *Demographic influences on American education*. Arlington, VA: Author.

Guido, M. (1992, March 8). Hard lessons in language: One in four new pupils can't speak English. *San Jose Mercury News*, p. 1A.

McCarty First, J., & Willshire Carrera, J. (1988). *New voices: Immigrant students in U.S. public schools*. Boston, MA: National Coalition of Advocates for Students.

National Association of State Boards of Education (NASBE) (no date). *The American tapestry: Educating a nation*. Alexandria, VA: Author.

National Center for Education Statistics (1992). *American education at a glance*. Washington, DC: United States Department of Education.

National Forum on Personnel Needs for Districts with Changing Demographics. (1990, May). *Staffing the multilingually impacted schools of the 1990s*. Washington, DC: United States Department of Education, Office of Bilingual Education and Minority Languages Affairs.

Nieto, S. (1992). *Affirming diversity: The sociopolitical context of multicultural education*. New York: Longman.

Numbers and Needs: Ethnic and Linguistic Minorities in the United States (1991, December). Washington, DC: Author.

Numbers and Needs: Ethnic and Linguistic Minorities in the United States (1992, May). Washington, DC: Author.

Numbers and Needs: Ethnic and Linguistic Minorities in the United States (1993, March). Washington, DC: Author.

Numbers and Needs: Ethnic and Linguistic Minorities in the United States
(1993, May). Washington, DC: Author.

O'Day, J. A., & Smith, M. S. (forthcoming). Systemic school reform and educational opportunity. In S. Fuhrman (Ed.), *Designing coherent education policy: Improving the system*. San Francisco: Jossey-Bass.

Olsen, L. (1990). *Embracing diversity: Teachers' voices from California's
classrooms*. San Francisco: California Tomorrow.

Pallas, A. M., Natriello, G., & McDill, E. L. (1989). The changing nature of
the disadvantaged population: Current dimensions and future trends.
Educational Researcher, 18 (5): 16–22.

Wolff, M., Rutten, P., & Bayers, A. F. (1992). *Where we stand: Can America
make it in the global race for wealth, health, and happiness?* New York:
Bantam.

Wong Fillmore, L., & Valadez, C. (1986). Teaching bilingual learners. In M.
C. Wittrock (Ed.), *Handbook of research on teaching*, 3rd ed. New York:
Macmillan.

Part I

Education Reform

INTRODUCTION

The 1980s precipitated "the most widespread, intense, public, comprehensive, and sustained effort to improve education in our history" (Murphy, 1991, p. viii). This section focuses on the impact of these reform efforts on students from language backgrounds other than English. In Chapter 1, Beverly McLeod creates a context for the book by discussing why such students have lagged behind and what kinds of changes in school and society would benefit them educationally. In Chapter 2, Patricia Gándara examines specific reform proposals and gauges their effect on these students. In Chapter 3, Hugh Mehan explores the implications of language for the reform of education.

McLeod examines the linguistic, cultural, and societal influences on the achievement of non-English language background students, and she discusses the changes in perspective and practice that have the potential to benefit these students. In contrast, Gándara's analysis concludes that the actual story of reform for students from non-English language backgrounds is a tale of neglect. Her survey of articles on school reform published in the *Phi Delta Kappan* during the past decade revealed that only 16 (4 percent) of 362 articles (fewer than 2 per year) mentioned such students at all, even though they comprise a large and growing percentage of the student body in

3

many schools. Her review of reform proposals implies that, at a time of increasing linguistic and cultural diversity in American schools, reformers believe that their proposals will benefit all types of students equally. This myth of a universal student contrasts with the reality of cultural and linguistic differences described in this book.

While Gándara faults reform efforts for ignoring the particular characteristics and special needs of different student groups, Hugh Mehan implies that some "new" reform proposals, such as school choice, have a reactionary basis. In Chapter 3, Mehan illustrates the importance of implicit metaphorical models of education. They determine the dominant discourse and thus the shape of reform. Mehan discusses three domains of language—teaching, schooling, and reform—and criticizes the ideal of the individual that emerges as the implicit model in all three. He presents two examples of teaching: (1) the traditional design, which constructs the classroom as an arena for individual achievement, directed by the individual-in-charge—the teacher—and (2) the new design, which constructs the classroom as a community of learners.

Reform proposals congruent with the second model have called for greater emphasis on complex knowledge and skills, to be developed through "whole language and literature-based approaches to literacy instruction, process approaches to composition, complex problem-solving in mathematics, and discovery and hands-on experimentation in science" (O'Day & Smith, forthcoming). These approaches are not just new instructional techniques; they embody a radical transformation of our conception of education away from acquiring information and skills and toward a goal of "learning for understanding" (Murphy, 1991).

The dominant discourse in schooling as presented by Mehan also asserts the primacy of individualistic explanations for achievement, an emphasis on innate talent rather than effort, and on the capability a child brings to school rather than the conditions of schooling. The dominant discourse embodied in the reform proposal that Mehan discusses—school choice—is that of an individual consumer in a free market system.

The similarity between the language of education reform and the language of the marketplace is no accident. Not only have corporate leaders been at the forefront of the education reform movement, but they have called for education to be remodeled along the lines of private enterprise. Because some companies have achieved success by becoming less hierarchical, by inviting workers to be partners in the corporate enterprise, by becoming closer to the customer, and by establishing rigorous standards for product quality

(Peters & Waterman, 1982), business leaders tout corporate reform as a blueprint for education (Murphy, 1991). The corporate strategies mentioned above are reflected in the educational restructuring movement as school-based management, teacher empowerment and professionalism, parent and community involvement, and competency and achievement testing.

What are the implications of viewing education as a corporate metaphor, characterizing students as individual consumers, pursuing individual self-interest, purchasing a product (schools) in a free market? A free market system may say more about the producers than the consumers, and some critics of school choice contend that it will enable schools to select students rather than students to choose schools. Free enterprise may in fact be an effective mechanism for competition among companies, an efficient unseen hand that allows the productive ones to thrive and the unproductive ones to fail. Using this reasoning, the inefficient and substandard school will not survive long. But what about inefficient consumers? If car buyers aren't careful, they end up with a lemon; if parents can't or won't assume the responsibility of becoming educated consumers, their children end up with a lemon education.

There is no guarantee in a free market system that the successful companies will produce quality products for all consumers. Why, for example, would private enterprise schools serve poor communities any better than private enterprise grocery stores, banks, clinics, or apartment houses now do? What guarantee is there that a private enterprise educational system won't end up like our private enterprise medical system, in which the poor get poor quality care?

School choice—whether including private schools or restricted to the public sector—clearly embodies individualism as a priority, and rests on the assumption that the sum of individual actions will eventually lead to the common good, improving education for all. This is not just a statement about education, but rather represents a certain vision of society. Larry Cuban (1990) comments that the recent round of reforms seems like "deja vu all over again." Educational problems are never "solved" because schools are social institutions, reflecting the changes and contradictions of the society at large; dilemmas and crises provoked by economic instability and moral uncertainty in the society are played out in the educational arena. The tension between individualistic and communitarian values was highlighted in the last presidential campaign, and is evident in reforms proposed for the classroom.

Whereas the Wave I education reforms of the early 1980s emphasized improvement of the existing system, the Wave II reforms now under discussion involve a restructuring of the entire system (Murphy, 1991). Along with changing how schools are organized and governed comes a fundamental metaphorical shift in our conception of learning and teaching, and of the role of the individual.

On the one hand, the new model that envisions the student as a worker and the teacher as a manager gives much more importance to the individual learner than the traditional conception of teacher as worker and student as product, or the classical idea of teacher as fount of knowledge and student as empty vessel. The "student as worker" model allows for a much more active role by students in their own learning. The new conception of learners emphasizes the importance of individual students' background knowledge and skills rather than viewing them as "tabulae rasae." Wave II reforms also stress the value of developing students' intrinsic motivation to learn, and of empowering them to direct their own learning.

On the other hand, this new concept views learning as a social activity, not a lone quest. Meaningful learning is viewed as occurring best in a social context, where experiences are planned collaboratively, ideas are defended before peers, and meanings are negotiated with others. Individual characteristics are to be respected and attended to, and individual learning is to be fostered and motivated, but in a communitarian atmosphere that encourages cooperation over competition.

How can this emphasis on empowering students and teachers to design and direct their own learning based on local characteristics be reconciled with the desire to hold all students and schools to common high standards? The only chance for universal improvement, some reform advocates (O'Day & Smith, forthcoming) contend, lies in systemic reform—encouraging specific changes from the highest levels of the educational establishment rather than counting on gradual or piecemeal change school by school. Larger entities such as states or professional groups of content area educators have been working to establish curricular frameworks and assessment instruments; these would be implemented, adapted, and augmented at the local level with flexibility for particular populations.

In order to assess the effect of education reform on students from non-English speaking backgrounds, the first question one must ask is: Which reforms? The sometimes congruent, sometimes conflicting discourse of reform reflecting the different values and goals of traditional schooling, corporate reform, and school restructuring goes to the heart of our assumptions about the purpose of education.

Are students to be viewed as economic resources to be developed for the growth of the economy? Even supporters of increased services to children talk in terms of "investing" in them with the expectation that the investment will pay dividends in the future. But the downside of using the language of investment is that it leads the public to expect a clearly measurable and immediate return for their tax dollars. This "quarterly report" mentality pushes educators to use standardized testing for public accountability, and this decision drives curriculum and instruction.

What are the implications of the metaphors we use for children? If children are economic resources, then the schools' role is to prepare them to be used productively in the economy. But what if children were viewed instead as future citizens? Then the role of the schools would be to teach students to practice the rights and responsibilities of citizens in a participatory democracy.

Or what if children were thought of as environmental resources, as whales, condors, and fur seal pups rather than as future workers? Then the role of schools would be to conserve and nurture students. The discourse of environmentalism provides a model for talking about children and their education in terms other than "developing economic resources." Environmentalists do not talk about rain forests as resources to be developed or exploited, but rather as global treasures to be protected. How would our concept of education be different if we thought of children, and the diverse cultural and linguistic groups they represent, as threatened ecological treasures?

The chapters in this section illustrate that reforms are always grounded in certain assumptions and metaphorical concepts. If language has the power to shape thought, then the reform of educational practice is inseparable from thought reform. The question is not only how education should be reformed, but what our idea of children should be. The question for this book is not only what kind of education should be given to students from non-English language backgrounds, but how the nation views these children.

REFERENCES

Murphy, J. (1991). *Restructuring schools: Capturing and assessing the phenomena*. New York: Teachers College Press.

O'Day, J. A., & Smith, M. S. (forthcoming). Systemic reform and educational opportunity. In S. Fuhrman (Ed.), *Designing coherent education policy: Improving the system*. San Francisco: Jossey-Bass.

Peters, T. J., & Waterman, R. H. (1982). *In search of excellence: Lessons from America's best run companies*. New York: Harper & Row.

✧ Chapter 1

Linguistic Diversity and Academic Achievement

Beverly McLeod

Despite the increasing linguistic diversity among students attending U.S. schools, education reform proposals of the 1980s have been addressed to the "universal" student, who is assumed to be a fluent, native speaker of English with a European American cultural background. As documented in Chapter 2 of this volume, the differential effect of reforms on various student groups has seldom been considered. Nor have reforms been tailored to the specific needs of different groups.

This chapter focuses on *why* there has been such a poor record of achievement for large numbers of students from non-English language backgrounds, and what schools can do to foster these students' success.

Reasons for Failure—Hopes for Success

While the reality of school failure for the majority of students from non-English language backgrounds is undeniable, the reasons for failure are less clear-cut. It is easier to demonstrate differential achievement among student groups than to account for it. The picture is also clouded by reports of superstars, students from non-English language backgrounds who, despite all odds, apparently succeed spectacularly.

Educational solutions depend on the definition of the problem; programs to counteract failure are always based on assumptions about the reasons for failure. Theories to explain differential achievement often conflict with each other, partly because educational success and failure, like other aspects of human behavior, are multiply determined. Several factors have been offered to explain the low academic achievement of these students, including:

- inadequate language services
- lack of access to standard curriculum
- cultural discontinuity
- outmoded instructional models
- inappropriate assessment and evaluation
- structural inequality
- insufficient student ability and motivation

Language Services

The Problem

The most obvious difference between students who are native English speakers and those from non-English language backgrounds is that the latter may lack sufficient proficiency in English to succeed in English-medium classes. It is not only common sense, but also a U.S. Supreme Court ruling (Lau v. Nichols, 1974) that such students require special assistance to help them overcome this obstacle.

But the Supreme Court did not mandate a specific remedy, and political arguments have hampered a comprehensive approach to developing language services (Padilla, Lindholm, Chen, Duran, Hakuta, Lambert, & Tucker, 1991). Proponents of bilingual education and those favoring English as a Second Language (ESL) instruction argue over which approach is more effective in helping students develop proficiency in English.

In addition to this major philosophical disagreement, practical problems of access and assessment plague the delivery of language services to students with limited English proficiency (LEP):

- Schools may be overwhelmed by the number, diversity, and high turnover of students needing special language services; at some schools a majority of students are not proficient in English. The number of LEP students in California alone has nearly doubled in the past five years (California State Department of Education, 1992).

- Title VII bilingual education programs serve only 5–7 percent of eligible students; a quarter of LEP students receive no extra educational services, most receive insufficient English language instruction and little native language support, and many are inappropriately placed in special education classes (Council of Chief State School Officers [CCSSO], 1990).

- Students may be receiving poor quality bilingual or ESL programs (Wong Fillmore & Valadez, 1986).

- Approximately three-quarters of LEP students receive most of their instruction from monolingual English-speaking teachers who lack special training in second language teaching (Ramirez, 1992).

- Students in good bilingual or ESL programs may be mainstreamed too early into regular English-medium classes; most students spend less than three years in these special programs, while experts estimate that children require at least 5–7 years to learn a second language (CCSSO, 1990).

- There are no nationally accepted criteria and procedures for identifying students with limited English proficiency (CCSSO, 1990).

- The progress of students in special language programs is not sufficiently monitored, and these programs are not well coordinated with the regular school program (CCSSO, 1990).

- Program evaluation is insufficient: "It appears that many more resources are being used to fund programs than to find out whether the programs are actually effective" (Rumberger, quoted in Chavez, 1991, p. 41).

- Laudable goals may work at cross-purposes with each other. "Before desegregation, . . . eight of San Jose [CA] Unified's 40 schools had bilingual programs. Now, those same resources serve 19 schools" (Guido, 1992).

Bilingual or ESL programs are only as good as the teachers who staff them, and the supply of trained teachers falls far short of the need. Despite offering higher salaries for teachers with bilingual certification, California alone could use 20,000 more such teachers (National Forum, 1990). Half of the bilingual teachers employed by the San Jose (California) school district are not fully certified, and the district has not been able to spend all the money in its budget for bilingual aides because it cannot find enough people who read and write two languages (Guido, 1992). While Hispanic students constitute two-thirds of those with limited English proficiency, only 15 percent of bilingual teachers are Hispanic (Nieto, 1992).

New Directions

The newer thinking about language development for students whose home language differs from the language of the school emphasizes two points: (1) learning a second language is difficult for children; and (2) language learning involves social-psychological as well as cognitive processes. (Part III of this volume explores these issues in depth.)

Contrary to popular belief, research (summarized in McLaughlin, 1992) has shown that young children do not learn a second language effortlessly, that they do not learn faster with more exposure to the new language, that their oral fluency outstrips their academic competence, and that they require many years to reach grade-level academic ability in the new language.

In practice, the most common special language programs available to students with limited English proficiency are ESL or structured immersion models, which offer minimal native language support. Bilingual programs vary widely, but most follow an early-exit model, which incorporates native language support for only the initial two or three years of elementary school. Late-exit and two-way bilingual models, which offer native language support throughout elementary school, are much less common.

In contrast, analyses of the sparse longitudinal research on bilingual learners have concluded that the more academic support students receive in their native language (in addition to high quality instruction in English), the higher their overall achievement as measured in English (Collier, 1992):

- In evaluating program models, it is important to measure language learning over the long term; short-term gains by students in ESL programs may not be sustained in later years (Collier, 1989b).

- Early-exit bilingual programs may offer no advantage over structured immersion programs, but late-exit bilingual programs may offer students the best chance of catching up with their native English-speaking peers (Ramirez, Yuen, & Ramey, 1991).

- Helping students develop their first language skills aids them in achieving competence in a second language (Hakuta, 1990).

- Continuing students' native language development through age 12 facilitates their acquisition of a second language, no matter when that language is introduced; discontinuing native language development before age 12 impedes competence in the second language (Collier, 1989b).

- Different approaches are required for students of different ages with different amounts of prior schooling in their native language; immigrant students under age 12 who have had at least two years of education in their native country reach average achievement levels in 5–7 years, but young children with no native language schooling and students older than 12 facing academically challenging subject matter in a second language may take as long as ten years to catch up (Collier, 1989b).

Instruction in their home language has several benefits for students. It prevents them from falling behind their peers in learning history, mathematics, science, and other subjects in the regular curriculum. It enables them to develop their native language competence so they can continue to communicate with their parents and build a foundation for adult fluency in two languages. And significantly, it does not retard—and may even accelerate—their acquisition of English (Ramirez, Yuen, & Ramey, 1991).

Students can succeed without native language instruction in school. For example, Caplan, Choy & Whitmore (1991) report that the children of the "Boat People" (refugees who escaped by boat from Vietnam) have attained remarkable success attending poor urban schools unlikely to offer exemplary bilingual programs. But the children's average achievement level is high only because of their superior scores in mathematics. Their scores on English language and reading tests are below average, and the students themselves cite language problems as a significant obstacle.

Caplan and colleagues do not report test scores by age of student, so it is impossible to confirm the findings of Collier discussed above. The Boat Children were studied after they had been in the United States for an average of only three and one-half years, so their long-term achievement is unknown. One of the most significant findings of the study is that children whose parents read to them, in Vietnamese or English, do better, indicating that academic-type support in the native language, whether at school or at home, may be a positive contributor to academic success.

The narrow focus on acquiring English fluency that has dominated the education of non-English language background students has aroused criticism from many quarters. Moll (1986) comments on the "overwhelming pressure to make students fluent in English at all costs. Learning English, not learning, has become the controlling goal of instruction for these students, even if it places the children at risk academically." The overriding assumption that learning English will lead to achievement has led educators to focus on teaching English and testing English proficiency. While Moll argues that this assumption impedes learning, Saville-Troike (1991) notes that it has also blinded us to more meaningful assessments of learning. Instead of asking how proficient a student's English is, perhaps we should be asking "what is really important to assess in regard to an LEP student's chances for succeeding in a regular English-medium classroom?" (p. 9). She advocates measuring achievement more directly, by testing content learning in the student's strongest language and by assessing predictors of academic success such as vocabulary development, rather than using English proficiency as a global proxy for achievement.

A second factor that has influenced thinking about language development for students learning a second language is a conception of language learning that goes beyond cognitive skill acquisition. This perspective views language as embedded in culture, and language learning as influenced by social and social-psychological forces (Snow, 1992). Farr (1986), in a discussion of the difficulty many students from ethnic minority communities have in learning to write in standard English, concludes that the task has profound psychological and social implications: "It is certainly possible . . . that experience with reading and writing mainstream academic prose induces cultural, as well as linguistic changes in students" (p. 215). Farr also cites evidence from the studies of Labov and his associates that speakers of Black English Vernacular acquire standard English only when they "interact meaningfully and frequently with standard English speakers" (p. 214).

There is no ideal blueprint of a language program for students from non-English language backgrounds. Each choice involves a dilemma; bilingual programs usually segregate students from their native English-speaking peers, and ESL programs may push students to abandon their native language while not guaranteeing them academic success. One model that offers both native language support and integration with majority language peers is the two-way bilingual program. The few studies that have evaluated such programs have shown favorable academic and attitudinal results for all students (Collier, 1989a, 1992; Cabazon, Lambert, & Hall, 1993).

As a practical matter, the kind of program offered depends not only on the philosophy adopted, but also on the number of students from each language group in a school, the availability of trained bilingual and ESL teachers and aides, the extent of native language support that parents and the community are able to provide, the age of the students and their level of literacy in their native language, and many other factors.

Most critically, program design depends on the goal of education for students with limited English proficiency. Programs with a narrow focus on English acquisition are often undergirded with the assumption (contradicted by evidence) that speakers of other languages do not, and do not want to, learn English. The goal of education then becomes replacing the students' native language with English, instead of adding English to their linguistic repertoire (Cziko, 1992).

The most important understanding to emerge from these new directions is a different way of viewing these students. Instead of seeing them primarily as deficient in English, and attributing their academic failure to that deficiency, the new perspective emphasizes that, while limited English presents them with difficulty in achieving in traditional schools, they are as linguistically competent as all normal children. Given the proper assistance, they will learn English. But in order to succeed academically, they must not only learn English, but be able to learn *in* English.

Access to Standard Curriculum

The Problem

The success of students from non-English language backgrounds is hampered not only by their limited command of English, but also by the challenge of simultaneously learning academic material. These students must spend time studying English while their English-speaking peers are studying mathematics, science, history, and social studies. Even when English instruction is combined with academic subject matter, programs for these students are often guided by a less rigorous curriculum. Students who are not fluent in English may be barred from regular classes; instead they are tracked into "remedial" or "compensatory" classes where instruction proceeds at a slower pace.

The assumption underlying tracking is that students learn best in groups that are homogeneous in ability, and that this method of dividing students into classes allows for enriched instruction for advanced students and intensive "catch-up" activities for slower learners.

The reality is that the instruction provided to students in the "slow" classes is often boring and repetitive, and does not prepare them to progress faster. Students may be consigned to a low-ability track for their entire schooling on the basis of a single test score, receiving an inferior education instead of extra help.

Oakes (1985) traces the entrenched practice of tracking to the beginning of the century, when schools faced the challenge of educating massive numbers of immigrant children. The prevailing belief that racial and ethnic groups differed in their innate capacity for intellectual achievement resulted in a stratified system that offered "appropriate" education for groups of varying ability. Although such racist assumptions have softened, students from non-English language backgrounds and from racial and ethnic minority groups are still more likely to be assigned to low-ability and special education classes and less likely to be placed in classes for gifted children (McCarty First & Willshire Carrera, 1988).

American schools have more extensive tracking than countries whose students achieve higher scores in mathematics. In an international comparison (McKnight, Crosswhite, Dossey, Kifer, Swafford, Travers, & Coney, 1987), nearly half of the variation in mathematics achievement scores of American students was accounted for by differences between classes, while in France and

Canada, only one-eighth of the variation was due to class differences. In Japan, differences among classes accounted for almost none of the variation in students' scores.

Whether because of tracking or for other reasons, students from non-English language backgrounds (with the exception of Asian language background students) take fewer advanced courses in mathematics and science (*Numbers and Needs*, 1991). At the secondary level, students from non-English language backgrounds may take only ESL courses plus electives, non-college prep courses, or watered-down content courses. One study of 27 California secondary schools found that only 6 gave LEP students access to the full core curriculum; half of the schools offered few or no content area classes at all to these students (BW Assoc., 1992).

Immigrant students who first enter the American school system at the secondary level may not have enough years left in high school to master both English and the academic material required for graduation or college entrance (Collier, 1992). Some students who might be able to succeed in regular high school courses are prevented from enrolling in them because the school requires a certain level of English fluency; such students may make diligent efforts to escape from the "ESL ghetto," feeling that these special efforts to help them are actually stigmatizing them and impeding their academic progress.

New Directions

New strategies have emerged to counter the problems created by programs with a compensatory emphasis and weak curricula. Some elementary schools have discarded the notion that low-achieving students benefit from simpler, slower instruction; instead they raise expectations and offer challenging material. The model of "accelerated schools" pioneered by Henry Levin and his colleagues (Levin & Hopfenberg, 1991) provides students from typically at-risk groups with the kind of enriching learning opportunities usually offered only to students in gifted programs, giving them a real chance to catch up.

This approach has also been successful in preparing low-achieving high school students from linguistic minority backgrounds for college. In the AVID "untracking" program, several high schools in San Diego, California, placed high-potential/low-performance students in college prep courses and gave them intensive support and assistance. Ninety-two percent of these students went on to a two- or four-year college, compared to 54 percent of all students in the San Diego high school system (Mehan, Datnow, Bratton, Tellez, Friedlaender, & Ngo, 1992).

At the secondary level, educators are questioning whether students who are not proficient in English should have to sacrifice their chance to learn academic material for the sake of studying English. Schools assisted by the staff of the Technical Education Research Center (TERC) (Rosebery, Warren, & Conant, 1992) have been successful in teaching science to Haitian students in their native language. Such programs value academic progress—in whatever language—more highly than competence in English. (Part IV of this volume explores new methods of teaching mathematics and science that emphasize linguistic and cognitive development and are compatible with this approach.)

Cultural Factors

The Problem

Another explanation for poor academic achievement is that students whose home language and culture differs significantly from that of the school find it difficult to succeed in the school environment. This thesis, which focuses on the mismatch between what students bring to, and find at, school, is explored in Part II of this book.

Children from different cultural backgrounds may learn and communicate differently. It has been suggested that children raised in European American families tend to have a field independent learning style (Witkin, 1962) that enables them to work well alone on analytic tasks and with abstract materials. In contrast, children raised in Mexican American, American Indian, or African American families tend to excel in field-dependent or field-sensitive (Ramirez & Casteneda, 1974) environments, where they can work in cooperation with others using materials with a social context.

If schools require individual competition and if the instruction is abstract rather than contextualized, students from cultures that emphasize cooperation over competition and prefer information in context may be at a disadvantage. Conversely, it has been suggested that the cultural congruence between the learning styles prevalent in some Asian societies and those emphasized in American schools accounts for the academic success of some Asian immigrant students (Stigler & Baranes, 1988–89; Caplan et al., 1991).

Conversational protocol, non-verbal behavior and gestures, and conventions of personal space and politeness differ greatly among cultures and may affect how students perceive and learn. When the majority of students from non-English language backgrounds are taught by teachers with European American backgrounds, the potential for misunderstanding is multiplied.

Students from immigrant families, who must adjust to a completely new language, culture, and school system, may also experience the anxiety, frustration, anger, and depression associated with culture shock (Adler, 1972; Foster, 1962). A nationwide project on immigrant children in U.S. schools (McCarty First & Willshire Carrera, 1988) "found culturally-based practices and behavior to be a major source of confusion and conflict for young immigrants" (p. 19).

Students from immigrant families who are adjusting to an alien language and curriculum rarely have assistance from a teacher who shares their own cultural and linguistic background. The growing diversity in the student population stands in stark contrast to the homogeneity of the teaching force. While one-third of students are from ethnic or racial minority groups, less than 10 percent of teachers come from these groups (McLaren, 1988). Of the new teachers in 1990, 93 percent are White (National Association of State Boards of Education [NASBE], no date).

Although it is logical to expect students to have academic problems if their home culture differs from the school culture, this conclusion is tempered by conflicting evidence. Overall, the dropout rates for Asian and Hispanic immigrants are extraordinarily high, as documented in the introduction to this book. However, some studies find immigrant groups achieving at higher than expected, and even higher than average rates.

One study (Matute-Bianchi, 1986) found that, among students from Spanish language backgrounds, recent immigrants and those who identified most strongly with their Mexican heritage were more successful in school than those with weaker emotional ties to the Mexican culture. Studies of Punjabi (Gibson, 1987) and Southeast Asian (Rumbaut & Ima, 1987; Caplan et al., 1991) immigrant students also found that academic success was correlated with maintenance of their culture of origin.

New Directions

The conclusion to be drawn from these studies is not that immigrants can succeed without special help, for that contradicts what we know about the majority of immigrants. Rather, these studies imply that cultural and linguistic assimilation are not prerequisites to educational success. They highlight the importance of cultural factors and the positive role they can play in educational achievement, and have led to a view that cultural differences can be educational resources instead of obstacles.

Caplan et al. (1991), who documented the unexpected success of the children of the Vietnamese refugee "boat people" in inner city schools, advocate that schools actively support and seek to strengthen the home cultures of their students in order to capitalize on the desire for success that parents from all cultures have for their children.

For students with limited English proficiency, their cultural "funds of knowledge" (Moll, 1992) can effectively be used as a foundation for teaching. Moll reports on a teacher who used the expertise of her students' families in construction-related occupations to teach about the history of dwellings, professions involved in construction, and mathematical concepts used in building.

Schools can bridge the cultural gap between home and classroom by reaching out to parents in their native language, by using curricula that include peoples of various cultures, and by modifying instructional methods to accommodate the cultural backgrounds of students. These approaches are discussed in detail in Part II of this volume.

Instruction

The Problem

All students, but particularly those not fluent in English, may suffer from the kind of "traditional" instruction labelled the "recitation script" (Tharp & Gallimore, 1988), in which teachers spend the majority of class time explaining, discussing, and quizzing students on assigned textbook readings. Even in homogeneous classes of White, middle class students taught by a teacher from a similar background, this method may work for only a minority of students. Successful students in such an environment are likely to:

- be motivated to get good grades by competing with other students, despite the dullness of the material or tediousness of workbook exercises

- be able to learn best by reading silently, working individually and listening to lectures

- be able to extract information quickly and accurately from printed text

- be test-wise and teacher-wise, knowing the kinds of answers that tests and teachers consider exemplary

- be able to work quickly, especially on timed tests

- submerge their own interests and curiosity in favor of the learning priorities of the teacher and textbook

- know how to acquire and remember information and perform well in this environment automatically, without needing much explicit instruction in how to learn

New Directions

Although "few reform reports have touched on the heart of the educational process, what is taught and how it is taught" (National Governors' Association, 1989, p. 1), most research on the education of students from non-English language backgrounds has focused on this area. In contrast to the assumptions underlying traditional teaching, it is now recognized that individuals have various learning styles and display different "intelligences" rather than there being a global cognitive ability (Gardner, 1983). As demonstrated in Chapter 5 of this volume, individual variation is compounded by language and cultural differences. Students whose reading and listening skills in English are not proficient may have difficulty learning in a class that delivers material only in these modes. Students whose cultural background encourages them to work with others may feel alienated by being required to work alone.

The only way to ensure that students with diverse learning styles have a real chance to learn is to offer a variety of teaching styles and learning environments in addition to the traditional whole class lecture/discussion.

- Cooperative learning assigns students to work collaboratively in small groups, allowing those whose English is not proficient to contribute their own strengths to a project. A review of 122 studies conducted between 1921 and 1981 (Johnson, Maruyama, Johnson, Nelson, & Skon, 1981) found that cooperative learning promoted higher achievement than competitive and individualistic learning experiences for all students, most particularly for the normally low achieving students.

• Mastery learning enables students to work at their own pace rather than being bored with a too-slow or frustrated with a too-fast lockstep curriculum. Given this time flexibility, students whose English is not proficient may nevertheless be able to learn the same material as others. Using a mastery learning approach enables about four-fifths of students to achieve at the same level as the upper one-fifth taught in the traditional manner by the same teacher (Bloom, 1981).

• Heterogeneous ability grouping allows advanced students to learn by teaching and by leading; it gives others a chance to learn from multiple "teachers." Studies of peer teaching have found that reading, mathematics, and self-concept scores increased for the students assisted and for the students doing the assisting (Richard-Amato, 1992).

• Multi-age grouping provides even more opportunities for individualizing the pace of learning and may capitalize on the strengths of sibling teaching common in some cultures.

• Experiential learning expands the range of learning modes beyond reading and listening. Students whose English is not proficient can still learn the material and simultaneously develop their English by using the language in context.

Re-designing teaching and learning for non-English language background students would mean incorporating opportunities for multiple learning modes into teaching. It would expand pedagogy beyond direct instruction to include active, student-directed learning, in which students and teachers are empowered as co-creators of the learning task.

This conception of pedagogy is based on a view of knowledge as constructed by the learner, rather than transmitted from expert to novice. The goal of teaching in this new view is not to impart information; rather it is to stimulate students' internal motivation and develop it into a lifelong drive to learn. The teacher's role in these innovative modes of instruction is as a coach or facilitator, an experienced and knowledgeable resource for students pursuing knowledge rather than the only source of that knowledge.

An additional departure from standard teaching methods would benefit students from non-English language backgrounds—making the implicit explicit. In addition to the factors already discussed, students from non-English language backgrounds may have difficulty in school because they lack familiarity with the "hidden curriculum" or "culture of the classroom." In a preliminary study of the effect of "untracking" classes on ethnic and linguistic minority students in San Diego public schools, Mehan et al. (1992) conclude that the success of the program is partly attributable to a support course that "explicitly teaches the implicit culture of the classroom and overtly exposes students to the hidden curriculum of the school" (p.32).

Along similar lines, Collins, Hawkins, & Carver (1991) advocate a "cognitive apprenticeship" approach for disadvantaged students, designed to teach not only subject matter but also strategies for approaching and solving problems and for learning new material.

Teachers can make their instruction more accessible to students not proficient in English by making simple alterations in the classroom and in the presentation of material:

- Non-verbal signs and cues can be used, such as a "speak no evil" monkey sign to indicate quiet areas, or a hat rack in the art center with as many painters caps as the number of students allowed to use the center at one time (Enright & McCloskey, 1992).

- Written text that contains cultural background information unfamiliar to immigrant students can be transformed into a visual presentation. For example, a history lesson on the first American colonies could be presented with a notated map of the east coast of the United States (Short, 1992).

- Lecture material can be restated in other ways, demonstrated visually, or recorded on tape for later review by students (Richard-Amato & Snow, 1992).

Assessment and Evaluation

The Problem

Students from non-English language backgrounds face their first assessment when the school must decide where to place them.

Many of these students are inappropriately placed in the wrong grade or type of class because they are not tested in their native language or because the extent and quality of their previous schooling is not taken into account.

Cognitive development in children is assumed to follow a universal sequence, but because this sequence was identified by European and European American researchers observing children from their own culture, Nieto (1992) questions whether our theories may be culture-bound. As a result, cultural differences in learning may be misinterpreted as cognitive delays. In many countries, including the United States, a disproportionate number of immigrant and language minority students are assigned to special education and vocational tracks (Cummins, 1984).

Once students from non-English language backgrounds have been placed, assessing their progress presents educators with a dilemma. Using standardized testing can have negative consequences, according to McCarty First & Willshire Carrera (1988) such as:

- Students may score poorly on tests because their English is limited; the exam tests their English rather than subject matter knowledge.

- Students who have not been instructed in their native language may be behind their age-mates in subject matter knowledge.

- Standardized tests contain cultural biases.

- Immigrant students may lack test-taking skills.

Recognizing these problems, many schools opt not to use standardized tests for students who are not proficient in English. But then such students are left outside the structure of accountability; educators and parents have no way to compare these students' progress against state or national norms.

Assessing student performance using standardized paper-and-pencil tests conflicts with a central tenet of reform advocates—that education should foster higher-order thinking and problem-solving abilities in a curriculum that integrates different skills and subjects. Standardized tests are designed not to provide feedback that will enhance instruction, but to sort students efficiently into tracks on the basis of supposed ability (Darling-Hammond, 1991).

Education reformers have advocated more meaningful methods of measuring authentic learning through student performance. Such assessments could include teachers' observations and notes, student portfolios, checklists and inventories, tests with open-ended questions, and student products (First, Kellogg, Almeida, & Gray, 1991). But Linn, Baker, & Dunbar (1991) caution that many of the assumptions about the benefits of performance-based assessment are unproven, that performance-based assessment is likely to widen the gap between advantaged and disadvantaged groups, and that such assessments are more susceptible to scorer bias than "objective" measures. Shavelson, Baxter, & Pine (1992) note that authentic assessments must be designed very carefully, and that poor quality assessment methods are likely to lead to poor quality teaching.

While standardized testing provides the means to compare students, it underestimates the achievement of students from non-English language backgrounds and often consigns them to compensatory programs. However, the relativity of performance-based testing means that such students may be held to lower standards than their peers.

New Directions

Murphy (1991) comments that reforms of the past decade have paid more attention to school governance than to teaching and learning. Even reformers who focus on instruction and assessment have often emphasized *how* to teach and test and neglected *what* students should be learning. Reforming assessment measures for students from non-English language backgrounds would mean addressing the content of instruction and solving the dilemma of standard vs. meaningful measures described above. One attempt to tackle this problem head-on is the New Standards Project, a partnership between state education departments and researchers at the Learning Research and Development Center at the University of Pittsburgh and the National Center on Education and the Economy in Rochester, New York. With the collaboration of hundreds of teachers, this project is developing internationally comparable achievement standards and designing innovative assessment methods that can be adapted to local student characteristics.

The New Standards Project advocates that students be evaluated on their individual portfolios, which would include three types of assessments: (1) performance exams such as writing samples that are administered and scored on a state, national or international basis; (2) common structured activities designed on a state or national basis but judged locally, similar to merit badges in scouting; and (3) tasks designed and evaluated in the local setting. This approach has the promise of combining comparability based on universal standards with the flexibility necessary to include students from diverse backgrounds while also responding to community priorities.

Underlying this and other attempts to reform assessment is a rethinking of the purpose of assessment itself. The new directions in assessment are guided by the following:

- Assessment is inseparable from instruction, both because teachers always teach with the test in mind and because the type of assessment used depends on one's definition and goal of education.

- Assessment has traditionally been used for accountability; it should also be used as pedagogy. Assessment tasks can teach as well as test, and can be used as feedback to help teachers plan their instruction.

- Assessment has traditionally measured what an individual person can demonstrate he knows, unaided, at a particular point in time. When assessment is used for teaching, the task may allow for collaboration, provide for feedback from peers and teacher, and give students the opportunity to revise, improve, and present their best work for judgment.

- The assessment of diverse students is best accomplished through a diversity in assessment, involving multiple definitions of competence and evaluation methods.

- Reform in assessment stresses tasks that are authentic and meaningful, and require reflection, analysis, and discussion.

The assessment activities designed by the New Standards Project incorporate many of these principles. Tasks given to elementary school students include the following: "Your class will be getting a 30-gallon aquarium. You will plan which fish to buy. You will have $25 to spend." Teachers usually provide information about the characteristics and cost of different fish species, or may require students to do the research necessary to respond. Students are asked to analyze, plan, calculate, and present their ideas in writing. Such a task has authenticity; a class may actually have to decide a similar question. It involves the students in an active learning process by which the teacher can also gain insight into their achievement in math and writing skills.

Other innovative methods of assessment can measure students' progress in the learning process more sensitively than standardized tests. For example, Dalton Miller Jones and colleagues (1993) have laid out a sequence that beginning readers follow, based on analyses of reading errors. Using this sequence, teachers can pinpoint students' progress and design appropriate instruction, something they can do much less effectively on the basis of student scores on standardized reading comprehension tests.

Structural Factors

The Problem

The factors discussed above focus on the within-school variables of curriculum and instruction. But the education of children from non-English language backgrounds is also affected by conditions in society. Many of these students are subject to the ills of poverty, substandard schools, and low expectations for success.

There is a significant overlap between economic status and language difference; more than 90 percent of students from non-English speaking homes in 1984 met official poverty guidelines (Garcia, in press). Overall poverty rates increased for children during the past decade, with a heavier impact falling on children from minority groups. While one in three young children in the United States are poor, three in five minority children are poor. Half of young African American children are poor, as are 40 percent of Hispanic children, compared to only 14 percent of non-Hispanic White children (National Center for Children in Poverty, 1992).

Living in poverty has several educational implications; children who are poor may be malnourished, may not have adequate health care, may live in substandard housing, may live in unsafe environments, are likely to have parents who have not progressed far in school, and are unlikely to have access to educational opportunities in the community such as preschools, libraries, music lessons and concerts, and after-school programs.

The school success of some groups of immigrant children, such as those from Cuba and some Asian countries, may be due in large part to the high educational level of their parents, whatever their current economic status.

Schools serving linguistically different or diverse student populations require more money than the average school for English language teaching programs; programs, teachers, aides, and materials that use the students' native languages; and social and counseling services. Yet such schools, if located in poor neighborhoods, often receive less than schools with fewer needs. Money from federal programs targeted for children disadvantaged by society is often denied to students from non-English language backgrounds in the erroneous belief that they cannot receive services from multiple programs (CCSSO, 1991).

The great variation in per-pupil spending from state to state and among school districts within states (ranging from $2000 to $13,000 per pupil in Ohio, for example, according to Wayson, 1991) means that urban schools with the greatest need often get the least money.

Thus, students from non-English language backgrounds have a high probability of attending a substandard (Kozol, 1991) and segregated (Espinosa & Ochoa, 1986) school. Studies in California and Texas found that as the proportion of Hispanic students increased, per-pupil expenditures (Valencia, cited in Chavez, 1991) and average achievement scores (Espinosa & Ochoa, 1986) decreased. The result is that, by the third grade, 80 percent of Hispanic, 56 percent of American Indian, and 53 percent of Asian-American students attend schools that are at or below average in reading and mathematics scores. The same pattern persists through high school (Espinosa & Ochoa, 1986).

Schools serving poor students emphasize basic computation skills and neglect mathematical concepts and applications (Porter, Floden, Freeman, Schmidt, & Schwille, 1988), have less experienced teachers and inadequate resources (Darling-Hammond & Green, 1988), and tend to have low expectations of their students' ability to learn (Good & Biddle, 1988). As Espinosa and Ochoa conclude (1986, p. 95), "A student of above-average potential in a Hispanic neighborhood would be very likely to attend a school with less challenging classmates and lower than average expectations than a similar Anglo student. . . . This may well point to one of the key mechanisms by which educational inequality is perpetuated and by which talented students are denied the opportunity for equal preparation for college."

New Directions

Solving the problems cited above depends on a broad scale societal effort, but guiding reform documents such as the National Education Goals are silent about making education and living conditions more equitable for all children. O'Day and Smith (forthcoming) trace the improvement in achievement scores of African American students during the 1960s and 1970s, and their subsequent decline during the 1980s, directly to the changes in socioeconomic conditions for African Americans during these periods.

Some critics of the education system (e.g. Kozol, 1991) contend that achievement patterns will not change until school funding is equalized. O'Day and Smith (forthcoming) argue that the equalizing should go beyond money; other factors may be crucial to ensuring that all students are offered an opportunity to learn challenging material. They advocate a system of standards and accountability that would measure inputs—the quality of a school's human and material resources, and the implementation of the educational program—as well as outcomes such as student achievement.

Even if schools cannot alter the socioeconomic and ethnic stratification of society, they can at least avoid perpetuating these differences within the school by no longer sorting students into different tracks. Some school districts have gone farther; La Crosse, Wisconsin, has embarked on a plan of socioeconomic desegregation, in which each school will reflect in its student body the socioeconomic make-up of the entire town, an approach endorsed by the National Coalition of Advocates for Students.

Schools that embrace the most radical form of multicultural education—one that aims for social change—see their purpose as leading toward the future rather than passively reflecting the status quo. This spirit is exemplified by the testimony that William Waxman, the principal of an elementary school confronted with an influx of Cambodian children, gave to the Immigrant Student Project of the National Coalition of Advocates for Students (McCarty First & Willshire Carrera, 1988). Waxman noted that the school's extraordinarily sensitive approach to welcoming and educating these children, in which each child was given an American "buddy," contrasted with the resentment expressed among adults in the community toward the newcomers. Waxman testified that "we've told the children that the elders will have to learn from them. Bring your friends home, introduce them to your parents" (p. 86).

Another way that schools can counteract societal inequity is to break the grip of low expectations for poor and minority students. Goldenberg and Gallimore (1991) document a process by which increased expectations led to higher achievement in a poor Hispanic school, resulting in an upward spiral of mutually reinforcing standards and achievement.

Student Ability and Motivation

The Problem

To explain the poor academic record of large numbers of students from non-English language backgrounds, this chapter first focused on characteristics of the school or educational program. In the last section, the discussion broadened to include the influences of society. Now we will consider the elements that students themselves bring to their education.

One explanation offered for the poor achievement of students from certain groups is that they are less intelligent or less capable of intellectual work. As the guiding assumption behind the tracking system established in the early part of the century to deal with immigrant students, this belief has become entrenched among educators and the public alike.

But while children from different ethnic, racial, and socioeconomic groups score differently on standardized tests of cognitive abilities learned at school, "there is no empirical basis for the hypothesis . . . that racial or socioeconomic groups differ in basic cognitive processes" (Oakes, 1991, p. 168). One of the few rigorous assessments of the cognitive abilities of preschool and kindergarten White and African American children (Ginsburg & Russell, 1981) found few differences. A few studies have found a negative relationship between field dependence—thought to be characteristic of the learning style of Hispanics—and mathematics achievement, and between Spanish as a primary language and mathematics performance, but the latter did not control for social class (Oakes, 1991).

Many educators who disavow innate qualities as an explanation for differential achievement among groups still ascribe educational failure to the "cultural deficits" of some groups. This is the rationale behind Head Start and other compensatory programs. But this is a retrospective analysis; when children from some ethnic groups do succeed, their cultural differences from the majority are often termed strengths rather than weaknesses.

While it is true that children from different groups have different cultural experiences, that the experiences provided by some cultural groups may be more conducive to success in the traditional school system, and that children from more favorable socioeconomic circumstances in fact succeed more often than others, there is no inevitable link between cultural difference and school failure. We have no way of knowing how students from traditionally low-achieving groups would fare if they were afforded the resources, same-culture teachers, native language development, culturally congruent curriculum and instruction, and high expectations routinely afforded to White upper middle class students, because the cases are so few.

While a great deal of attention has been paid to student characteristics derived from their cultural background as influencing ability, the most important student contribution to achievement is probably effort. Students are more likely to succeed if they have a positive attitude toward school and the motivation to study.

The feelings that students develop toward school may be shaped in large part by their perception of how much the school and society values them. One of the greatest disadvantages of attending a poor school in a poor neighborhood is a negative school climate. All students are influenced by the appearance of the school and by the way that the people at the school treat each other. If teachers demonstrate by attitude or word that they have low expectations and low opinions of students from non-English language backgrounds, if students from minority groups are considered troublemakers by the administration, if students from different ethnic groups are frequently in conflict, if school is a dangerous and unpleasant place, students who are not native English speakers can feel afraid and demeaned, decreasing their motivation and interest in school.

More than half of the students in inner city schools become "turned off" and drop out (McLaren, 1988), many because of racial discrimination, negative attitudes by teachers, and punitive school policies (Felice, 1981). Some studies have found that dropouts leave school not because they cannot do the work but because they are pushed out by an intolerable atmosphere (Raywid, 1987).

The motivation of students can be dampened not only by the low expectations of teachers, but also by their view of their opportunities in society. What they observe in their neighborhoods may reflect official statistics indicating that poverty rates for adults with equivalent education are higher for Hispanics and Blacks than for Whites. While 19 percent of Whites with a high school diploma are

poor, 33 percent of Hispanics and 52 percent of Blacks who gradu-
ated from high school live in poverty. Only 5 percent of Whites with
more than a high school education live in poverty, compared to 20
percent of Hispanics and 25 percent of Blacks (National Center for
Children in Poverty, 1992).

A more significant obstacle for non-English language background children than cultural or linguistic difference per se may be
society's disparagement of those differences. The academic motivation of these students can be negatively affected in the following
ways:

- Native languages other than English are often devalued by
  schools (Nieto, 1992); this "linguicism" (Skutnabb-Kangas,
  1988), or discrimination based on language, can be felt as
  deeply as racism.

- Cultural differences are often viewed as an obstacle to
  learning. Students feel forced to abandon their language
  and culture in order to be successful in American society
  (Ogbu, 1992).

- Teachers may have low expectations of culturally different
  students, which students "live down to" (Rosenthal &
  Jacobson, 1968) in a self-fulfilling prophecy (Merton, 1948).
  (On the other hand, the academic success of some students
  from Asian backgrounds may in part be due to the positive
  expectations of teachers, based on the stereotype that Asian
  students are industrious and excel in mathematics.)

- A curriculum that excludes non-European American people
  and cultures or includes only negative stereotypes of them
  can lead students to feel devalued and rejected, resulting in
  their refusing to learn (Ogbu, 1986).

Ogbu's (1986) distinction between voluntary and involuntary
immigrants to the United States provides an explanation for the
differential success rates of minority groups by highlighting the reciprocal influence of dominant culture opinion and the self-image of
minority group members. Ogbu argues that involuntary immigrants—groups that have been conquered or colonized, such as
African Americans, Native Americans, or Hispanics—are more stigmatized than newer groups of voluntary immigrants, who sometimes outperform even U.S.-born Americans of European ancestry.

The prejudicial attitudes of American society toward non-

European American cultures are perpetuated by the schools. Dominated groups can experience academic disadvantage *because of* their subordinate relationship in society (Nieto, 1992). Involuntary minority groups, such as Koreans in Japan, Finns in Sweden, Irish Catholics in Northern Ireland, and Maoris in New Zealand, do poorly in their own country but often succeed academically if they immigrate to the United States or Australia (Nieto, 1992). Similarly, it has been argued that Mexicans, Africans, and Puerto Ricans newly arrived in the United States often do better in school and have higher self-esteem than their counterparts born in the United States (Nieto, 1992).

As societal institutions, schools reflect societal values. The prejudices of the larger society are conveyed to students in subtle ways, even by school personnel who sincerely believe themselves to be unbiased:

- A study that analyzed a videotaped class found that the White teacher made eye contact more frequently with her White students. Her Black students "had to strain three times as hard to catch the teacher's eye, looking for approval, affection, and encouragement" (Nieto, 1992, p. 21).

- Several studies have documented that teachers pay more attention to White and male students than to students of color and female students (Nieto, 1992, p. 25).

- Even students of superior ability may be neglected by teachers if they are not White males; according to Shakeshaft (1986), teachers direct the least attention to high-achieving female students.

- One study (cited in Nieto, 1992) found that African American and Mexican American students performed equally to European Americans in an objective measure of language development, but the same children were rated as inferior to European Americans by teachers who used subjective criteria.

- Student assignments to different tracks are often based on ethnic background and social class rather than valid assessments of ability (Rist, 1971).

- The terms used to refer to students and the programs designed for them, such as "cultural deprivation" and "compensatory," send a strong message of inferiority.

- Some school personnel are overtly biased; a New York City teacher testified that "in general, the reception given to immigrant children was so negative and hostile that many of them were so turned off to their new society that they were never able to learn how to speak English. Bilingual students were called animals, garbage, jerks, idiots by many teachers . . . and this unprofessional and inhumane treatment of children was condoned by the administration" (McCarty First & Willshire Carrera, 1988, p. 60).

- In many multi-ethnic schools, hostility between groups is the norm, and immigrant students are at the very bottom of the ranking order, subject to verbal and physical abuse from fellow students (McCarty First & Willshire Carrera, 1988).

What is the effect of interpersonal and structural discrimination on student learning? One study of the influence of racial prejudice on African American college students (Gougis, 1986) concluded that racism adversely affected their performance by increasing emotional stress and decreasing motivation. Even if a direct link is difficult to prove, Ortiz (1988) contends that discrimination creates an inferior education for Hispanic students because it results in more remedial-focused instruction, tracking, lower teacher expectations, and less positive teacher involvement with students.

While all poor and minority students may be negatively affected by societal attitudes, students from different cultural groups may be even more heavily influenced by the particular attitude toward academic achievement demonstrated by their own peer group. Ogbu (1992) has written about the dilemma faced by academically inclined African American students; their cultural peer group compels them to choose between being accepted by the group and succeeding in school. In that group's cultural value system, achievement stands in opposition to ethnic identity. For other groups, achievement may not be problematic; the peer group may endorse school success as congruent with ethnic identity.

Reviews of studies assessing the effects of cooperative learning (cited in Educational Research Service [ERS], 1990) found that the performance of African American and Hispanic students improved more than White students. One of the authors (Slavin, 1983) hypothesized that "there is something in black and Hispanic cultures that supports cooperation as a motivational system. Black and Hispanic

children's self-esteem seems to depend more on how they see themselves getting along with their peer group than how they are doing
academically, while the reverse is true for whites" (p. 62).

New Directions

While schools cannot change the society around them, they can
serve as model communities for socializing young people who will
create the society of the future. One of the National Education
Goals is to make every school a drug-free, violence-free, disciplined
environment conducive to learning. But the National Coalition of
Advocates for Students recommends more than simply removing
negative influences; they advocate the creation of a school climate
of inter-ethnic tolerance and understanding.

Caplan et al. (1991) recommend that schools build bridges
with the ethnic communities from which their students come so as
to help parents reinforce achievement aspirations in their children.
Ogbu (1992) also believes that communities of African Americans
and others whose children do not work seriously enough in school
need to play an active role in re-defining ethnic identity in ways
compatible with school success.

Schools also need to understand the powerful pull of the peer
group on students, and to experiment with altering the conditions
of instruction. Some teachers have had success in channeling the
motivation of African American students toward greater learning
by capitalizing on the peer group interactional style of challenge
and public display of talent (Williams, 1981).

Education Reform Trends and Linguistic Diversity

Murphy (1991) describes the education reform movement as two
distinct phases. Wave I, launched by the 1983 report, *A Nation at
Risk*, focused on repair, Wave II on reconstruction. In the early and
mid-1980s, reform proposals aimed to fix the sagging schools by
shoring them up—holding teachers and students to higher standards, increasing teacher's salaries, providing better books and
materials. By the latter part of the decade, educators, commis-
sioned panels, business leaders, and politicians were calling for
more drastic reform—restructuring the educational system.

A parallel evolution has occurred in the thinking about education for students from non-English language backgrounds. The first wave of programs was intended to overcome these students' presumed linguistic and cultural "deficits" by teaching them English and providing compensatory programs. The emphasis has now shifted from fixing the students to fixing the schools. In this newer way of thinking, these students are fully competent linguistically and cognitively; they just happen to know a different language, have different cultural knowledge, and perhaps learn best in a different manner from the students that American schools were designed for. The challenge is not how to make these students fit the traditional mold, but how to remold the traditional school to fit the educational needs of these students.

Organizing for Diversity

The lack of English fluency is only one obstacle to academic achievement faced by students from other language backgrounds, and it may not be the most formidable. It is naive to expect English instruction to remove all the barriers to educational excellence. A person who cannot walk has the potential for mobility with a wheelchair, but that potential will not be realized if there are no wheelchair ramps on sidewalks, buildings, or buses. Similarly, learning English will not remove the barriers of poverty and discrimination faced by many students from non-English language backgrounds.

Reforming schools to enable these students to succeed requires much more. A report on the challenge of diversity for colleges and universities (Smith, 1989) concludes that such institutions will fail to truly engage students and faculty of both genders and those with diverse ethnic heritages, economic backgrounds, and disabilities if they continue to perceive the concerns and needs of these groups as peripheral to the central educational enterprise. Programs for categories of students with special needs represent a necessary "institutional accommodation." But "specific programmatic and policy responses by themselves are not sufficient to make major strides." They "run the risk of simply helping students 'adjust,' 'manage,' or 'survive' in an alien environment" (p. 54).

More comprehensive organizational shifts are necessary. "By asking *how* an institution begins to educate and create a climate that is involving for all its members, the question is focused on fundamental aspects of the institution and its ability to embrace diversity, rather than on its ability to simply add programs or make modest changes" (Smith, 1989, p. 54). What is required, at the elementary and secondary as well as college level, is the commitment, backed up by strong leadership, to make school a truly diverse community of learning to which all students and teachers feel that they belong and in which they can all participate fully.

If one of the major purposes of an education is to prepare students to become responsible citizens in a democratic and ethnically diverse nation, then schools should incorporate a democratic and multicultural ethic in every aspect of their functioning. Too often, students are exposed to democracy only in civics class, and to multiculturalism only as a unit of study. Good citizenship is learned best when students practice democratic ideals of self-government as members of the school community. Respect and appreciation for other cultural heritages is best absorbed as students interact with diverse members of the school community and as they learn about the contributions of people from various cultures to science, art, and literature.

Organizing schools for diversity will involve special challenges for the majority of the nation's teachers and administrators. They will require opportunities for expanding their cultural knowledge and sensitivity beyond that provided by their monolingual and monocultural background. Even more important for educators than acquiring specific knowledge and skills useful for working with diverse learners is developing a reflective frame of mind that will enable them to create challenging learning environments for all students (Milk, Mercado, & Sapiens, 1992).

An analysis of effective schooling practices for Latino and other language minority students (Garcia, 1991) echoes many of the recommendations in this chapter, and highlights the crucial role of teachers and administrators. Principals in successful programs supported and gave autonomy to teachers. Teachers emphasized communication with and among students, encouraged collaborative learning, allowed students to progress naturally from native language to English, and organized instruction around themes influenced by the students' interests. Teachers worked cooperatively with parents, and, perhaps most important, were committed to their students' high achievement. "They were proud of their students—academically reassuring but consistently demanding. They rejected any notion of academic, linguistic, cultural, or intellectual inferiority in their students" (p. 6). Teachers with such positive attitudes may be the most important key to the success of all types of students.

REFERENCES

Adler, P. S. (1972). *Culture shock and the cross cultural learning experience: Readings in intercultural education* (Vol. 2). Pittsburgh: Intercultural Communication Network.

Bloom, B. S. (1981). *All our children: A primer for parents, teachers, and other educators.* New York: McGraw-Hill.

BW Associates. (1992). *Meeting the challenge of language diversity: An evaluation of programs for pupils with limited proficiency in English.* Berkeley, CA: Author.

Cabazon, M., Lambert, W. E., & Hall, G. (1993). *Two-way bilingual education: A progress report on the Amigos program.* Santa Cruz: The National Center for Research on Cultural Diversity and Second language Learning.

California State Department of Education (CSDE). (1992). *Language census.* Sacramento, CA: CSDE.

Caplan, N., Choy, M. H., & Whitmore, J. K. (1991). *Children of the boat people: A study of educational success.* Ann Arbor, MI: The University of Michigan Press.

Chavez, C. A. (1991, May). *"State of the play" in educational research on Latino / Hispanic youth.* Unpublished manuscript.

Collier, V. P. (1989a,). Academic achievement, attitudes, and occupations among graduates of two-way bilingual classes. Paper presented at the annual meeting of the American Education Research Association. San Francisco, March, 1989.

Collier, V. P. (1989b). How long? A synthesis of research on academic achievement in a second language. *TESOL Quarterly, 23* (3): 509–531.

Collier, V. P. (1992). A synthesis of studies examining long-term language minority student data on academic achievement. *Bilingual Research Journal, 16* (1&2): 185–210.

Collins, A., Hawkins, J., & Carver, S. M. (1991). A cognitive apprenticeship for disadvantaged students. In B. Means & M. S. Knapp (Eds.), *Teaching advanced skills to educationally disadvantaged students.* Final Report. Data Analysis Support Center (DASC) Task 4. Washington, DC: U.S. Department of Education, Office of Planning, Budget, & Evaluation.

Council of Chief State School Officers (CCSSO) (1990). *School success for limited English proficient students: The challenge and state response.* Washington, DC: Resource Center on Educational Equity.

Cuban, L. (1990). Reforming again, again, and again. *Educational Researcher, 19* (1): 3–13.

Cummins, J. (1984). *Bilingualism and special education: Issues in assessment and pedagogy.* Clevedon, England: Multilingual Matters.

Cziko, G. A. (1992). The evaluation of bilingual education. *Educational Researcher, 21* (2): 10–15.

Darling-Hammond, L. (1991). Measuring schools is not the same as improving them. In *Voices from the field: 30 expert opinions on 'America 2000,' the Bush administration strategy to 'reinvent' America's schools.* Washington, DC: William T. Grant Foundation Commission on Work, Family, and Citizenship and Institute for Educational Leadership.

Darling-Hammond, L., & Green, J. (1988, Summer). Teacher quality and educational equality. *College Board Review*, 16–41.

Educational Research Service (ERS). (1990). *Cooperative learning.* Arlington, VA: Author.

Enright, D. S., & McCloskey, M. L. (1992). The physical environment. In P. A. Richard-Amato & M. A. Snow (Eds.), *The multicultural classroom: Readings for content-area teachers.* White Plains, NY: Longman.

Espinosa, R., & Ochoa, A. (1986). Concentration of California Hispanic students in schools with low achievement: A research note. *American Journal of Education, 95* (1): 77–95.

Farr, M. (1986). Language, culture, and writing: Sociolinguistic foundations of research on writing. *Review of Research in Education, 13*, 195–223.

Felice, L. (1981). Black student dropout behavior: Disengagement from school rejection and racial discrimination. *The Journal of Negro Education, 50*, 415–424.

First, J., Kellogg, J. B., Almeida, C. A., & Gray, R. (1991). *The good common school: Making the vision work for all children.* Boston, MA: National Coalition of Advocates for Students.

Foster, G. M. (1962). *Traditional cultures.* New York: Harper & Row.

Garcia, E. (1991). *Education of linguistically and culturally diverse students: Effective instructional practices.* Santa Cruz, CA: The National Center for Research on Cultural Diversity and Second Language Learning.

Garcia, E. (In press). *Understanding and meeting the challenge of student cultural diversity*. Boston, MA: Houghton Mifflin.

Gardner, H. (1983). *Frames of mind: The theory of multiple intelligences*. New York: Basic Books.

Gibson, M. A. (1987, December). The school performance of immigrant minorities: A comparative view. *Anthropology and Education Quarterly, 18* (4): 262–275.

Ginsburg, H. P., & Russell, R. L. (1981). *Social class and racial influences on early thinking*. (Monographs of the Society for Research in Child Development). Chicago: Society for Research in Child Development.

Goldenberg, C., & Gallimore, R. (1991). Local knowledge, research knowledge, and educational change: A case study of early Spanish reading improvement. *Educational Researcher, 20* (8): 2–14.

Good, T. L., & Biddle, B. J. (1988). Research and the improvement of mathematics instruction: The need for observational resources. In D. A. Grouws & T. J. Cooney (Eds.), *Perspectives on research on effective mathematics teaching*. Reston, VA: National Council of Teachers of Mathematics.

Gougis, R. A. (1986). The effects of prejudice and stress on the academic achievement of Black Americans. In U. Neisser (Ed.), *The school achievement of minority children: New perspectives*. Hillsdale, NJ: Erlbaum.

Guido, M. (1992, March 8). Hard lessons in language: One in four new pupils can't speak English. *San Jose Mercury News*, p. 1A.

Hakuta, K. (1990). *Bilingualism and bilingual education: A research perspective. Focus No. 1*. Washington, DC: National Clearinghouse for Bilingual Education.

Johnson, D. W., Maruyama, G., Johnson, R., Nelson, D., & Skon, L. (1981). Effects of cooperative, competitive, and individualistic goal structures on achievement: A meta-analysis. *Psychological Bulletin, 89* (1): 47–62.

Kozol, J. (1991). *Savage inequalities: Children in America's schools*. New York: Crown Publishers.

Levin, H., & Hopfenberg, W. N. (1991). Accelerated schools for at-risk students. *Principal, 70*, 11–13.

Linn, R. L., Baker, E. L., & Dunbar, S. B. (1991). Complex, performance-based assessment: Expectations and validation criteria. *Educational Researcher, 20*, 8.

Matute-Bianchi, M. E. (1986, November). Ethnic identities and patterns of school success and failure among Mexican-descent and Japanese-American students in a California high school: An ethnographic analysis. *American Journal of Education*, 233–255.

McCarty First, J., & Willshire Carrera, J. (1988). *New voices: Immigrant students in U.S. public schools*. Boston, MA: National Coalition of Advocates for Students.

McKnight, C. C., Crosswhite, F. J., Dossey, J. A., Kifer, E., Swafford, J. O., Travers, K. J., & Coney, T. J. (1987). *The underachieving curriculum: Assessing U.S. school mathematics from an international perspective*. Champaign, IL: Stipes Publishing.

McLaren, P. (1988). Broken dreams, false promises, and the decline of public schooling. *Journal of Education, 170* (1): 41–65.

McLaughlin, B. (1992). *Myths and misconceptions about second language learning: What every teacher needs to unlearn*. Santa Cruz, CA: The National Center for Research on Cultural Diversity and Second Language Learning.

Mehan, H., Datnow, A., Bratton, E., Tellez, C., Friedlaender, D., & Ngo, T. (1992). *Untracking and college enrollment*. Santa Cruz, CA: The National Center for Research on Cultural Diversity and Second Language Learning.

Merton, R. (1948). The self-fulfilling prophecy. *The Antioch Review, 8*, 193–210.

Milk, R., Mercado, C., & Sapiens, A. (1992). *Re-thinking the education of teachers of language minority children: Developing reflective teachers for changing schools*. Washington, DC: National Clearinghouse for Bilingual Education.

Miller Jones, D. (1993). Talk given at Conference on Assessment and Diversity, University of California, Santa Cruz, February 17–20.

Moll, L. C. (1992). Bilingual classroom studies and community analysis: Some recent trends. *Educational Researcher, 21* (2): 20–14.

Murphy, J. (1991). *Restructuring schools: Capturing and assessing the phenomena*. New York: Teachers College Press.

National Association of State Boards of Education (NASBE). (no date). *The American tapestry: Educating a nation*. Alexandria, VA: Author.

National Forum on Personnel Needs for Districts with Changing Demographics. (1990, May). *Staffing the multilingually impacted schools of the 1990s*. Washington, DC: United States Department of Education, Office of Bilingual Education and Minority Languages Affairs.

National Governors' Association (1989). *Results in education 1989*. Washington, DC: Author.

Nieto, S. (1992). *Affirming diversity: The sociopolitical context of multicultural education*. New York: Longman.

Numbers and Needs: Ethnic and Linguistic Minorities in the United States. (1991, December). Washington, DC: Author.

Oakes, J. (1985). *Keeping track: How schools structure inequality*. New Haven, CT: Yale University Press.

Oakes, J. (1991). Opportunities, achievement, and choice: Women and minority students in science and mathematics. *Review of Research in Education, 16*, 153–222.

O'Day, J. A. & Smith, M. S. (forthcoming). Systemic school reform and educational opportunity. In S. Fuhrman (Ed.), *Designing coherent education policy: Improving the system*. San Francisco: Jossey-Bass.

Ogbu, J. U. (1986). The consequences of the American caste system. In U. Neisser (Ed.), *The school achievement of minority children: New perspectives*. Hillsdale, NJ: Erlbaum.

Ogbu, J. U. (1992). Understanding cultural diversity and learning. *Educational Researcher, 21* (8): 5–14.

Ortiz, F. I. (1988). Hispanic-American children's experiences in classrooms: A comparison between Hispanic and non-Hispanic children. In L. Weis (Ed.), *Class, race, and gender in American education*. Albany: State University of New York Press.

Padilla, A. M., Lindholm, K. J., Chen, A., Duran, R., Hakuta, K., Lambert, W., & Tucker, G. R. (1991). The English-only movement: Myths, reality, and implications for psychology. *American Psychologist, 46* (2): 120–130.

Porter, A., Floden, R., Freeman, D., Schmidt, W., & Schwille, J. (1988). Content determinants in elementary school mathematics. In D. A. Grouws & T. J. Cooney (Eds.), *Perspectives on research on effective mathematics teaching*. Reston, VA: National Council of Teachers of Mathematics.

Ramirez, J. D., Yuen, S. D., & Ramey, D. R. (1991). *Final report: Longitudinal study of structured English immersion strategy, early-exit and late-exit transitional bilingual education programs for language-minority children*. San Mateo, CA: Aguirre International.

Ramirez, J. D. (1992). Personal Communication, March 30.

Ramirez, M., & Casteneda, A. (1974). *Cultural democracy: Bicognitive development and education*. New York: Academic Press.

Raywid, M. A. (1987). Making school work for the new majority. *Journal of Negro Education, 56* (2): 221–228.

Richard-Amato, P. A. (1992). Peer teachers: The neglected resource. In P. A. Richard-Amato & M. A. Snow (Eds.) *The multicultural classroom: Readings for content-area teachers*. White Plains, NY: Longman.

Richard-Amato, P. A., & Snow, M. A. (1992). Strategies for content-area teachers. In P. A. Richard-Amato & M. A. Snow (Eds.), *The multicultural classroom: Readings for content-area teachers*. White Plains, NY: Longman.

Rist, R. C. (1971). Student social class and teacher expectations: The self-fulfilling prophecy in ghetto education. *Challenging the myths: The schools, the Blacks, and the poor*, Reprint Series #5. Cambridge, MA: Harvard Educational Review.

Rosebery, A. S., Warren, B., & Conant, F. R. (1992). *Appropriating scientific discourse: Findings from language minority classrooms*. Santa Cruz, CA: The National Center for Research on Cultural Diversity and Second Language Learning.

Rosenthal, R., & Jacobson, L. (1968). *Pygmalion in the classroom*. New York: Holt, Rinehart, & Winston.

Rumbaut, R. G., & Ima, K. (1987). *The adaptation of Southeast Asian refugee youth: A comparative study*, Final Report. San Diego, CA: Office of Refugee Resettlement.

Saville-Troike, M. (1991). *Teaching and testing for academic achievement: The role of language development. Focus No. 4*. Washington, DC: National Clearinghouse for Bilingual Education.

Shakeshaft, C. (1986, March). A gender at risk. *Phi Delta Kappan*, 499–503.

Shavelson, R. J., Baxter, G. P., & Pine, J. (1992). Performance assesments: Political rhetoric and measurement reality. *Educational Researcher, 21* (4): 22–27.

Short, D. J. (1992). Adapting materials and developing lesson plans. In P. A. Richard-Amato & M. A. Snow (Eds.), *The multicultural classroom: Readings for content-area teachers*. White Plains, NY: Longman.

Skutnabb-Kangas, T. (1988). Multilingualism and the education of minority children. In T. Skutnabb-Kangas & J. Cummins (Eds.), *Minority education: From shame to struggle*. Clevedon, England: Multilingual Matters.

Slavin, R. E. (1983). *Cooperative learning*. New York: Longman.

Smith, D. G. (1989). *The challenge of diversity: Involvement or alienation in the academy?* Report No. 5. Washington, DC: School of Education and Human Development, The George Washington University.

Snow, C. E. (1992). Perspectives on second-language development: Implications for bilingual education. *Educational Researcher, 21* (2): 16–19.

Stigler, J. W., & Baranes, R. (1988–89). Culture and mathematics learning. *Review of Research in Education, 15*, 253–306.

Tharp, R. G. & Gallimore, R. (1988). *Rousing minds to life: Teaching, learning, and schooling in social context*. New York: Cambridge University Press.

Wayson, W. W. (1991). Steaming backward to 2000. *Voices from the field: 30 expert opinions on "America 2000," the Bush administration strategy to "reinvent" America's schools*. Washington, DC: William T. Grant Foundation Commission on Work, Family and Citizenship & Institute for Educational Leadership.

Williams, M. D. (1981). Observations in Pittsburg ghetto schools. *Anthropology & Education Quarterly, 12*, 211–220.

Witkin, H. A. (1962). *Psychological differentiation*. New York: Wiley.

Wong Fillmore, L., & Valadez, C. (1986). Teaching bilingual learners. In M.C. Wittrock (Ed.), *Handbook of research on teaching*, 3rd ed. New York: Macmillan.

✧ Chapter 2

The Impact of the Education Reform Movement on Limited English Proficient Students

Patricia Gándara

There is no question that the 1980s ushered in a decade of educational reform of unprecedented proportions. Many hundreds of reports have been issued (Alliance for Achievement, 1989), more than a thousand education reform initiatives have been launched in the state legislatures (Darling-Hammond and Berry, 1988) and no state has been untouched by the movement (Bridgman, 1985; Fuhrman, Clune and Elmore, 1988). Unlike the last reform effort which began in the mid-1960s, however, this one has been less about equity and access than about "stemming the tide of mediocrity" (Fuhrman, et al., 1988).

The first wave of the 1980s reforms focused on increasing standards and assessments for both students and teachers, and in creating more incentives for teaching, while the second wave shifted to the "restructuring" of constituent relationships (Smith and O'Day,

1990). While calls to overhaul the educational system went out from all quarters, most of the efforts of the last decade were initiated by the states, with some prodding, but little funding by the federal government (Dougherty, 1986; Fuhrman, et al., 1988).

The 1990s, however, have seen a new agenda developing, one stimulated by the federal government, whose central themes are accountability and efficiency. The new agenda, as spelled out in the Bush administration's America 2000 plan, incorporated the six education goals delineated by the nation's governors at the 1989 Education Summit meeting in Charlottesville, but emphasized national testing and school "choice" as cornerstones of the plan (U.S. Department of Education, 1991; Stedman and Riddle, 1992). The Clinton administration has indicated that it will continue to push the national goals developed under the previous administration but that its support of "choice" will probably be confined to the public sector (Miller, 1992).

Demographic Change

During this same period of reform activity, another change has been occurring in American education. Fueled by high levels of immigration and social and economic policies designed to benefit the most economically advantaged, the proportion of the nation's students who are poor, minority, and limited English proficient (LEP) has increased dramatically in recent years (Phillips, 1990). In 1980 approximately one-fourth of all U.S. students were minorities, in 1990 nearly one-third were (NCES, 1992). Poverty has accompanied diversity, with one out of every four American children living under the poverty line (CED, 1987). While data on the numbers of LEP students are notoriously difficult to obtain, an estimated 3.5 to 5 million American students were sufficiently limited in English in 1990 to qualify for special programming (CCSSO, 1990). In California, where the nation's highest concentration of LEP students resides, the numbers doubled between 1984 and 1991, from just under 500,000 to almost one million students (California State Department of Education, 1992). LEP students are among the most at risk of all students for dropping out of school (Blinde, Steinberg, and Chan, 1982; CCSSO, 1990), performing below grade level (Baratz-Snowden and Duran, 1987), and being enrolled in non-academic courses (Baratz-Snowden and Duran, 1987; CCSSO, 1990). Nonetheless, while LEP and other "at risk" students are frequently cited as *justifications* for why reforms are needed, they are rarely included in any specific way in the reforms themselves (Bliss, 1986; Valadez, 1989).

Reform Objectives

Student-Oriented Reforms

The first wave of educational reform initiatives can be roughly divided into three large groups: student-oriented reforms, teacher-oriented reforms, and reforms in governance and administration. All of the major reform reports called for changes in the curriculum that students study and the standards to which they are held accountable (Stedman and Jordan, 1986). Notable among these are the extensive curricular recommendations made in *A Nation at Risk* (NCEE, 1983), which laid out a course of study referred to as "The New Basics." The authors recommend that it be undertaken by all students seeking a diploma, and that it include increased requirements in English, mathematics, science, and social studies. Additionally, the report called for stricter college admission standards, with the belief that this would act as a catalyst for strengthening the secondary curriculum.

The Paideia Proposal (Adler, 1982) went a step further and carefully delineated not only *what* students should be taught, but *how*, insisting that teaching should consist of three pedagogic strategies: teaching for acquisition of knowledge (e.g., lecture), development of skills (e.g., coaching), and an enlarged understanding of ideas and values (e.g., socratic method). Goodlad (1984), in *A Place Called School*, also emphasized strengthened academic requirements coupled with a different pedagogy. He suggested that students should be taught through mastery learning approaches, eschewing the strict lock-step of age/grade divisions. This, he felt, would assure that students are not only exposed to the curriculum, but that they would absorb it.

The National Science Board Commission's report, *Educating Americans for the 21st Century* (1983), predictably exhorted the schools to increase requirements for science and mathematics study for all students, as did Ernest Boyer's work, *High School* (1983), which also emphasized the importance of a central core of English studies, and two years of foreign language. Foreign language study is, ironically, mentioned in several of the reports (Adler, 1982; NCEE, 1983; Berman Weiler Associates, 1988) as well as being alluded to as an objective in the National Goals (National Education Goals Panel, 1991), suggesting the recognition of a need for multilingual skills. Yet, with the exception of the Berman Weiler report, none makes mention of the possibility of nurturing the language skills that America's students bring to the classroom.

Horace's Compromise (Sizer, 1984) takes a somewhat different tack, suggesting that the curriculum is overly comprehensive and that the study of foreign language, as well as other subject areas, ought not to have the same priority as the study of English and the core academics. Sizer's chief concerns are that the educational system is overregulated and that it stifles learning by setting standards that are too low.

While Boyer does make a plea for the full funding of Chapter One so that "disadvantaged" students can also meet the strengthened requirements, none of the reports suggests how the millions of U.S. students who do not speak sufficient English to access the core curriculum might accomplish this, nor how these reformed schools might create greater avenues of access for such students.

Following the recommendations of a number of these reports, many states instituted or strengthened their student accountability systems, and minimum proficiency testing also came into wider use during the period (Bridgman, 1985). However, through the 1980s this type of testing remained under the purview of the states and the local education agencies with little regard for standardization across localities.

Teacher-Oriented Reforms

All of the reports already mentioned also touch on topics of teacher standards and rewards. A common theme is inadequate teacher preparation. Goodlad (1984) cites a survey of teacher feelings of preparedness to teach in various subject areas. Nearly one quarter of the elementary school teachers contended that they felt unprepared to teach science, and almost a third made the same statement about art. What may be more surprising is that only five percent felt they lacked the preparation to teach mathematics, and only eight percent felt similarly about teaching science in the upper grades, when the data suggest that future teachers score lower on tests of mathematics ability than other college-bound students (Carnegie Forum, 1986), and many mathematics and science teachers are teaching these subjects without the appropriate credentials (Rumberger, 1985).

The teacher preparation issue is attacked on two fronts by the bulk of the reports: pre-service training, and increased testing for teacher certification. A common theme in the area of pre-service training is the notion that teachers should be more broadly educated in the liberal arts (Adler, 1982; Sizer, 1984) as well as in mathematics and science (NSBC, 1983; Carnegie Forum, 1986), and that courses in pedagogy ought to be reserved for a fifth year of post-baccalaureate study (The Holmes Group, 1986; Carnegie Forum, 1986).

There is also broad agreement among the reports that teachers who are well-prepared in the manner recommended ought to be well-compensated and given greater autonomy in the classroom and a greater voice in the curriculum. Virtually all of the reports suggest that teacher pay ought to be increased, and some even specify the amount (Twentieth Century Fund Taskforce, 1983; Boyer, 1983; Carnegie Forum, 1986). Many also recommend greater opportunities for job mobility and differentiation, such as the development of career ladders (Boyer, 1983; NCEE, 1983), and the option of taking on different roles at different times (Sizer, 1984). While there has been little real progress in the area of building career ladders, states have invested considerably in bringing up teacher salaries and instituting other teacher-related reforms. Most reform dollars have been spent on teacher reforms (Dougherty, 1986) and teacher salaries climbed by almost 20 percent between 1980 and 1990 (NCES, 1991).

There is great consensus among the reports that properly prepared teachers should have greater control over both curriculum and methodology, with some reports even suggesting that teachers might have ultimate control over what is taught in their classrooms (Adler, 1982; Sizer, 1984). There is no mention, however, of how teachers might be prepared to adapt their curricula to the needs of a diverse student body, many of whom may not speak the language of the classroom.

Governance and Administrative Reforms

Ironically, while the would-be reformers wrote at great length about a new flexibility in the classroom and greater autonomy for teachers, the reform thrust in the area of governance was set in a different direction. The source of political power necessary to take control of these reforms shifted away from the local level and toward the state. Increased graduation standards, longer school days and years, the testing of teachers, have all been state-level activities that have given little voice to local concerns. In many states, new tax laws and increased investment in schooling shifted the locus of responsibility for schools toward the state and resulted in a greater concentration of policy-making power at that level. By the end of the decade of the 1980s the states had increased their budgets by more than 25 percent, with the additional dollars going to reform-oriented spending (Firestone, Fuhrman, and Kirst, 1991) With the extra dollars came the heavier hand of the state in the business of education. This coupling of the loss of control over teaching policies and a perception that not very much had actually changed in America's classrooms became the impetus for the second wave of reform, "restructuring" (Fuhrman, et al., 1988; ETS, 1990).

Restructuring

Restructuring was to involve "a fundamental break with the organizational, governmental, and pedagogical practices of the past and included the proposition that change should start from the bottom, that there should be room to exercise discretion at the school building level . . . " (ETS, 1990, p. 2). "Yet, for all the effort, evaluations of the reforms indicate only minor changes in the typical school, either in the nature of classroom practices or achievement outcomes" (Smith and O'Day, 1990, p. 233). Restructuring came to be more of a catch phrase for incorporating more voices into the planning and, sometimes, the decision-making at the school site level. But even this more modest notion of change has not been realized in the schools serving the most "at risk" students. As Jonathan Kozol points out in his book, *Savage Inequalities*, after having surveyed schools serving poor Spanish speakers in Texas, as well as other inner city schools,

> to the extent that school reforms such as "restructuring" are advocated for the inner cities, few of these reforms have reached the schools that I have seen . . . what is termed "restructuring" struck me as very little more than moving around the same old furniture in the house of poverty. (Kozol, 1991, p. 4)

A New Reform Agenda

On the heels of these often disappointing, and as Seymour Sarason (1991) would note, highly "predictable failures of educational reform," the Bush administration launched its new initiative: America 2000, a plan to realize the aims of the national goals by the turn of the century. The six goals are: (1) that every child will come to school ready to learn; (2) that 90 percent of students will graduate from high school; (3) that all students will learn to use their minds well; (4) that U.S. students will be first in the world in science and mathematics; (5) that all Americans will be literate; and (6) that all schools will be free of drugs and violence (U.S. Department of Education, 1991). Exactly how this was all to be accomplished by the year 2000 has been left to the Congress to sort out. However, the Bush administration made clear that certain elements must be included in the plan: a network of "New American Schools" to be funded in each of the congressional districts to serve as "lighthouses" for reform; a new system of national student testing, "The Nation's Report Card"; and the public funding of private schools through a voucher system, otherwise known as "choice" in schooling (Stedman and Riddle, 1992). While Congress continued in 1993 to debate the ultimate form that the initiative will take, little, if any, mention has been made of the plight of limited English speakers. While OBEMLA, the Office of Bilingual Education and Minority Language Affairs, has continued to try to position itself for a role in the National Goals strategy, whatever form it may eventually take (US Department of Education: OBEMLA,1992), the Department of Education, as a whole, has been notably silent on the issue of LEP students and programs targeted to their needs (Stedman, 1992). Inasmuch as the new administration has warned that "a new agenda will not be set for some time," no changes in the status quo are yet evident (Miller, 1992, p.1).

Who is Benefitting from Reform?

Who have been the beneficiaries of the reforms of the past decade, and who stands to benefit from the current crop of new reform initiatives? There are many who would argue that the reform movement has been largely confined to the middle class, as a direct result of the inequities in resources made available to implement these policies (Smith and O'Day, 1990; Kozol, 1991; ETS, 1991). Others contend that unless the special, and substantially different needs of LEP (and other "at risk") students are specifically taken into account, educational reform will remain out of their reach (Galvan, 1987; Valadez, 1989).

   The evidence is mounting in favor of these critics of the reform movement. As the rapidly shifting demographics of the nation result in an increasing proportion of students who are poor, minorities, and LEP, little progress has been noted. After a decade of reforms targeted to increasing achievement, wide gaps between the performance of white students and those of color remain, especially for Hispanics (ETS, 1991). In California, which receives the largest portion of the nation's immigrants and educates one of every nine U.S. students, and where almost one of every three children arriving in kindergarten is LEP (Bizjak, 1992), the disparities in performance can be startling.

> In 1990, for example, white students scored on average 79 points higher than black students, and 77 points higher than Hispanic students, in reading across the grade levels . . . [Average reading score for all students was 261 . . .] Generally, these gaps increase as students move through school, that is, from grades 3 to 12, and the gap has widened over time. (PACE, 1991, p. 116)

Unfortunately, it is impossible to know to what extent LEP students, as a group, may have benefitted from any of the educational reforms of the past decade because they have essentially been left outside the structure of accountability. A recent study of testing practices with LEP students in California demonstrated that, even in exemplary programs, very few districts or schools tested these students consistently in any language (Gándara and Merino, 1993). If we were to take Hispanic students as a proxy, however, inasmuch as they form the largest percentage of limited English speakers, we would have to conclude that there has been little, if any, positive impact. High school completion rates have remained static and college enrollment has declined for this group over the reform period (ETS, 1990; De La Rosa and Maw, 1990).

The Reform Trade-offs for LEP Students

Inasmuch as LEP students have apparently been left on the sidelines of the educational reform movement, one question has been conspicuously absent from the discourse: Are the reforms, *at least*, benign with respect to their impact on LEP (and other poor and minority) students? In fact, there is evidence that there may be serious educational trade-offs for LEP students in the case of many of the reforms.

The centerpiece of the first wave of educational reforms—increased high school graduation requirements—may have a far-reaching impact on LEP students. There is a relatively common belief that LEP students will "catch up" to rising educational standards as soon as they acquire English proficiency. Yet the data suggest otherwise. A recent study of programs for secondary LEP students demonstrated that those students who entered secondary schools without sufficient English to be mainstreamed were at great risk of being tracked into courses which often did not yield credit for university admittance, and would not even count toward high school graduation (Minicucci and Olsen, 1992).

Similarly, the focus on increasing course requirements for teacher certification and the introduction of new licensing exams weigh heavily on (language) minority candidates (Murnane, Singer, Willett, Kemple & Olsen, 1991). In California, which suffers from tremendous shortages of bilingual teachers, many bilingual teacher candidates, after successfully completing an undergraduate baccalaureate degree and a one-and-a-half-year bilingual teacher preparation program, are unable to pass the state's certification exam (Majetic, 1992). These individuals, with five-and-one-half years of college or university education, are often rerouted into other occupations where they are highly coveted. The schools, on the other hand, are left to fill the increasing need for trained bilingual teachers with English-only teachers who lack the specialized training needed to work with LEP students, but who have passed the certification test.

The new reform initiatives associated with America 2000 are particularly fraught with danger for LEP students. The "choice" initiative, which was central to the Bush administration's reform strategy, has been shown in several demonstrations to provide more "choice" for the most affluent and well-informed sectors of the public education system (Elmore, 1990; Echols, 1992). Given the evidence on choice programs which have been implemented to date, there is little reason to believe that large numbers of excellent private schools would spring up to serve the needs of LEP students whose parents are unable to supplement the basic government education allowance. More likely, these students would be left behind in the financially gutted public schools, along with the other students whose parents were unable to make up the difference between private tuition and government vouchers, or who were unable to transport their children out of the neighborhood, or who were, because of their own educational disadvantage and language difference, uninformed about, and unable to evaluate the options for their children (Elmore, 1990; Smith and O'Day, 1990). Even where "choice" is limited to the public schools, LEP students can be seriously disadvantaged. Dispersion of students from a single language group to schools outside the neighborhood, whether for desegregation or development of magnet and choice schools, can deplete the critical mass of students required to mount an effective language program. On the other hand, LEP students are not likely to meet the criteria for admission to a district's selective magnet programs which may offer better opportunities for the educational advancement of students with limited English skills. "School choice," unless its implications are thought through very carefully, could well prove to be the most educationally devastating for LEP students of all the proposed reform initiatives.

National testing, another major initiative in the America 2000 plan, likewise warrants careful monitoring. In the report of the National Council on Education Standards and Testing (1992), the council outlined the five objectives of national testing, to:

1. exemplify for students, parents, and teachers the kinds and levels of achievement expected;

2. improve classroom instruction and learning outcomes for all students;

3. inform students, parents, and teachers about student progress;

4. measure and hold students, schools, school districts, states, and the Nation accountable for educational performance; and

5. assist education policymakers with programmatic decisions (NCEST, 1992).

No one would argue that these are not noble goals: the issues lie in their implementation. Many experts on student assessment have warned of the potentially negative effects of testing on student performance (Linn and Baker, 1992). Among the concerns raised are the insensitivity of national tests to local curriculum, the potential conflict between state-determined curricula and federally-mandated tests, and the potential for the tests to drive the curriculum in exactly the opposite direction from what reformers have campaigned for: away from teacher-designed curricula that emphasize higher-order thinking skills towards a curriculum that reflects that

which is easily testable. To the extent that such issues are important for English-speaking test-takers, they can only be more
acutely so for LEP students. And, since the Department of Education has not directly addressed these issues with respect to LEP
students, one can only speculate on the possible options which may
await them.

Most obviously, and most consistent with current practice,
LEP students could be left out of the accountability system altogether. Or, they could be recipients of a test that is ill-constructed to
tap their knowledge, or that is modified to provide an inadequate,
and most probably inaccurate, profile of their skills and potential.
The greatest danger would be in the ways national tests might be
applied. If they are used to sort and track students, to provide the
basis for special program admission or exclusion, or if they are used
by school personnel to make judgments about students' intellectual
potential or likelihood for success in other academic endeavors,
then these tests could become tools to further academic inequality.
On the other hand, if students are not included in the testing
process, the outcome can be equally disadvantageous in terms of
equity of access to the full range of options provided by the schools.
In either case, if the specific issues surrounding the construction of
tests and the curriculum to which LEP students are exposed are
not adequately addressed, it is unlikely that nationwide testing will
yield information that would be helpful in setting an agenda for the
education of LEP students.

Missed Opportunities

The failure to address the specific needs of LEP students in any of
the reform agendas or reports has resulted in a number of missed
opportunities. With little guidance at the federal level and considerable misinterpretation of the law at the state level, many state education agencies (SEA's) have specifically prohibited LEP students
from being served by categorical programs which might enhance
their opportunities to more rapidly join the educational mainstream. It is not uncommon to find LEP students in need of special
academic help who are denied access to Chapter One programs, or
who need the services of a special education teacher, but who are
refused such aid because of the mistaken belief that they are ineligibile for multiple programs (CCSSO, 1990). Failure to coordinate
services for LEP students in the schools often results in situations

where the English as a Second Language instructor is the only person available to help struggling LEP students, even though these teachers may have no specific training in working with students with learning problems. Worse yet, a significant number of LEP students—estimated at 25 percent—receive no additional educational services at all; they are simply placed in regular classrooms (CCSSO, 1990).

In spite of the growing consensus that insufficient progress has been made towards narrowing the performance gaps between the advantaged and the disadvantaged in our schools, the national agenda, spurred most recently by the America 2000 initiatives, has shifted the discourse ever further from a focus on specific groups of students. The six national goals, as they have been articulated in the America 2000 strategy, speak to schools *generally,* not any particular kinds of schools, and to students *generally,* as though all students faced the same, or even similar, challenges. Allusions are made in the America 2000 document to the need to close the gap between minority and majority students, but the former administration was careful to avoid any discussion of different responses to different needs. Of course, the reality is that unless attention is paid *specifically* to special needs of LEP students, as well as to others who have been left on the margins of the reform movement, their educational problems will remain intractable to those initiatives.

> Limited English proficient children have a formidable task facing them as they enter school. If they are to succeed in school, they must overcome the obstacles caused by poverty and assignment to low-achieving schools, learn to deal successfully with an institution and individuals from a culture other than their own, master all the subjects taught in the regular school curriculum, and become completely proficient in a second language—English. (La Fontaine, 1988, cited in CCSSO, 1990)

Signs of Hope: A Tentative Agenda for Education Reform for LEP Students

While the "official" stance of the educational establishment has been relative silence on the topic of LEP students and education reform, some researchers, educators, and policymakers have moved forward with their own, albeit fragmented, initiatives.

Bilingual Education

The most obvious "reform" targeted to LEP students is, or would be, bilingual education. However, this initiative is neither a product of this era, nor has it been wholeheartedly endorsed by any of the major education reform reports. In spite of an established body of literature which points to the consistent advantages of using the primary language for academic instruction whenever possible (Valadez, 1989; CCSSO, 1990; Garcia, 1991), the reform movement of the 1980s and now the 1990s has been conspicuously silent on this issue. This is particularly ironic in light of the fact that many of the major education reform reports have commented on the need to strengthen foreign language instruction (Adler, 1982; NCEE, 1983; Boyer, 1983), and even strive for multilingualism (Adler, 1982). Nevertheless, considerable work has been done in the area of curriculum and methodology development for bilingual education in recent years.

Rubio (1987) reports on a "restructured" program model for serving Spanish-speaking LEP students in the Los Angeles area. The development of the model (known as the Eastman model) was supported by the California Department of Education (CDE). It provides for a developmental use of primary language across the core of academic subjects and integration of LEP students with English-only speaking students for non-academic portions of the day in its early phases, gradually shifting the proportion of the day spent in English-only classes, until the students are completely mainstreamed, usually after the fourth grade. It also incorporates a strong ESL instruction component. Because LEP students are grouped for academic instruction in their primary language, the school can take maximum advantage of bilingual teachers, using them where they are most urgently needed, and allow English-only teachers to provide instruction for students who are already fluent English speakers, and for those periods when LEP students are integrated into English-only class settings. The coherent program, that in all respects parallels the English curriculum, has produced test results for these students that are higher than for any school in the surrounding area. The program has been so successful that the district has expanded it into a number of replication sites, and several other school districts have adopted it as well.

Milwaukee, Wisconsin (NCAS, 1991) and Napa, California (Lindholm, 1989) report on two highly successful models of two-way bilingual education. In these schools, LEP students are integrated with English-only speakers throughout the day and for all subject matter. The goal is for all students to become bilingual and biliterate. Instruction is language-rich and the curriculum is structured thematically so that all the basic content areas (mathematics, science, language arts, and social studies) are woven into a single theme. In this way, academic content and language development are mutually supported. Such schools not only produce impressive test scores, but they reinforce the notion that bilingual instruction can be an additive process and that bilingual education can be a form of enrichment rather than remediation.

Bilingual Education Handbook: Designing Instruction for LEP Students (CDE, 1990) is a break-through document that demonstrates how educators can combine instruction for LEP students with the core academic curriculum developed for all students. The handbook weaves the objectives of the highly touted (Smith and O'Day, 1990) California curriculum frameworks in mathematics, science, social science-history, language arts, and visual and performing arts into a bilingual program—indicating how the two may mesh into a single, coherent curriculum for LEP students. This is a key example of the way in which educational reform for all students can be adapted to the special needs of the LEP school population.

Curriculum Reform

While bilingual education, which incorporates the primary language of the student into content instruction, is a generally preferred mode of instruction whenever possible, it alone is not the solution to the continuing educational disadvantage of LEP students. Bilingual education is essentially a methodology, a way of delivering instruction; it does not necessarily treat the issue of the content of instruction that is delivered. However, some recent innovative studies suggest the viability of potentially powerful modifications in curriculum for LEP and other educationally disadvantaged students.

DeAvila (1984) has developed an integrated program of science/mathematics education that focuses heavily on engaging students in their own learning through highly motivational activities which also emphasize the development of language. *Finding Out / Descubrimiento (FOD)* is a bilingual program for Spanish speakers that allows the students to become actively involved in a higher-order thinking skills curriculum while they are acquiring their second language. Unlike more traditional approaches, it neither defers more sophisticated learning until the student is fluent in English, nor does it focus on the acquisition of English language skills to the exclusion of other content areas. DeAvila contends that students learn English (or any language) best through the practice and manipulation of language in content-rich learning environments. And science and mathematics, according to DeAvila, are the most authentically motivating of the content areas—all children have questions that can be answered, and which they can learn to answer for themselves, through science and mathematics experiments. The apparently paradoxical aspect of the program, as reported by DeAvila, is the very large gains in English language scores demonstrated by the students even though the ostensible focus of the program is not on language. He maintains that this is further evidence of the ready transferability of concepts between languages, such that material learned in any language automatically transfers to the student's other languages.

In a similar vein, Henry Levin (1991) has developed, and implemented in more than 50 schools, a program of *Accelerated Learning* for educationally disadvantaged and LEP students. Levin contends that remedial educational strategies for students who are functioning below average will never achieve the result of bringing them up to the level of their on-grade peers. Remediation only increases the performance gap between educationally disadvantaged and other students by watering down the curriculum and slowing the pace of instruction. What is needed, he believes, is acceleration—gifted education for the educationally disadvantaged. Levin's schools incorporate a variety of enrichment-oriented methodologies for teaching students, focusing on whole-community efforts to build a total learning environment for students and making more effective use of time. In a controlled study of one of the project schools that serves a high percentage of LEP students, the school has progressed from one of the lowest scoring schools in the district to being the highest (Levin, 1992).

Another attempt at modifying the curriculum for "at risk" students, and one which has specifically addressed the needs of LEP students, is the *Success for All* program (Slavin, Leighton, Yampolsky, 1990). The program has been used with Asian-American LEP students attending a school where resources for bilingual education were not available. Hence, the focus of instruction was the acquisition of English reading skills.

Success for All emphasizes increased resources at the early school years with a particular focus on reading instruction. Slavin et al. contend that acquisition of good reading skills in the early grades is key to bringing "at risk" students into the educational mainstream. The program attempts to increase the opportunities for one-on-one instruction through tutoring and through grouping strategies that allow teachers to focus on smaller units of children than the whole class.

An evaluation of the effects of the program was inconclusive because of the limitations of the data—a chronic problem in evaluation of LEP programs (Gándara and Merino, 1993). However, by second grade, the program's students appeared to be outperforming their control group by a fair margin. While the authors cite the advantages of a bilingual approach to instruction with LEP students, they acknowledge the reality that circumstances do not always allow for such an approach, and other strategies must be developed for meeting the needs of students with limited English. *The Success for All* program may represent one of these viable alternatives.

The programs cited here are illustrative only of the kinds of approaches being used to adapt—and enrich—curriculum for LEP students. These programs are mentioned because they have received considerable attention in the literature and they have been replicated in sites around the country.

Teacher Preparation

While considerable emphasis was placed on the need to strengthen teacher preparation and certification in the reform literature of the past decade, virtually no attention has been paid to the need to prepare teachers for teaching linguistically different students. Some reports called attention to the need to recruit more minority teachers (Carnegie Forum, 1986), but none focused on the need to develop specialized skills for working with LEP students. Not surprisingly, California, with nearly one million LEP students, has gone beyond the reform reports to take the lead in developing new programs and certification criteria for teachers who will teach LEP pupils.

In November 1989 the California Commission on Teacher Credentialing took the interim step of requiring that all teachers certified to teach in the state would have to meet competencies in multicultural education and the knowledge of the processes of second language acquisition (CTC, 1989). Since that time the Commission has continued to develop a new credentialing structure for teachers of LEP students. Effective in 1992, in order to qualify for a credential as a cross-cultural, language and academic development (CLAD) teacher the following competencies must be met:

1. Knowledge about the nature, structure, use and acquisition of first and second language, including the theories and factors in language and literacy acquisition.

2. Bilingual and ESL models and methodologies . . .

3. Knowledge of culture, learning styles, and cross-cultural communication . . .

To further qualify as a bilingual CLAD teacher, all the above competencies must be met in addition to knowledge of the following:

4. Bilingual methodology for content and literacy instruction including the language of emphasis . . . selection, adaptation, and use of primary language materials.

5. Culture specific knowledge, including culture of the home country(ies), culture of emphasis in the United States . . . and . . . (its) contributions . . . to the United States and global society.

6. Demonstrated ability to use the language of emphasis, including speaking, listening, reading and writing proficiencies (CTC, 1992).

Because nearly one of every three students entering kindergarten in California is an LEP student, it is unlikely that many teachers in California will find themselves teaching in a classroom that does not have LEP students. Hence, the Commission anticipates that the majority of California teachers will seek one of the CLAD credentials. It is virtually certain that school districts will place a premium on hiring teachers with these credentials since almost all of the state's school districts are being challenged by the need to provide educational services to LEP students. Other states which are heavily impacted by LEP students are reportedly studying the California plan.

School Climate Reforms

There is some literature on schools that appear to have been particularly effective with LEP students (Carter and Chatfield, 1986; Steffens, 1988; Gándara, 1989; NCAS, 1991; McLaughlin, Minicucci, Nelson, and Parrish, 1992). These reports tend to be largely descriptive of practices that foster a high level of student achievement in LEP students and can be clustered under the category of studies of school climate. While the schools they describe differ considerably in detail, all of the studies point to certain common features of schools with good climates for learning for LEP students. All such schools have comprehensive programs designed to meet both the language acquisition and academic needs of the LEP students. All have high levels of parent and community involvement, though each may envision different kinds of roles for these groups. All purport to hold high expectations for LEP students and to maintain high academic standards. In all of these schools, the leadership of a strong principal who has the capacity to unite faculty in a common vision for the school is noted. Importantly, while many of the features of these schools are the same as those found in effective schools for non-LEP students, the schools have adapted these aspects of their program to meet the specific challenges of a non-English speaking community. Hence, while the school may hold high standards for its students, it also makes allowances for students to meet those standards in more than one language, and while the faculty and principal may have a shared vision for the school, that vision is also shaped by the particular concerns of the community in which the school resides.

Technology and LEP Students

Educators interested in the application of technology to issues of school reform have been slow to realize the potential of this effort for LEP students. The massive literature on educational technology yields few examples of innovative approaches in this area. However, DeVillar and Faltis (1991) review several studies on the use of computers with implications for LEP students. It is clear from a number of studies cited in DeVillar and Faltis that computers can be important allies in the development of English language skills for LEP students. Planned interaction around a computer, in cooperative learning settings, appears to stimulate the natural use and development of language among students with varying levels of English proficiency. Hence, computers can be an important catalyst for English language learning.

　　Perhaps more significant, though, are the ways in which computers—and other technology—can be used as a primary vehicle of instruction themselves. The Orillas project (Cummins and Sayers, 1990) provides the opportunity for Spanish-speaking LEP students to increase proficiency in both English and Spanish, improve academic achievement, and enhance self-esteem through an interactive program that allows students to communicate with others in Spanish-speaking countries. The students compose their own informational articles in both languages and share these with readers in the United States and abroad. They also critique and respond to the work of others. In this context, computers are seen as vehicles for students to use and develop language arts competencies in a naturally motivating environment.

The potential for computers, video, and other distance learning technologies to allow LEP students to access the core curriculum even where there are shortages of bilingual teachers, and where enriched and specialized curricula may not be available in the primary language of the student, is just beginning to be realized. In April of 1992 the California Planning Commission for Educational Technology presented to the Legislature a Master Plan for Educational Technology (CPCET, 1992) which includes the following elements:

> A Golden State Education Network [consisting of]...a statewide integrated voice, video, and data link...using the resources...to address the needs of all learners who are not proficient in the use of English. This plan will describe a strategy and an infrastructure to support the delivery of learning resources and services to learners who have limited English proficiency...[to] be fully implemented by August 1994. (p. 12)

Conclusions

The thrust of the education reform movement of the past decade has been to increase U.S. competitiveness in the global marketplace and to restore the nation's role as the preeminent world economic power. To this end, reform has focused on a theme of excellence through increased standards for both students and teachers. Issues of equity and access have not only been omitted from the reform agenda, they have been consciously eschewed at the national level as indicative of the kind of policy-making activity that led to the "rising tide of mediocrity" which some claimed threatened to engulf our entire educational system.

In this climate, the needs of LEP students were largely ignored by the plethora of reports pointing the way to a reformed system that would salvage our position in the world economy. Nonetheless, disappointing results from the extensive reform efforts, and demographic shifts in the composition of the school-age population, have forced schools to come to terms with those students who were left on the margins of the movement. Cities such as Los Angeles, New York, Chicago, Houston, and San Francisco which have traditionally been home to large language minority communities have also been greatly affected by an immigration wave that ranks as the largest in this century. In some schools and districts in these communities, the majority of students are language minorities (NCAS, 1988).

In the absence of any guidance at the national level, and at the impetus of school personnel who have sometimes felt overwhelmed by the task of educating diverse groups of LEP students, these schools, districts, and their SEA's have pioneered new practices for educating language minority students. Some of those programs and practices have been highlighted above. Though the initiatives are fragmented—not coordinated by any oversight agency or stimulated by any nation-wide movement—they represent the seeds of a reform effort of enormous potential. All of these programs and practices have been designed to respond to real needs—of students, teachers, and communities. They are "bottom-up" reforms that continue to be implemented in schools and classrooms by virtue of the fact that they work in the settings in which they have been developed. They are the product of the thinking and collaboration of practitioners, school-based researchers and, in some cases, those state agencies which are directly responsible for providing materials and personnel to serve the schools. These are all the elements of reforms that have historically worked and remained in place after the rhetoric of the movement has faded (Elmore and McLaughlin, 1988; Tyack, 1991).

Reform in the education of LEP students has had a slow start and remains without any national focus. However, it has grown roots in those states and local communities that are most impacted by the dramatic growth in the LEP population. As American schools continue to diversify, the nation can no longer ignore the enormous unmet needs of LEP students, nor can it ignore the innovative responses being developed locally to meet those needs, not as a part of the reform movement, but in spite of it.

REFERENCES

Adlor, M. J. (1982). *The Paideia proposal: An educational manifesto*. New York: Macmillan Publishing Company, Inc.

Alliance for Achievement. (1989). *Community schools*. Chicago, IL: Alliance for Achievement.

Baratz-Snowden, J., & Duran, R. A. (1987). *The educational progress of language minority students*. Princeton, NJ: National Assessment of Educational Progress (NAEP).

Berman Weiler Associates. (1988). *Restructuring California education: A design for public education in the twenty-first century. Recommendations to the California Business Roundtable*. (R/112–2). Berman, Weiler Associates.

Bizjak, T. (1992). English foreign for one-third of State. *Sacramento Bee*, May 12.

Blinde, P., Steinberg, L., & Chan, K. (1982). *Dropping out among language minority youth: A review of the literature*. Los Alamitos, CA: National Center for Bilingual Research.

Bliss, B. (1986). Literacy and the limited English population: A national perspective. In C. Simich-Dudgeon (Ed.), *Proceedings of the symposium held at Trinity College, June 6–7* (pp. 17–24). Washington, DC.

Boyer, E. L. (1983). *High school: A report on secondary education in America*. New York: Harper and Row Publishers.

Bridgman, A. (1985). A changing course. *Education Week, 4* (20): 12–29.

California Department of Education (CDE). (1990). *Bilingual education handbook: Designing instruction for LEP students*. Sacramento, CA: CDE, Office of Bilingual Education.

California Department of Education (CDE). (1992). *Language census*. Sacramento, CA: CDE.

California Planning Commission for Educational Technology (CPCET). (1992). *California's master plan for educational technology*. Sacramento, CA: CPCET.

Canales, J. (1989). Assessment of language proficiency: Informing policy and practice. *Focus*. San Antonio, TX: Southwest Educational Developmental Laboratory.

Carnegie Forum on Education and the Economy Task Force on Teaching as a Profession. (1986). *A nation prepared: Teachers for the 21st century* . New York: The Carnegie Forum.

Carter, T., & Chatfield, M. (1986). Effective bilingual schools: Implications for policy and practice. *American Journal of Education, 95*, 200–232.

Commission on Teacher Credentialing (CTC). (1989). *Standards of program quality and effectiveness for the multiple and single subject teacher education programs*. Sacramento, CA: CTC.

Commission on Teacher Credentialing (CTC). (1992). *Overview of the design for the preparation and credentialing of teachers for limited-English-proficient students*. Sacramento, CA: CTC.

Committee for Economic Development (CED). Research and Policy Committee. (1985). *Investing in our children: Business and the public schools*. The Research and Policy Committee of the Committee for Economic Development.

Council of Chief State School Officers (CCSSO). (1990). *School success for limited English proficient students. The challenge and state response*. Washington, DC: CCSSO.

Cummins, J., & Sayers, D. (1990). Education 2001: Learning networks and educational reform. In C. J. Faltis & R. A. Devillar (Eds.), *Language minority students and computers*. Binghamton, NY: Haworth Press.

Darling-Hammond, L., Berry, B. (1988). *Evolution of teacher policy*. Santa Monica, CA: The Rand Corporation.

De Avila, E. (1984). Science and math: A natural context for language development. In *delivering academic excellence to culturally diverse populations*. Conference Proceedings, December 7–8, Fairleigh Dickinson University, Saddle Brook, NJ, 19–35.

De LaRosa, D., & Maw, C. (1990). *Hispanic education, a statistical portrait*. Washington, DC: National Council of La Raza (NCLR).

DeVillar, R. A., & Faltis, C. J. (1991). *Computers and cultural diversity: Restructuring for school success*. Albany: State University of New York Press.

Dougherty, V. (1986). *Funding state education reforms*. Denver, Colorado: Education Commission of the States.

Echols, F. (1992). *Parent choice and education equity in Scotland*. Paper presented at the Sociology of Education Conference. Asilomar, CA, February 22.

Education Commission of the States. (1983). *Action for excellence: A comprehensive plan to improve our nation's schools from the Task Force on Education for Economic Growth*. The Commission.

Educational Testing Service (ETS). (1990). *The education reform decade*. Princeton, NJ: ETS.

Educational Testing Service (ETS). (1991). *The state of inequality*. Princeton, NJ: ETS.

Elmore, R. (1990). Choice as an instrument of public policy. In W. Clune & J. Witte (Eds.), *Choice and Control in American education, vol. I*. New York: The Falmer Press, 285–317.

Elmore, R., & McLaughlin, M. (1988). *Steady work: Policy, practice, and the reform of American education*. Santa Monica, CA: The Rand Corporation.

Firestone, W., Fuhrman, S., & Kirst, M. (1991). State educational reform since 1983: Appraisal and the future. *Educational Policy, 5,* 233–250.

Fuhrman, S., Clune, W. H., & Elmore, R. F. (1988). Research on education reform: Lessons on the implementation of policy. *Teachers College Record, 90* (2): 237–257.

Galvan, J. (1987). Promising practices: Integrated content language approach. In *Making schools work for underachieving minority students: Next steps for research, policy and practice. Proceedings of the Conference*. Washington, DC: U.S. Department of Education, OERI, 129–132.

Gándara, P. (1989). Those children are ours: Moving towards community. *Equity and Choice, 5,* 5–12.

Gándara, P., & Merino, B. (1993). Measuring the outcomes of LEP programs: Test scores, exit rates and other mythological data. *Educational Evaluation and Policy Analysis, 15,* 320–338.

Garcia, G. (1991). Bilingualism: Second language acquisition and the education of Chicano language minority youth. In R. Valencia (Ed.), *Chicano school failure and success*. Bristol, PA: Falmer Press, 93–118.

Goodlad, J. I. (1984). *A place called school: Prospects for the future*. New York: McGraw-Hill Book Company.

Holmes Group. (1986). *Tomorrow's teachers*. East Lansing Michigan: The Holmes Group.

Kozol, J. (1991). *Savage inequalities: Children in American schools*. New York: Crown Publishers.

Krashen, S. (1986). Bilingual education is good for English. *California School Boards Journal, 44*, 6–9.

Levin, H. (1992). *Accelerated schools: A restructuring option.* Paper presented at the Sociology of Education Conference. Asilomar, CA, February 22.

Levin, H., & Hopfenberg, W. N. (1991). Accelerated schools for at-risk students. *Principal, 70*, 11–13.

Lindholm, K. (1989). *The Washington Elementary School bilingual immersion program: Student progress after three years of implementation.* San Jose, CA: California State University, San Jose.

Linn, R., & Baker, E. (Winter 1992). *Testing as a reform, true?* The CRESST Line, Newsletter of the National Center for Research on Evaluation, Standards and Student Testing. University of California, Los Angeles.

Majetic, R. (1989). *California Basic Educational Skills Test: Annual report.* Sacramento, CA: CTC.

McLaughlin, B., Minicucci, C., Nelson, B., & Parrish, T. (1992). *Meeting the challenge of diversity. Volume III.* Berkeley, CA: BW Associates.

Miller, J. (1992). Standards and aid bill seen as top Clinton priorities, *Education Week, 13* (1): 17–18.

Minicucci, C., & Olsen, L. (1992). *Meeting the challenge of language diversity. Volume V. An exploratory study of secondary LEP programs.* Berkeley, CA: BW Associates.

Murnane, R., Singer, J., Willett, J., Kemple, J., & Olsen, R. (1991). *Who will teach?* Cambridge, MA: Harvard University Press.

National Center for Education Statistics (NCES). (1991). *Digest of education statistics.* Washington, DC: U.S. Department of Education.

National Center for Education Statistics (NCES). (1992). *American education at a glance.* Washington, DC: U.S. Department of Education.

National Coalition of Advocates for Students (NCAS). (1988). *New voices. Immigrant students in the U.S. public schools.* Boston: NCAS

National Coalition of Advocates for Students (NCAS). (1991). *The good common school.* Boston: NCAS.

National Commission on Excellence in Education. (1983). *A nation at risk: The imperative for educational reform.* Washington, DC: U.S. Government Printing Office.

National Council on Education Standards and Testing (NCEST). (1992). *Raising standards for American education*. Washington, DC: NCEST.

National Education Goals Panel (1991). *The national education goals report: Building a nation of learners*. Washington, DC: Author.

National Governors' Association, Center for Policy Research and Analysis. (1986). *Time for results: The governors' 1991 report on education*. National Governors' Association, Center for Policy Research and Analysis.

National Science Board Commission on Precollege Education in Math, Science and Technology. (1983). *Educating Americans for the twenty-first century: A plan of action for improving mathematics, science and technology education for all American elementary and secondary students so that their achievement is the best in the world by 1995*. National Science Foundation. National Science Board Commission on Precollege Education in Mathematics, Science, and Technology.

Olsen, L. (1988). *Crossing the schoolhouse border*. San Francisco: California Tomorrow.

Olsen, L., & Dowell, C. (1988). *BRIDGES: Promising programs for the education of immigrant children*. California Tomorrow.

Phillips, K. (1990). *Politics of rich and poor*. New York: Random House.

Policy Analysis for California Education (PACE). (1991). *The condition of education 1990*. Berkeley, CA: PACE.

Rubio, B. (1987). Promising practices: The Eastman success story for helping limited English proficient students succeed. *Proceedings of the conference*. Washington, DC: U.S. Department of Education, OERI, 133–137.

Rumberger, R. (1985). The shortage of mathematics and science teachers, a review of the evidence. *Educational Evaluation and Policy Analysis. 7*, 355–369.

Sarason, S. (1991). *The predictable failure of educational reform*. San Francisco, CA: Jossey-Bass.

Sizer, T. R. (1984). *Horace's compromise: The dilemma of the American high school*. Boston, MA: Houghton-Mifflin.

Slavin, R. E., Leighton, M., & Yampolsky, R. (1990). *Success for all: Effects on the achievement of limited English proficient children* (Report No. 5). Baltimore, MD: Center For Research on Effective Schooling for Disadvantaged Students: The Johns Hopkins University, ED 331 585.

Slavin, R. E., Madden, N. A., Karweit, N. L., Livermon, B. J., & Dolan, L. (1990). Success for all: First-year outcomes of a comprehensive plan for reforming urban education. *American Educational Research Journal, 27* (2): 255–278.

Smith, M., & O'Day, J. (1990). Systemic school reform. *Politics of Education Association Yearbook*, 233–267.

Stedman, J. B. Congressional Research Service. Personal Communication, May 1, 1992.

Stedman, J., & Jordan, K. F. A. (1986). *Education reform reports: Content and impact* (Report No. 86–56 EPW). Washington, DC: The Library of Congress, Congressional Research Service.

Stedman, J. B., & Riddle, W. (1992). *National education goals: Federal policy issues* (Report No. IB92012). Congressional Research Service: The Library of Congress.

Steffens, H. (1988). Turning a school around. *NEA Today, February*, 4–5.

Twentieth Century Fund Task Force on Federal Elementary and Secondary Education Policy. (1983). *Making the grade*. Twentieth Century Fund.

Tyack, D. (1991). Public school reform: Policy talk and institutional practice. *American Journal of Education, 100* (1): 1–19.

U.S. Department of Education (1991). *America 2000. An education strategy*. Washington, DC: U.S. Department of Education.

U.S. Department of Education (1992). *The condition of bilingual education in the United States*. Washington, DC: Office of Bilingual Education and Minority Language Affairs of USED.

Valadez, C. M. (1989). Language-minority students and educational reform: An incomplete agenda. In S. Cohen & L. Solmon (Eds.), *From the campus: Perspectives on the school reform movement*. New York: Praeger.

✧ Chapter 3

The Role of Discourse in Learning, Schooling, and Reform[1]

Hugh Mehan

Language has power. Discourse plays a vital role in learning, schooling and reform because the language we use in the classroom and the way we talk about education in everyday life makes a difference in the way we think and the way we act about education. This sentiment is captured by Tom Stoppard in his play, *The Reality*:

> If you can get the right words in the right order, you can nudge the world a little.

Stoppard is saying that words have constitutive power: they make meaning of things. And when we make meaning, the world is changed as a consequence. This power is subtle. It does not hit like a hammer or fist. It is "mysteriously ambiguous," as Vaclav Havel, the leader of the "velvet revolution" in Czechoslovakia, has so elegantly stated.

Havel, when awarded the *Friedenpreis des Deutschen Buchandels* (the Peace Prize of the German Booksellers) in 1989, reflected on the mysterious link between words and peace. Words have the power to change history, he said, reciting a litany of examples in which dissident writers in Czechoslovakia were imprisoned for raising questions about the oppressive regime under which they lived. Those speeches, those *samizdat* texts and recordings of nonconformist singers and bands rocked the system. So too, have the liberating words of Walesa, the alarm-raising words of Sakharov and Rushdie.

But the words of a Khomeini, a Stalin, a Hitler also have power: they have mesmerized and electrified, reminding us that words can have a diabolic as well as a liberating power. Havel went on to say that the young dissidents in his country—members of Charter 77 and the Independent Peace Association—rehabilitated the meaning of the word 'peace.' Under the communist regime, it had meant ever mightier armies arrayed to keep the people down. But the actions of dissidents not only "saved a word," they saved something far more important, the realization that:

> All important events in the real world—whether admirable or monstrous—are always spearheaded in the realm of words.

Havel's reflections on the mysterious power of words in human history orient this chapter. The settings of this chapter may seem much more mundane than Havel's: classrooms and schools, not prisons and parliaments. But upon reflection, I think we will find that the words we use when we talk about education and teach our students are every bit as powerful as the words political leaders use to energize political action.

In the next three sections, I discuss the power of language in classroom instruction, in schools, and in educational reform. In the fourth and final section, I address the power of language in research on education.

The Power of Language in Instructional Discourse

The language teachers use with students is constitutive. The way in which teachers ask questions and engage in discourse with students both constrains and enables the ways in which they can display what they know. Because of the co-occurrence relationships which operate in conversation, what students can say in lessons depends on the frames established by what teachers say and the questions they ask.

Here is an all too familiar example of that constraint:[2]

23. Teacher: Make a red flower under the tree. Make a red flower under the tree. Ok. Let's look at the red flower. Can you tell me where the red flower//

24. All: = right here, right here//

25. Teacher: = is, Dora?

26. Dora: Under the tree

27. Teacher: Tell me in a sentence

28. Dora: It's under the tree

29. Teacher: What's under the tree? Dora? Tell me, the flower . . .

30. Dora: The flower, the flower is under the tree

31. Teacher: Where is the red flower Richard?

32. Richard: Under the tree

33. Teacher: Can you tell me in a sentence?

34. Richard: The flower is under the tree

35. Teacher: Cyndy, where is the red flower?

36. Cyndy: The flower is under//

37. Richard: = Hey, that's not red//

38. Cyndy: = the tree

Let me set the scene: This snippet of teacher-student discourse is extracted from a lesson in a first grade classroom. The teacher told me that she wanted to teach the children about locatives—prepositional phrases which express relative location. In the moments before this excerpt, the teacher had asked the children to draw a number of objects on the paper before them: trees, grass, flowers. Now she was asking them to report on the results of their drawing activity.

Although this segment is brief, it contains the main ingredients of the 'recitation script' (Tharp & Gallimore, 1989) which is so prevalent in classroom lessons (Mehan, 1979). First is their sequential structure. While everyday conversations seem to be organized into two-part sequences (Sacks et al., 1974), classroom lessons are organized into three-part sequences; a teacher's initial query induces a student's reply, which in turn evokes a teacher's evaluation. This three-part structure seems to be the function of the kinds of questions teachers ask. Teachers' questions often test students' knowledge rather than elicit new information. These "known information questions" are responsible for the presence of the evaluation act in the third slot in the syntax of classroom lessons.

This lesson fragment displays another feature common in lessons which conform to the lesson script: the search for correct answers. Because there is often a single correct response to known information questions, and the teacher knows this answer before initiating questioning, bizarre sequences of interaction can develop wherein students present trial responses seeking validation for the correct answer.

Unbeknownst to the students, the teacher wanted them to report on the results of their drawing in a complete sentence, i.e., "The red flower is under the tree." The first time she asked the question "Can you tell me where the flower is?" (see line #23 above), the students responded in unison with an answer that described quite adequately the location of the flowers on their pages: ("right here"). The teacher wanted complete sentences, however, and so continued questioning Dora, who provided a more elaborate answer, "under the tree." That answer, too, functions to communicate the location of the flower. But since her answer was not in a complete sentence, the teacher continued questioning her:

27. Teacher: Tell me in a sentence

28. Dora: It's under the tree

At this point, Dora has answered the teacher's question. But since she provided a pronoun instead of a noun in the subject position, the teacher continued to question her. In doing so, she reduced the cognitive complexity of her question to the lowest level; Dora is only to fill in the blank in the teacher's question. The teacher, by inviting Dora to complete her sentence, supplied her with the answer she had been seeking all along. In effect, the teacher ventriloquized the desired answer to her question through Dora.

The tempo of the lesson picked up at this point. Richard was asked the same question (line #31), and one more question-answer exchange was sufficient to induce Richard to produce the appropriate information in the correct form. The teacher then turned to Cyndy, who provided the answer that the teacher had been looking for in her first response (see line #36). Although Cyndy provided the correct form of the answer the teacher wanted, Richard pointed out that it did not accurately reflect what she had drawn. Cyndy had, in fact, used a crayon of a different color. Perhaps prompted by the cues provided in the students' answers, and the structure of the preceding sequences, Cyndy was able to provide an answer with the desired form, but without the appropriate content.

As a result of this teacher's search for the one correct answer to her question, a bizarre sequence ensued. In recitation scripts, with their known information questions and concern for the one correct answer, students can be trapped into anticipating teacher's questions rather than participating in genuine thinking and reasoning.

Teachers may, of course, frame lessons in another way. Here is a contrasting example:

> **26. Teacher:** . . . The problem I'm going to have you work on with your partner is to figure out how many red rods it would take to stretch across the table, how many white rods it would take to stretch across the table, and how many blue rods it would take to stretch across the table. I'm going to ask you to do this, not by measuring, but by using what we now know about how many light green rods and how many dark green rods it takes. With you and your partner I'd like you to record on one piece of paper, so I'd like an answer from you that is an estimate of how many blue, red and white rods it takes. And for each estimate that you come up with, I'd like an explanation that tells how you figured out that that estimate makes sense.

Before I present more transcript from this lesson, let me explain this situation. This teacher is teaching ratio and proportion. She does so, not by direct instruction, but by eliciting different ways of making estimations which the students generate from their work with Cuisenaire rods. After this introduction, the students are sent off to work in small groups. When they reassemble, she explains the purpose of the lesson and its rationale:

> **27. Teacher:** So, what I'm interested in hearing now is how you figured out how many blue, red and white rods it took to stretch across the table. And I'm also interested in hear-

ing how many different ways there were to think about that. So, Craig, how many blue rods does it take to stretch across the table and how did you figure that?

28. Craig: 6 and 2/3.

29. Teacher: And how did you figure that out?

30. Craig: Because, um that there is three light greens that fit into the blue and then you go '3 3 greens times 6' that would be 18 and that won't be a full rod so you take off 2 so you put 2 down and take out one green, that would be 2/3, that would be 6 2/3.

31. Teacher: And Nathan, how many blue rods do you think stretch across the table?

32. Nathan: About 6.

33. Teacher: And explain to me how you got that answer.

34. Nathan: We took the blues and then took the light greens and compared how many would stretch across and worked our way down and we got up to 20 green and we just stuck these on top to see how many of these would fit on 20 green.

35. Teacher: Kim, how many blue rods do you think it takes to stretch across the table, and how did you figure that out?

36. Kim: 6 and 3/4. We just like laid 'em out and then laid about half on the table lengthwise and if we didn't have enough we just like used some bigger one and like added them together.

37. Teacher: So when I ask this question, I wind up getting 3 different answers. I get 6 and 2/3 from Craig and I get 6 and 3/4 from Kim and I get 6 from Nathan, and so it shows me that there still are some differences of opinion but everybody is quite close with that. And now what I need to hear as a teacher is what you thought about the other rods. That will give me more information about your understanding and help me decide what sorts of questions to ask you next. So, Melissa, tell the class about how many red rods you and Eva figure would stretch across the table and explain how you got that.

38. Melissa: We figured about 30 red rods would stretch across the table because dark green rods go across the table 10 times and it takes 3 red rods to make one dark green rod, so you multiply 3 times 10 and we got about 30.

39. Teacher: Someone else have another way of explaining that. Jorge?

40. Jorge: We got 30 and since 3 reds fit into two greens, we divided the green by 2 then times them by 3

This lesson segment has a different sequential structure than the "orientation lesson" discussed above: the teacher asks questions, students reply, but the teacher evaluation which is so ubiquitous in the recitation script is absent. In its place is a further question (see lines 27, 28, 29), and it is a different type of question. It asks for explanations, not just the facts of the matter (as in line #35). It assumes that there is more than one answer to the question, and encourages that divergence (as in #39).

The teacher's treatment of students' answers is also interesting. Not all of the students' answers are elegant; they are hardly masterpieces of the mathematical register, yet she encourages the students' pursuits and does not sanction their bumbling.[3] In fact, this teacher's interest seems to be in generating variety; at the end of the lesson, the teacher does not demand that the students find one correct way to make estimations. She validates the many different ways of making estimations which the students generate:

53. Teacher: I've been teaching math for many years and I've spent a lot of time trying to explain things to students and knowing they don't understand. The important thing is to be able to figure it out for yourself. I believe Yvette knows what she did, and she understands what the process is that she and Elissa did. What's most important is that each one of you can figure out a process that makes sense to you.

As I close this section, let me underline this point: I am not stating that one lesson format is necessarily better than another, that 'collaboration scripts' should replace 'recitation scripts.' Lectures have their place in academic discourse, as do drill and practice (we need only watch musicians or athletes repeat their actions over and over again in their practice sessions to understand the importance of properly contextualized drill and practice). Getting children to recall information is important, as is getting them to provide explanations. My point is not an advocatory one, it is a constitutive one: the structure of questioning influences the structuring of answering.

A more general point follows: If instructional discourse is constitutive in that it constrains and enables the ways in which students can talk and, hence, reveal what they know, then what the teacher says makes a difference in the classroom. The way in which the teacher organizes a lesson (as whole group, as small group), the task (one at a time, many simultaneously) and allocates turns (in groups, by naming individuals) influences the possibilities of learning.

This means that teachers can not take the features of classroom instruction for granted. They need to reflect on them and be aware of the consequences of one form of organization vs another. The "reflective practitioner" idea, in turn, is part of a larger issue: the goals of education, and the teacher's role in that construction. As Courtney Cazden has said many times (e.g., 1988) the recitation script is the "default condition" of classroom instruction. It is what will always appear unless teachers make a concerted effort to change the parameters of instruction. If the recitation script will appear by default, then teachers have to examine their teaching practices critically, and insure that their discourse facilitates the kinds of goals they want to achieve.

The discourse of the classroom is connected to the organization of society. Are the ways in which teachers talk to students and organize their classrooms related to the kinds of students our educational system produces? Is it possible that students taught to respond passively, conform to externally imposed rules, and obey external authority in classrooms, will become passive participants in democratic institutions and the workplace? By the same token, is it possible that students who are taught to participate actively in their learning will be guided by internalized authority and become active participants in society?

The Power of Language in Schooling

History is a story we tell which captures what we like to believe about ourselves. One important ingredient in our historical script is the theory of success and failure. The conventional wisdom about success and failure in the United States is a personal, individualistic one. It says that a person's place in life is a function of the hard work and effort that person invests. This 'achievement ideology' is evident in the conventional wisdom about school success/failure in the United States. The student is responsible for what he or she achieves or doesn't achieve: if a student is successful in school and in life after school, it is because of individual effort; if a student fails, it is because he or she didn't work hard enough.

Achievement ideology is encapsulated in the idea of progress towards a more meritocratic education system and society. It is true that in our nation's past, decisions about people, their access to schools, public facilities, and jobs were based on ascribed characteristics—socioeconomic status, gender, race, ethnicity. But now things are getting better. More and more, it is what you do—your actions—not what you are—your characteristics—that matter. Civil rights legislation in the areas of education and housing, as well as gains in the occupational achievement of women and minorities, are cited as evidence to support this shift from ascription to achievement.

Achievement ideology and progressive ideology are optimistic. They celebrate the power of human action (agency) over structural limitations. Nurture defeats nature in this script. People may be born into oppressive conditions: poor families, or members of oppressed groups (women, minorities), but by manipulating their social conditions, they can overcome the constraints initially imposed upon them.

The individualistic representation of success and failure has been opposed by a discourse which emphasized collective actions. The civil rights movement changed the dynamic of educational theory, policy and practice, because it changed the agent of action—the actor—from the individual to groups. In *Brown vs. Board of Education*, for instance, the courts decided that segregation was wrong because an entire collective, Blacks, had been wronged. The effects of a separate but equal educational policy on a single student or family was not at issue; the effects of segregation on an entire race was at issue. Affirmative action, too, shifts the basis of agency away from individuals and toward collectives. The argument used to justify affirmative action is that "women," "minorities" as groups, not Bill Smith or Mary Jones, have been victims of discrimination.

The Baake case and recent decisions by the Rehnquist Court argue against the collective move, and attempt to return issues of discrimination to individual cases. In the firemen's case, the Supreme Court said that discrimination could not be assumed just because groups of people were underrepresented in a particular occupation or profession. Discrimination would have to be proved in an individual case against the company. This line of legal thinking marks a significant shift away from collective agents and a return to individual agents.

This tension between individual and collective agency is also apparent in discussions about the reasons for the educational difficulties of linguistic and ethnic minority youth. John Ogbu (1978, 1982, 1987), in his provocative thinking about differential school performance, distinguishes the responses that different kinds of immigrant groups make to the undisputed fact of discrimination. He notes that minorities such as Jews and the Amish adopt a strategy which keeps them outside the structures of discrimination, while voluntary immigrant groups such as the Japanese and the Chinese have adopted strategies which buy into the achievement ideology. By contrast, involuntary immigrant groups such as Hispanics, African Americans and Native Americans, Ogbu notes, have adopted a collectivist strategy. They invoke collective civil rights, rail against systems of oppression, and demand that the government instigate and enforce policies to rectify past wrongs. And because Blacks and Hispanics are not successful in school, Ogbu says their reliance on a 'collective' discourse strategy has been unproductive.

Linda Chavez (1990), in a recent essay on the education and occupational achievement of Hispanics, makes a similar argument. She says that the move by Hispanic political leaders in the late 1960s to attach Hispanics' fate to the civil rights movement led by Blacks was a mistake. Developing an ethos of dependency, it undercut individual initiative. By questioning the viability of collective action, Chavez and Ogbu implicitly affirm the primacy of achievement ideology built on its individualistic base.

There is accumulating evidence which suggests that individualism is being pushed further inside people in the public discourse about education. When discussing special education, issues don't just center *on* the individual; they are placed *inside* the individual. Problems are located in the body, between the ears, beneath the skin, of the special education student.

This internalist bias has been prevalent throughout the history of the discourse of special children. The locus of trouble has been inside the child since the 1800s, although its exact place has changed. First, it was in the soul: problems in school were seen as a sign of bad morality. "Restless," "passionate" children observed at the Royal College of Physicians at the turn of the century, were said to be suffering from an "abnormal defect of moral control" (Kohn, quoted in Christy, 1990: 13). Then it was in the heart; troubled children come from the families of immigrants who have given them inadequate socialization (Gordon, 1988).

From the turn of the 20th century the problem has been medicalized,[4] a search for an underlying, biological, basis for the school troubles of special children. In more recent times, the move toward medicalization has been exemplified by the 'mental retardation' designation. Retardation is seen as a special form of illness. When special children are represented in a medical discourse, then the practices and policies which accompany the medical model follow. Hence, we get "examinations," "diagnoses," and "treatments." The IQ test is used like a thermometer; it is inserted into the child's mind so that a 'reading' can be taken of the patient. Equating educational testing with a medical exam is justified by the theory of IQ testing: the IQ test is assumed to be measuring genetically, biologically, 'naturally' given intelligence (Jensen, 1981).

More recently, and partially in response to sociological criticisms (e.g., Mercer, 1974), the mental retardation label has been expanded to include "educational handicaps" and "learning disabilities." To be sure, these are more benign terms, but they are still based on a medical model which places the locus of difficulty within the child.

Let's look closely at the metaphor of 'handicap' and the educational practices which are affiliated with it. Proponents of federally supported special education programs in the 1960s were critical of the segregationist tendencies in schools which placed children in wheelchairs in isolated classrooms near boiler rooms and left them there virtually without recourse. They wanted students with physical handicaps to be educated in environments which were not as restrictive, which were not isolated from the mainstream. Political action led to laws favoring the mainstream education of physically handicapped students. Soon the physical handicaps metaphor was stretched to include not only students with visible, physical symptoms, but those with *educational* handicaps. According to the federal law governing special education (PL 94–142, "The Education for All Handicapped Students' Act"), handicapped students are

> mentally retarded, hard of hearing, deaf, orthopedically impaired, other health impaired, speech impaired, visually handicapped, seriously emotionally disturbed, *or [are] children with specific learning disabilities who by reason thereof require special education and related services* [PL 94 142–Sec 4(a) (1)]. (emphasis added)

But there is a logical and discursive conundrum affiliated with the attempt to extend 'handicaps' from physical to educational. The power of speaking about the special educational needs of students with physical handicaps comes from the affinity to the medical relationship between symptoms and their underlying cause. Educators who say children suffer from physical handicaps can appeal to visible symptoms: legs which have been paralyzed, eyes or ears which don't work, and link these symptoms to an underlying cause located in the body, at the neurological or biological level.

That semeiotic relationship does not hold with *educational* handicaps. There may be symptoms (children staring into space or falling asleep in class), which are coded as "inattention." Children may interrupt lessons with noisy comments or hit each other (which are coded as 'behavioral difficulties"), but such symptoms do not necessarily index damage, a disorder on the underlying biological level. No necessary connection between learning disabilities and neurological or biological damage has been demonstrated. In other words, symptoms and their underlying cause do not stand in a symptomatic or indexical relationship. Instead, they stand in a 'counts as' relationship: the piece of behavior counts as an instance of a category. So, we get a circular definition: a learning disabled child is one who requires special education.

Both educational handicaps and physical handicaps are defined by the power of language. In both cases, there is a constitutive relationship between behavior and its interpretation. A discursive system and institutionalized practices (such as testing, tracking, placement opportunities) establish the relationship between mode of representation and subsequent practices, and maintain that relationship in schools (Mehan et al., 1986). In special education generally, then, this way of talking about educational difficulty locates the problem *within* the student while simultaneously pushing into the background such issues as classroom organization, school structure, relationships between home and school, disparities in the economics of school funding and cultural variation.

There are significant educational and social consequences associated with this discourse move: it *naturalizes* the educational process. Development and achievement become the product of natural forces. When the educational handicaps of special education students and the 'gifts' and 'talents' of their cousins at the other end of the Gaussian curve are defined as biological, it means they are unchangeable, unmalleable. People either have intelligence or they do not. People have talents or they have handicaps. These conditions are treated as given. The naturalizing move is not exclusively internal, however; it can be external as well. Consider the case of poverty (Fine, 1991). If the impoverished conditions in which people live are taken as inevitable, then poverty has been naturalized. We can find evidence of the naturalization of poverty when social analysis or everyday people treat poverty as a natural feature of everyday life [as did Vice-President Dan Quayle in his commentary on the Los Angeles violence in the aftermath of the Rodney King verdict (Quayle, quoted in Rosenthal, 1992)].

The naturalizing move, whether it is expressed in achievement ideology or special education, justifies and rationalizes a 'do nothing' social policy. While the hierarchy of educational attainment and the stratified system of occupational success may be acknowledged, it is said to be the result of natural forces, which implies that interventionist social programs will have little or no success. This way of talking justifies the *status quo*. The ranking and stratification we observe in society becomes an inevitable consequence of underlying natural forces. That is the danger of the naturalizing move: it justifies and rationalizes a social policy that keeps existing systems of inequality in place, and blunts the urge for change and transformation. When talent and poverty are natural states, it means there is nothing that can be done about them

The Power of Language in Reform

Since the early 1980s and the publication of *A Nation At Risk*, we have had an often highly charged and emotional debate about public education. We have seen scathing criticism of public schools, and their products, the students, using measures of everything from performance on the SAT to international comparisons of academic achievement as the shibboleth.

A Nation At Risk sparked wave upon wave of recommendations for the reform of education, including calls for a longer school day and year, and for the assignment of more homework. The reforms demanded also included higher standards for college admissions, more professional standards for teachers, more rigorous grading, better textbooks and a nationwide system of achievement tests.

Underlying all of this, and not often examined, is the language of reform. The metaphor which has dominated this reform movement is 'excellence.' Its logic is this: If we increase the numbers of courses students take and the standards teachers and students must meet, then we will improve the quality of education and its graduates. This way of thinking and talking often translates into an exclusive concern for the elite of the educational system, the upper echelon of its graduates.

Lost in this discussion is the hidden underside of the recommendations: calls for excellence, increased standards and the like, often leave out significant segments of the society, especially low income families and students from underrepresented backgrounds. This point can be made more strongly by comparing the rhetoric of the current reform effort with the last significant educational reform effort, that of the 1960s. Then the metaphor was quite different: it was one of equality, not excellence. In the 1960s, educational reformers wanted to broaden the base of inclusion; the idea was to expand the option of educational opportunity to groups excluded from the educational and political process. And so, under the banner of equity/equality, students who had been denied access to schooling were admitted. Those who had been admitted earlier, but who had been excluded from specialized programs, were advanced.

My fear is that in answering the calls for excellence in the 1980s and 1990s, we are overlooking our obligations to equity and equality. Equity and excellence are pitted against each other in ways which can be divisive. In the final analysis, one does not preclude the other.

A particularly telling example of the exclusionary aspects of the excellence reform movement that demands careful attention is President Bush's *America 2000* proposal for the expenditure of public funds for private schooling, aka: 'parental choice' or 'the voucher plan.' Proponents of choice maintain that a voucher plan will give parents freedom, and will drive weak schools out of the market, while students will be attracted to strong schools. For example, David Boaz (1991) (Executive Vice President of the Cato Institute) says that schools can benefit by applying the principles of efficiency developed in the business community:

> Within a few years, parents may have a wide array of corporate schools to choose from. Mom-and-Pop schools might bring back the one-room school house in an entrepreneurial form. One company's schools might be efficient enough to give your child a full high school education in an hour a day, while another might promise to stay open from 6 A.M. to 6 P.M. to accommodate working parents.
>
> Profit-making companies are beginning to go into the school business, confident that they can provide better and less costly education than government schools and still make a profit.
>
> We will not see innovation, cost cutting and creativity in our schools until profit-making firms get into the business of education.

In this scenario, parents will "shop" for the best schools for their children:

> The idea behind choice is that a free market system can work as well for schools as it does for private businesses; the good schools will attract more students and the ones which fall short will have to improve or perish. (*LA Times*, 1992)

Further, it is argued "bad" schools will be closed down and "good" schools will flourish because of "market forces":

> [parental choice] is an idea whose time has come . . . which will introduce cleansing competition to the stolid monopoly that is now the public system. The money follows the children and the children follow the good schools. Competition, not monopoly, is the American way; we have seen it work and produce. In schooling, let bad schools fail; close them, guarantee their students access to successful schools. Then revamp some of the failed schools, open them under new management to put competitive pressure on the others. (Safire, 1991: A17)

The voucher plan has found support not only among "free market" proponents, but also among African American educational leaders disenchanted because they feel their children have not been well served by public schools. They see a voucher plan as an economic tool to strengthen Black schools (Khalada Salaam, Principal of the Community Preparatory School and the Rev. George McKinney, Bishop, St. Stephens Church, in interviews with the author).

Opponents of choice, on the other hand, have highlighted issues concerning the separation of church and state:

> There is "something inherently unfair and potentially dangerous in having state money go to private schools that would not have to follow the same rules that apply to public schools." (Marcia Viger, Vista USD School Board Member, quoted in Gaw, 1991: B3)

Critics are afraid that Blacks and Whites, rich and poor will be resegregated. For example:

> In many instances, public school choice is becoming a new form of segregation, creating multitiered and unequal educational opportunities. (Moore, 1989)

Del Weber, president of the California Teachers' Association, called the California constitutional amendment to legalize choice 'evil' because it would not require private schools to accept low income students or those with disabilities (quoted in Trombley 1992: A13).

Others see the voucher plan as a cynical trick to pass public funds to private schools:

> Davis Campbell (Executive Director of the California School Boards Association) denounced the measure as "a fraud," saying "it is intended to subsidize private schools and nothing more." (quoted in Trombley 1992: A13)

Albert Shanker, president of the American Federation of Teachers, says "school choice [is a] fig leaf for giving public funds to private schools. . . . Most of its emphasis is on providing financial aid for private schools rather than helping public schools achieve the national education goals" (quoted in deWitt, 1991: A7).

> Our already financially starved public schools will lose at least $1.3 billion, about $8,500 per classroom. . . . That amount will be shifted to private (and church run) schools beginning with the 1995-96 fiscal year. (Graham-Caso, 1992: 1)

The specter of "Karl Marx Schools" or separatist schools run by the likes of the Ku Klux Klan also pepper the counterarguments:

> You'll have no way of knowing what they're doing, you could end up with 'David Duke Academies'. (California State Superintendent Bill Honig, quoted in Trombley, 1991: A1)

> Tax dollars could go to schools operated by special interest groups intent on teaching their own political philosophies and religious principles. (California Congress of Parents, Teachers and Students, 1992)

While these arguments are captivating, I think there is a more fundamental issue beneath the surface level of the debate. That issue is the very concept of education, the way we talk about (and, hence, act upon) schooling. The issue centers on whether we represent schooling as a public good or as a private commodity.

In pro-school-choice arguments, education is being represented as a commodity that can be bought and sold. Education, or at least 'quality' education becomes available to the highest bidder, or to those with the most capital to purchase it. This discourse move reduces schooling to an economic activity.

As in other economic models, the actor depicted in pro-school-choice arguments acts based on enlightened self-interest. A parent or student is presumed to be 'rational' in the sense that he or she has access to the information needed to make choices among goals or ends, has access to those goals or ends, has access to the means to make those choices and knows the possible consequences of those choices in advance (Schutz, 1962). In short, this is a discourse of self-interested rational actors. Insofar as there is a common good, it is understood as the sum of individual interests.

This discourse, in which schooling is equated with an economic activity in which self-interest prevails, has important educational and sociological consequences. The discourse of self-interest runs up against the discourse of the common good in which schooling is seen as one of those activities that not only benefits individual participants, those who go to school, but benefits the society as a whole. Society as a whole benefits because education increases the general welfare of the society. As people gain more knowledge, they learn to take the role of the other in problem solving and conflict resolution; they lead healthier lives because they are more likely to use medical and dental facilities; they are less likely to engage in criminal behavior; they participate in democratic institutions, such as voting for elected officials, and they are less susceptible to demagoguery, more resistant to rule by force, and more tolerant of those who are less fortunate.

The "common good" principle is a difficult one however, because it requires the citizenry to recognize that education is 'a good thing' even though each individual citizen doesn't necessarily benefit directly. This point can be exemplified by reference to taxes. Under the 'common good' principle, all citizens are taxed for education, even though they do not have children in school. The money is distributed to schools so that all children can attend without paying money out of pocket. This way of making education available does not limit access to the privileged elite; a concern for the common good is assumed.

What makes 'personal interest' arguments appealing? Arguments which appeal to self-interest carry weight and succeed, because they are concrete, immediate, and local, while arguments that appeal to collective interest are abstract, potential and distant. Self-interest arguments require citizens to imagine a course of action that has immediate benefits, while common good arguments require citizens to imagine a future course of action that has the potential to benefit everyone, not just themselves.

Again, this point can be clarified by reference to the issue of taxation and choice. When people begin to talk about the government making vouchers available to parents which can be spent at different schools, an appeal is being made to people's self-interest. For the person with children, concerned about securing the best possible school, the voucher plan is appealing because that person can seemingly choose among options. For the person not paying taxes, the voucher plan is appealing, because it seems to lessen the tax burden, an important factor given Census Bureau data which indicates the proportion of the U.S. population with children in school is declining significantly, from 45 percent in 1970 to 35 percent in 1990 (Richter, 1991).

The public debate about vouchers and parental choice stands for much more than the question of whether the state should give money to private schools or sponsor schools which may have outrageous curricula. It is about a course of action which has the potential to undermine some of the basic principles of the common good.

The Power of Discourse in Research: Resisting the Politics of Despair

In this final section, I shift my attention away from discourse in the classroom, school and reform movements and toward the role of discourse in research. Therefore, these comments are aimed more at researchers in education than practitioners in schools. They are a reflexive commentary on the role of theory and research in reform. Let me start with a biographical observation.

When I started conducting close analyses of educational testing and classroom teaching in the late 1960s and early 1970s, I had a political motive as well as a theoretical interest. I had the belief that exposing the subtle and often overlooked practices of sorting and stratifying could have a positive effect. Information about how testing (unwittingly?) operated against poor students, or children from ethnic or linguistic minority backgrounds, or girls, or "unattractive" students, could be used, I hoped, to resist the misclassification of students and to assist the development of more democratic educational practices.

I know this orientation was shared by others conducting "microethnographies" of schooling (e.g., Ray McDermott [McDermott & Gospodinoff, 1981] and Fred Erickson [Erickson, 1975]). This "sociological imagination" (Mills, 1964) was also apparent in the sociolinguistic research of the era, the research that showed that the communicative competence of linguistic and ethnic minorities was every bit as functional as that of their White, middle income contemporaries. The sociolinguistic and microethnographic work also had an affinity to those ethnographic studies of school practices (e.g., Metz, 1983; Oakes, 1985) which revealed how tracking and segregation operated against poor and ethnic minority children. A similar tone was heard in larger scale surveys (e.g., Jencks, 1972; Coleman, 1966) which indicated that educational opportunities were often distributed more on the basis of students' characteristics than on their merit. All of this contributed to a "critical pedagogy" (Apple, 1985; Giroux, 1988), the goal of which was democracy and social justice.

This research was conducted against the underlying assumptions of the progressive agenda. Democracy and equity were tacitly assumed to be the goals of society and schooling was assumed to play a vital role in achieving those goals. People were assumed to have the capacity to resist oppression in the name of liberty, or at least they had the ability to be aware of their historical situation and its contingency (Diggins, 1992).

If there was a general finding from the work of that era it was that the progressive goals had not yet been met. More work had to be done, certainly, but improvement was possible. This sense of cautious optimism about the ongoing possibility of progress was captured nicely by the title of a report written by Kati Haycock & Suzanna Navarro for the Achievement Council: "*Unfinished* Business: *Fullfilling* Our Children's Promise" (emphasis added).

While optimistic about the idea of progress, this research was not blindly obedient to the tenets of modernism. First (as I have described in this chapter), there was the recognition that language and the way it is used constitutes the social world. Second, there was the belief that knowledge is limited, rationality is bounded, reasoning is contextualized. Third, there was the belief that objectivist claims to disinterested truth had to be replaced by perspectival claims to contingent truth. Fourth, there was the recognition that claims to a centralized authority were not natural or given.

Over the past decade, a different mentality has been developing in social commentary and social research: A politics of despair seems to permeate much of the discourse about the possibility of action in public life in general, and in education in particular. Sometimes called "post modern," but really *unti*-modern (Berbules

& Rice, 1991), this discourse seems to reject the very possibility of democracy and proclaims the end of the era of progress.

When research was conducted against the assumed background of a progressive agenda, teachers, students, and parents were depicted as people who made things happen. They organized community groups, staffed innovative educational innovations such as Headstart, marched for civil rights or boycotted segregated stores. The children who provided alternative interpretations to established canon, the Black English vernacular speakers who were even more logical than elaborated code users, the teachers and parents who restructured schools were celebrated for improving dreary lives. These people were not passive objects, but active subjects engaged in resisting oppression and dedicated to constructing a moral community.

But when the *anti*-modernist studies schooling, all possibility of human freedom and morality seems to disappear: freedom and virtue are eclipsed; human agency fades into the structures of domination and the discourses of power. Oppression cannot be escaped. Even discourse and practices established for progressive purposes wind up being oppressive. Cherryholmes (1988: 165), for instance asks: "is emancipation categorically distinct from oppression?"

Ellsworth (1989) maintains that the discourse of critical pedagogy—ostensibly constructed to fight oppression and to achieve a critical democracy—is oppressive in actual practice. Because critical theorists fail to provide a clear statement of their agendas, they hide the fact that they are seeking to appropriate public resources to further one particular political agenda—progressivism—which they believe serves the public good, but may only serve certain specialized interests. She is particularly hard on the idea of "empowerment," because it depends upon rationalist principles, equalizing teacher-student relations, and because it doesn't challenge the paternalism she finds inherent in education.

Cherryholmes (1988: 162ff) finds masked power and selfish interests in recent reform movements. The reform packages of the 1980s, which seemingly accord more professionalism and status to teachers, really serve conservative political ends because the state's surveillance over teacher education is expanded via increased testing and certification requirements. So, too, the restructuring movement which seems to give teachers more freedom and authority in decision making, is but a "liberal illusion of social autonomy" because the locus of the discourses of power have merely been shifted, not removed.

MacLaren (1992) finds hidden modes of power even in the seemingly benign ethnographic research strategies which are the staple approach of anthropological and critical pedagogy. Researchers engage in certain practices in order to gain entry into the field site, establish an ongoing rapport with subjects, establish reciprocal trust, and report authentically the lived practices of the people studied. MacLaren (1992) sees in those practices a "policing structure," which exploits a "sovereign discourse" and promotes an insider politics that often "freezes and ossifies difference."

For the anti-modernist, then, *every* discourse move is saturated with stifling power, even those which were organized for liberty. Freedom, too, is an illusion. Actions taken, even those in the name of freedom, merely reproduce existing structures of power, or cruelly create new ones.

Willis's (1977) interviews of disaffected White working-class males in a British secondary school can be read this way. He found the "lads," a group of high school dropouts who rejected achievement ideology, subverted teacher authority, and disrupted classes. Willis says that the lads' rejection of the school is partly the result of their deep insights into the economic condition of their social class under capitalism. But their cultural outlook limited their options; equating manual labor with success and mental labor with failure prevented them from seeing their actions led to dead-end, lower paying jobs. Blind to the connection between schooling and mobility, they *chose* to join their brothers and fathers on the shop floor, a choice apparently made happily and free from coercion. Thus, what begins as a potential insight into the social relations of production is transformed into a surprisingly uncritical affirmation of class domination. Their identification of manual labor with masculinity ensures they will accept their subordinate economic fate, and ensures the successful reproduction of the class structure.

MacLeod's (1987) ethnography of two groups of U.S. high school boys in depressed socioeconomic circumstances lends itself to this interpretation as well. "The Brothers" (predominantly Black), and "the Hallway Hangers" (predominantly White) lived in the same housing projects, attended the same school and experienced the same environment where success was uncommon. Despite the similarity of their environment, they did not respond evenly to their circumstances. The Hallway Hangers reacted in ways reminiscent of the lads in Willis's account: cutting classes, disrupting the few they attended, dropping out, smoking, drinking, using drugs, committing crimes. In short, they took every opportunity to oppose the regimen of the school and resist its achievement ideology. By contrast, the Brothers tried to fulfill societally approved roles: attending classes, conforming to rules, studying hard, rejecting drugs, playing basketball, cultivating girl friends.

We learn from MacLeod that the Brothers and the Hallway Hangers have different hopes and beliefs. But, are there differences in material outcome? Do the Brothers actually get ahead—further than we would expect, further than they wish? MacLeod returned to the scene of his study a few years later, only to find that the Brothers' academic achievement and occupational attainment were not all that special. Even though they had a new ideology, a new consciousness, their actual performance looked similar to others in a similar plight. Therefore, instead of a revitalized ideology leading to an improved course of action, MacLeod gives us a more sophisticated version of cooling out the mark, wherein a limited opportunity structure secures the self-selection of Black workers into the urban underclass.

The discourse move into anti-modernism abandons the enlightenment challenge to further knowledge in order to achieve freedom (Diggins, 1992). That impulse is dangerous. Like the naturalizing move (described above), it lends itself to a justification of the *status quo*. Wittingly or unwittingly, anti-modernist thinking and research plays into an apologist agenda. By denying the possibility of *any* positive action, human agency disappears into the structures of domination and anti-modernism rationalizes and legitimizes existing status distinctions and inequalities.

The challenge for researchers is a difficult one when we realize that political action must pass through the cloudy medium of language which renders possibilities obscure. But when we realize that discourse is constitutive, knowledge is limited and action is contingent, it is not necessary to conclude that life is meaningless. Understanding that meaning is constructed does not imply that the meaning-construction process is evil or wrong. Realizing that the grounds for claims to authority are contested and unnatural does not necessarily mean that *all* claims to authority are groundless. We must find ways to take progressive political action without giving into the politics of despair or we will be trapped in the infinite regression of nihilism which renders actions impossible.

NOTES

1. The critical commentary by Sharon Hays improved the paper immensely. I appreciate her keen insight and theoretical acumen.

2. A comment on 'constraints'. It is not impossible for students to 'break frame,' and in this lesson, for example, provide a long exegesis on relative location. But because the dynamics of classroom lessons (like the dynamics of the turn-exchange systems of which they are a part) are so powerful, frame-breaking is done only at a cost: a cost of energy, but also a normative cost, in that such behavior is often interpreted as breaking the rules, as deviant, as a sign of a disruptive student.

3. This lesson also illustrates another point: the mathematical register must be learned; it is akin to a second language (Pimm, 1987; Lemke, 1990; Rosebery et al., 1992). Seeing the math or science register as akin to a 'second language' has implications for recent immigrants. We have the stereotype that students from Southeast Asia, for instance, are mathematical whizzes with some sort of natural skill. Their excellent performances in mathematics may not be as much due to natural talent as much as the 'cultural capital' (Bourdieu & Passeron, 1977) they bring with them from their native lands. If students migrate from lower SES backgrounds, they may not have that 'natural' ability. All of this means we need to be aware of the discursive constraints as well as the structure and grammar of language when teaching mathematics and science to ESL speakers.

4. This move in educational discourse is parallel to discourse in related domains, such as deviance (See Foucault, 1978).

REFERENCES

Apple, M. (1985). *Education and power*. New York: Routledge & Kegan Paul.

Berbules, N. C., & Rice, S. (1991). Dialogue across difference: Continuing the conversation. *Harvard Education Review, 61* (4).

Boaz, D. (1991). For profit schools would deliver. *Los Angeles Times*. June 27, 1991, B8.

Bourdieu, P., & Passeron, C. (1977). *Reproduction*. Los Angeles: Sage Publishing Co.

California Congress of Parents, Teachers and Students, Inc. (1992). *Fact sheet for education*. Los Angeles: Author.

Cazden, C. B. (1988). *Classroom discourse*. New York: Heineman.

Chavez, L. (1990). *Out of the barrio: Toward a new politics of Hispanic assimilation*. New York: Basic Books.

Cherryholmes, C. H. (1988). *Power and criticism: Poststructural investigations in education*. New York: Teachers College Press.

Christy, T. (1991). When children move out of synch: The social construction of the hyperactive disorder with social and educational consequences for diagnosed children. Senior Honors Thesis, Department of Sociology, UCSD.

Coleman, J. et al. (1966). *Equality of educational opportunity*. Washington, DC: U.S. Government Printing Office.

DeWitt, K. (1991). Union chief assails Bush school plan. *New York Times*, July 11, 1991, A7.

Diggins, J. P. (1992). *The rise and fall of the American left*. Boston: W. W. Norton & Co.

Ellsworth, E. (1989). Why doesn't this feel empowering? Working through the repressive myths of critical pedagogy. *Harvard Educational Review, 59* (3): 297–324.

Erickson, F. (1975). Gatekeeping and the melting pot: Interaction in counseling encounters. *Harvard Education Review* (45): 44–70.

Fine, M. (1991). Interrupting the structured silence: Trying to talk about race and class in education. Paper presented at the annual meetings of the American Anthropological Association, Chicago, IL, November 21, 1991.

Foucault, M. (1978). *Discipline and punish: The birth of the prison*. New York: Vintage Books.

Gaw, J. (1991). Doctor says he has cure for education's ills. *Los Angeles Times*, July 21, 1991, B1–B3.

Giroux, H. (1988). *Schooling and the struggle for public life: Critical pedagogy in the modern age*. Minneapolis: University of Minnesota.

Gordon, L. (1988). *Heroes of their own lives: The politics and history of family violence*. New York: Viking Press.

Graham-Caso, F. (1992). The voucher initiative: Disaster for schools. *The San Diego Review, 2* (24): 1–2.

Havel, V. (1990). Words on words: Acceptance speech upon presentation of the peace prize of the German Booksellers Association. *The New York Review of Books,* January 18, 1990, 5–8.

Jencks, C. et al. (1972). *Inequality*. New York: Basic Books.

Jensen, A. (1981). *Straight talk about mental tests*. New York: The Free Press.

Lemke, J. (1990). *Talking science: Language, learning and values*. New York: Ablex.

Los Angeles Times. (1992). Elements of educational choice (Editorial).

McDermott, R. P., & Gospodinoff, K. (1981). Social contexts for ethnic borders and school failure. In H. T. Trueba, G. P. Guthrie, K. H. Au (Eds.) *Culture and the bilingual classroom: Studies in classroom ethnography*. Rowley, MA: Newbury House Publishers.

MacLaren, P. (1992). Collisions with Otherness: "Travelling theory, postcolonial criticism, and the politics of ethnographic practice—the mission of the wounded ethnographer." *Qualitative Studies in Education*, 5 (1): 77–92.

MacLeod, J. (1987) *Ain't no makin' it: Leveled aspirations in a low-income neighborhood*. Boulder, CO: Westview Press.

Mehan, H. (1979). *Learning lessons: The social organization of the classroom*. Cambridge, MA: Harvard University Press.

Mehan, H., Hertweck, A., and Meihls, J. L. (1986). *Handicapping the handicapped: Decision making in students' educational careers*. Stanford, CA: Stanford University Press.

Mercer, J. (1974). *Labeling the mentally retarded*. Berkeley, CA: The University of California Press.

Metz, M. H. (1983). *Classrooms and corridors*. Madison, WI: University of Wisconsin Press.

Mills, C. W. (1964). *The sociological imagination*. New York: Ballantine Books.

Moore, D. (1989). *The new and improved sorting machine*. Chicago: Designs for Change.

National Commission for Excellence in Education. (1983). *A nation at risk: The imperative for educational reform*. Rochester NY: NCEE.

Oakes, J. (1985). *Keeping track: How schools structure inequality*. New Haven: Yale University Press.

Ogbu, J. (1978). *Minority education and caste: The American system in cross-cultural perspective*. New York: Academic Press.

Ogbu, J. (1982). Cultural discontinuities and schooling. *Anthropology and Education Quarterly, 13* (4): 290–307.

Ogbu, J (1987). Variability in minority school performance: A problem in search of an explanantion. *Anthropology and Education Quarterly, 18* (4): 312–334.

Pimm, D. (1987). *Speaking mathematically*. London: Routledge.

Richter, P. (1991). Unwillingness to finance public schools feared. *Los Angeles Times*. September 12, 1991, A1–A23.

Rosebery, A. S., Warren, B., Conant, F., and Hudicourt-Barnes, J. (1992). Cheche Konnen: Scientific sense making in bilingual education. *Hands On!, 15* (1): 1, 16–19.

Rosenthal, A. (1992). Quayle says riots arose from burst of social anarchy. *New York Times*, May 20, 1992, A1.

Sacks, H., Scheggloff, E., & Jefferson, G. (1974). A simplest systematics for the organization of turn taking in conversation. *Language* (50): 696–735.

Safire, W. (1991). Abandon the pony express. *New York Times,* April 25, 1991, A17.

Schutz, A. (1962). *Collected papers*. The Hague: Martinus Nijhoff.

Tharp, R., & Gallimore, R. (1989). *Rousing minds to life: Teaching, learning and schooling in social context*. Cambridge: Cambridge University Press.

Trombley, W. (1991). Major fight looms over initiative on vouchers. *Los Angeles Times*, November 15, 1991, A1 and A32.

Trombley, W. (1992). Education groups call school voucher ballot proposal 'evil.' *Los Angeles Times*, A3 and A13.

Willis, P. (1977). *Learning to labour: How working class kids get working class jobs*. Farnborough, Eng.: Saxon House.

Part II

Culture and Learning

INTRODUCTION

The increasing diversity among America's students has led researchers and educators to consider the role of culture in education. What is culture? "Culture can be understood as the ever-changing values, traditions, social and political relationships, and world-view shared by a group of people bound together by a combination of factors that can include a common history, geographic location, language, social class, and/or religion" (Nieto, 1992, p.111).

People who share a common linguistic heritage usually share a cultural tradition as well. The students who are the concern of this book come from families who speak languages other than English. That means that their cultural background is likely to differ from that of English-speaking families, and from the prevailing culture of most American schools.

This section will focus on the implications of culture differences for teaching and learning. The chapters in this section address the two halves of this topic. In Chapter 4, Christine Sleeter discusses the cultural content of the curriculum—*what* students are taught. In Chapter 5, Roland Tharp examines *how* children from different cultures learn, and how they are best taught. Sleeter advocates multicultural education, based on a culturally inclusive curriculum. Tharp argues for a culturally sensitive pedagogy that is congruent with culturally patterned learning styles.

In a monocultural society, the cultural aspects of schooling may be invisible; teachers and students share the same assumptions, background knowledge, values, learning styles, and patterns of interaction because they were raised in the same culture. When a European American teacher has students read about Dick, Jane, and Spot, or about Halloween, she doesn't have to explain why a brother and sister play together, live with only their parents in a house, and keep a dog as a pet. She doesn't have to explain why children wear costumes and go from house to house asking for candy. She doesn't have to explain why stories begin, progress, and end in a certain predictable pattern. She assumes that the story is a neutral context for teaching students to read and comprehend.

In culturally diverse societies, one would expect cultural factors to leap into the foreground. But they don't always identify themselves clearly. As Tharp illustrates, cultural differences may be the unrecognized force behind misunderstanding and hostility between teacher and student, resulting in students' disengagement from school. A student who misinterprets Dick and Jane's relationship with Spot because her culture has no notion of a pet animal, or who has different cultural associations with ghosts and witches, may seem to the teacher merely to be a poor or unmotivated reader.

In addition to these kinds of cultural differences in assumptions and background knowledge, there are the differences in cognitive approach, communication styles, social interaction patterns, and motivation that Tharp examines in detail. For example, Native Hawaiian children are used to conversing animatedly in multi-age groups with an adult participating but not directing, and there is evidence that they learn best when this pattern is duplicated in the classroom. On the other hand, Navajo children spend long periods alone, converse in a slow-paced pattern, and learn by observing and not questioning adults. They too learn best when their distinctive cultural styles of interaction are reproduced in the classroom.

Sleeter tackles the issue of curricular content, arguing that American society, and schoolchildren in particular, would benefit from acquiring a multicultural perspective. She views different cultures, and their unique wisdom, as endangered species which we should be encouraging to flourish. Although many multicultural education programs aim to improve the achievement of children from ethnic minority groups by teaching them about their own heritage, Sleeter advocates that all students become multiculturally educated, familiar with the histories and traditions of groups outside their own.

Sleeter has written elsewhere that, in practice, multicultural education takes several forms. Some programs focus on learning about other cultures and/or learning to get along with children from various groups. Other programs redesign the entire educational enterprise to reflect cultural diversity in staffing, curriculum, teaching styles, and grouping of students. Other programs encourage students to take a critical or reformist stance toward social injustice based on group differences.

But even in its "mild" form, multicultural education is revolutionary. As Sleeter's chapter makes clear, if knowledge is power, then being able to decide which knowledge is important enough for schoolchildren to study is the ultimate power. The positions taken by both Sleeter and Tharp embody a powerful and radically new role for schools. They both imply that schools should *create* a new society within their walls, not merely reflect the larger society. Just as feminists are questioning the inevitability of a "boys will be boys" attitude that demeans and disadvantages girls, Sleeter contends that multicultural education can overcome the "kids will be kids" attitude that tolerates racial slurs and animosity among ethnic groups.

Sleeter's chapter redefines what it means to be an educated person. A truly educated person, she implies, would have a broad knowledge of other cultures, would act toward members of other groups with tolerance and understanding, and would work for social justice. Similarly, Tharp's vision of a new education based on culturally sensitive pedagogy entails a redefinition of the educational experience. Instead of viewing learning as acquiring knowledge, Tharp characterizes it as experiencing, discussing, and thinking about something new. Instead of viewing knowledge as something that teachers transmit to students, Tharp sees teachers and students as becoming knowledgeable by forming a community of learners.

Sleeter sees the classroom as a special place where teacher and students can create their own society. Through multicultural education, students from different groups can work together amicably toward common goals of education and social justice. Tharp also sees the classroom as a special place where teacher and students create a unique society. Despite his emphasis on the importance of matching instructional approaches to students' cultural learning styles, Tharp advocates universal strategies for teaching all students. Reading about how sharply divergent different cultures are, one may wonder how the differences can be integrated into a single classroom, and how universal strategies can address particular cultural learning styles. But though Tharp presents universal teaching strategies, he does not envision a universal student. He advocates adapting these strategies to the needs of the particular students in the class, and creating a class culture that all students can relate to and participate in. Just as researchers who study the different learning styles of girls and boys argue that this understanding can be used to create a coeducational learning climate favorable to both, Tharp argues that understanding cultural learning styles is a prerequisite for creating a multicultural classroom conducive to learning for the particular mix of students it contains.

The chapters in this section raise several questions about the theory and practice of multicultural education:

- Tharp cites a comparative study of Japanese, Chinese, and White American fifth graders that concluded that all three showed similar cognitive styles. How can we account for this? Certainly these three cultures are very different, and their philosophies of education are different. If fifth grade students in these three countries demonstrate similar cognitive styles, does it say more about their schooling than about their cultures?

- Most of the research on the degree of congruence between the school and different cultures has been conducted by comparing speech and interactional styles of standard American schools with the home and community environments of various minority groups. What is needed to complete the picture are studies of home-school congruence in other countries. One would expect that Mexican schools are compatible with Mexican culture, and would reflect the cognitive styles and other features of students of Mexican ancestry in the United States. But do we really know this for sure? We also need studies of same-culture teaching contexts outside of formal education, for example, African American Sunday school classes, Hispanic confirmation classes, weekend Chinese language and culture schools. Would the learning styles of African American, Hispanic, and Chinese students gleaned from research in public educational settings also be demonstrated in these within-culture teaching contexts?

- Tharp cites evidence that the "standard" verbal/analytic mode of presentation of material used in most schools impedes learning for Native Americans, whose cultural learning style is more visually oriented. Because of this,

presenting material to Native Americans in culturally compatible wholistic/visual modes improves learning. It also
appears to improve their analytic/verbal skills. Why should
presenting material in one mode improve functioning in
another mode? Assuming that the empirical evidence is
solid, what is the theoretical explanation for this?

- Cognitive research presents another paradox in this area.
Exposing European American and Asian children to material presented in a wholistic/visual mode can expand their
cognitive styles. But if that mode is culturally incompatible,
why wouldn't it impede learning for them? In other words,
if there are two basic modes, why is using the non-preferred
mode beneficial and enriching for one group, but detrimen-
tal to learning for the other? And, if using the culturally
compatible mode for Native Americans improves their
skills in the non-preferred mode, does the same thing happen for European Americans and Asians—does instructing
them in the preferred verbal/analytic mode somehow
increase their visual/wholistic skills? Why or why not?
What is the relationship between these two modes, when
influence between the two seems to move only in one direction? And what would happen if American schools used
more visual/wholistic instruction—would schools produce
more artists and poets?

- Both Sleeter and Tharp make a strong case for the importance of cultural differences. But authors elsewhere in this
book argue that cultural differences are less important
than differences in social power, and that actual cultural
differences are less important than society's attitude
toward those differences. How can we sort out the relative
importance of culture, power, and attitude, and what implications can be drawn for education?

- Because differences among cultural groups seem to be obvious, there is a danger of overattributing the behavior of
individuals to cultural explanations. While information
about various cultures can useful to educators, they should
remember that there is diversity within cultures, and that
most cultural traits are optional rather than obligatory.
How can schools balance curriculum and instruction to
address the universal, culture-specific, and individual characteristics and needs of students?

The vision of multicultural education presented in this section is not only revolutionary but idealistic, and the practical challenges are many. They include:

- Is culturally sensitive pedagogy equally important across all grade levels, or it is more crucial in the early grades? If the vision illustrated in this section is to be implemented in secondary schools, is it realistic to expect teachers to create a special learning environment based on a knowledge of the students' backgrounds under the current structure—five or six classes of 50 minutes each?

- The authors in this section argue that changing schools will benefit students from linguistic and cultural minority groups. It is less clear that changing schools will benefit those who perform well in the current schools. If researchers are convinced that changing instruction and curriculum will be advantageous for all students, how can they convince parents?

- If multicultural education means changing the prevailing view of history, then we can expect resistance from groups favored by the current accounts. People treat their history as property, and will fight to preserve their version of history as the truth as strongly as they will fight for physical property. How can favored groups be convinced to relinquish their power over the telling of history?

- Teachers can learn about the cultural traditions of students in their class, they can implement varied instructional styles, and they can learn to interpret and respond appropriately to children from different backgrounds. But how can they alter their sociolinguistic style, something that is so ingrained? Can they reasonably be expected to be able to carry on a fast-paced overlapping conversation with one group of students and then switch to a slow-paced exchange with long wait times with other students?

- Where should the balance be struck between offering children instruction in a manner that is compatible with their cultural learning styles and working to expand their cognitive styles and knowledge beyond their own culture?

- What role should explicitness play in multicultural classes? Would students benefit by classroom discussions of different modes of learning or communication styles? Would they benefit by being made privy to the teacher's conscious lesson planning? For example, suppose a teacher wanted to develop both analytic and wholistic skills in students. Would she do better to present material sometimes in one mode and sometimes in another, or to tell the students what she was doing and why? The first approach may bewilder students, if for example, on Monday she read a story straight through and admonished the students not to interrupt, and on Tuesday she read another story but encouraged them to interrupt and interrupted the story herself to ask questions. If an explicit approach makes more sense, how should it be designed?

The vision of education presented in the following chapters is ambitious and exciting, but translating it into reality will require facing these and other hard questions.

REFERENCES

Nieto, S. (1992). *Affirming diversity: The sociopolitical context of multicultural education*. New York: Longman.

✧ Chapter 4

The Value of a Multicultural Education
for All Students

Christine E. Sleeter

Joanna (fictitious name) teaches in a highly multicultural school: students are Anglo, African American, and Mexican American, and about 8 percent speak Spanish as their native language. Joanna enrolled in a graduate course in Multicultural Education to learn how to teach her students more effectively. Initially she viewed multicultural education as good for "those" students, meaning students who are not Anglo. Over the semester, however, she began to ask why she, an Anglo who had grown up in a small town in Wisconsin, had never had a multicultural education herself. She became critical of the fact that her teachers had assumed that she and her classmates would inhabit a monocultural world, and prepared her accordingly. Her most substantive encounter with another culture had been three years of Spanish, a language she had never actually mastered and had subsequently forgotten. In retrospect, she felt that the schools she had attended had never actually expected her to become bilingual since only an elementary level of language learning had been demanded; and they had never prepared her to conceptualize the American population and American culture as pluralistic. Now here she was, trying to work in a setting for which her 17 years of schooling had not prepared her. She began to ask: Wouldn't an education that is multicultural and multilingual be good for all students?

In the flurry of debates over multicultural education during the 1980s, a degree of consensus seems to have emerged about one thing: the United States is a multicultural society. Its diversity is increasingly difficult simply to ignore or deny. Even in the small towns of the rural Midwest, ethnic and racial diversity become part of daily life through television and movies (distorted though that image may be) and through travel, sometimes only to the next town. Further, debates about sexism, poverty, and the rights of people with disabilities crop up virtually everywhere. Many educators see some value in connecting the culture of the school with the home culture of non-Anglo students in order to maximize their achievement. Of what value is a multicultural, multilingual education to all Americans?

In this chapter I will argue that such an education has value for everyone for four main reasons: (1) to prepare all of us to interact constructively with Americans who differ from ourselves culturally; (2) to provide multiple funds of human wisdom for addressing issues and problems we face today; (3) to provide the insights necessary for resolving persistent social injustices; and (4) to cultivate rather than destroy the talents of diverse students who are in the schools now.

Preparation to Live in a Pluralistic Society

Demographic changes in the United States have been well-publicized; the introduction to this book summarizes current population shifts well. The demographic changes alone increase the likelihood that any American child today will grow up working and possibly living with other Americans who differ culturally, linguistically, and/or racially. Technological advances in communication and transportation also enhance the possibility for cross-group contact.

Joanna, whose story introduced this chapter, is not alone. Teachers across the nation confront the difficulty of teaching students whom they, the teachers, had never been prepared in their own educations to understand. Businesses, too, over the past decade, have instituted programs to teach their employees how to understand culturally diverse employees, clients, and consumer communities (Riche, 1991). EuroAmericans are not the only group who struggle with effects of their own cultural insularity, ethnocentrism, and ignorance of other groups. For example, journalism schools in predominantly minority as well as predominantly White institutions of higher education are grappling with the need to prepare all reporters for diversity: "When you look at the racial composition of this country, we might as well start figuring out how to train racial ethnic minorities to cover each other's community" (Hawkins, 1992, p. 24).

The gaps in ignorance across groups are too large and deep to bridge in a workshop or a single university course, as those who investigate effects of such training on adults document (Sleeter, 1992). Communication and understanding can break down (or fail to develop in the first place) on many levels, some of which are discussed in detail in other chapters in this volume. Failure to understand someone else's language is an obvious example; failure to understand language nuances and shades of meaning also occurs, such as when a Latino envisions "la familia" as including extended family members, translates this into the word "family," and is understood by a non-Latino to mean the nuclear family. People also commonly misread the behavior of others. For example, non-Black teachers often read active behavior of African American children as defiant and aggressive rather than as enthusiastic and participatory (Shade, 1990); non-Indian teachers often misinterpret Indian children as withdrawn and uncommunicative due to a lack of understanding of Indian communication processes (Philips, 1983).

Diverse experiences, viewpoints, and frames of reference also lead to misunderstanding. For example, people who are unfamiliar with Maxine Hong Kingston, Nellie Wong, Yoshiko Uchida, Ron Takaki, Chinese exclusion acts, and Japanese American relocation will have difficulty understanding conversations that include reference to Tule Lake, Vincent Chin, "white ghosts," or poverty in Chinatown areas. People who are unaware of the history of Jim Crow and lynchings during the first half of the twentieth century have great difficulty understanding why racial equality did not result shortly after the Emancipation Proclamation.

Adults who find themselves in culturally diverse contexts often seek information or workshops to help them cope. How much better prepared would they be if their entire education, from kindergarten forward, had provided them with a knowledge base that affirmed America's cultural diversity? For example, even if an individual's first face-to-face contact with a Mexican American does not occur until adulthood, that individual is better prepared to communicate effectively if she or he has read a history text such as *Occupied America* (Acuna, 1988) and literary works by authors such as Sandra Cisneros, Tomas Rivera, and Gary Soto, and has learned that there are several North American dialects of Spanish that have as much linguistic integrity as Castilian.

Human Wisdom in a Multicultural Society

Virtually everyone agrees that schools should transmit the best of human wisdom from one generation to the next, but we disagree on a definition of what counts as wisdom. Debates often become trivialized into discussions of which (and how many) pieces of factual information about which cultural groups to include in textbooks, which themselves provide a single, standardized narrative to impose on all children. Many EuroAmericans perceive discussions about multicultural curricula as attacks on Western culture, a perception that assumes only one cultural tradition can have value. Or, EuroAmericans argue that non-White children should learn something of "their own" cultural heritage, without perceiving its value to the rest of us. Such conceptions of multicultural curriculum entirely miss the value of multiple funds of human wisdom in a multicultural society.

Humanity is perpetually confronted with life's universal problems, which manifest themselves in particular locations and points in time. Americans moving into the twenty-first century face problems such as ecological survival, the quest for life's meaning, the development of ideals of democracy and equality, search for community, and so forth. Our conception of what culture means, however, limits what we regard as worthwhile sources of knowledge. As Rosaldo (1989) argued, most Americans regard culture as a way of life other people have, that is interesting to study, but frozen in the past: "Social analysts sat at the 'postcultural' top of a stratified world and looked down at the 'cultural' rungs to its 'precultural' bottom" (p. 209). But it is much more useful to regard culture as a dynamic repertoire of possibilities that can be combined, remade, and synthesized to address the present and the future. Western culture offers one valuable fund of wisdom; the world offers multiple funds that Westerners have tended to destroy rather than learn from. I will briefly discuss two issues confronting twenty-first century Americans—erosion of the natural environment, and loss of family and community—to suggest diverse cultural repertoires from which we can learn in order to create better answers than we have at present.

Destruction of the natural environment is increasingly becoming a publicized concern. The range and scope of what is being destroyed has grown considerably in my lifetime, as I have witnessed concern for an increasingly lengthy list of endangered forms of nature, such as some species, rainforests, the ozone layer, natural erosion control, clean water, and clean air. Scientists debate possible long-range effects of environmental destruction, as evidence of short-run effects accumulates. As EuroAmericans scramble about for solutions to potential environmental disaster, it continues to amaze me how little attention they give to Native American perspectives about how humans should relate to the natural world. For thousands of years Indian people lived in such excellent harmony with the natural world that Europeans, as they arrived, apparently did not recognize civilization when they encountered it, because it was structured so differently. What Indian people can teach non-Indians is not just techniques for wildlife management or cleaning water, but a worldview that does not lead humankind down the path of global destruction.

> Today the species of Man is facing a question of the very survival of the species. The way of life known as Western Civilization is on a death path on which their own culture has no viable answers. When faced with the reality of their own destructiveness, they can only go forward into areas of more efficient destruction. (Hau do no sau nee, 1977, p. 9)

Western perspectives contrast markedly with Indian perspectives about the universe. Non-Indians generally conceptualize the world in a hierarchical order with humans at the top, other life forms, then non-life forms, rank ordered below humans (P. G. Allen, 1986, p. 58). Within this worldview, humans have conceptualized the non-human environment as something to be mastered and tamed. The Western hierarchical worldview was coupled with capitalism's drive for material accumulation, which "led men, such as Columbus, to set sail across the Atlantic" (Hau de no sau nee, 1977, p. 7). Europeans and EuroAmericans have now spent about 500 years taking from the natural environment of the Americas as much as possible, continually developing consumptive appetites and industries to both produce consumer goods as well as convince us to consume. But destructive results are increasingly difficult to ignore. For example, based on an analysis of smog in the Los Angeles area, Mann (1991) wrote,

> Smog and air toxins are primarily a result of 1) our dependence on an automobile centered, fossil-fuel burning transportation system dominated by the auto, oil, and rubber-tire industries; 2) factories using and emitting dangerous chemicals; and 3) consumer goods produced by the petrochemical industry that pollute our environment. After decades of failed efforts to regulate these industries more fundamental change is needed. (p. 35)

Ironically, today people of color—including Indian people—are disproportionately targets of pollution and toxic waste disposal (*Minority Trendsletter*, 1991).

In contrast, the Indian worldview emphasizes circular connectedness of all existence, and defines the purpose of life as the attainment of harmony with the universe, rather than control and consumption of it. Decisions made today are evaluated in terms of their impact seven generations into the future (Hau de no sau nee, 1977). For example, Weatherford (1988) described complex farming processes that Indians developed over thousands of years that maximized food production without contributing to erosion and chemical poisoning, and that widely diversified strains of many plants for varied uses. In his description of farming techniques used by Indians he visited, he frequently remarked that a farm looked "like an abandoned area after a forest fire" (p. 83) or some other natural arrangement. Indian agricultural processes work *WITH* nature, Indians maintaining a clear understanding that their relationship with the natural world is one of reciprocal give-and-take; the natural world rather than the human world establishes the rules for existence.

EuroAmericans generally approach the problem of how to reverse planetary destruction without reference to the wisdom that Native people have. For example, the publication *Environment 92/93* (J. L. Allen, 1992) contains 35 articles discussing issues and potential solutions to environmental destruction, not one of which acknowledges Indian knowledge. And EuroAmericans approach the study of Indian culture as a brief foray (usually at the elementary school level) into historic artifacts that are presented as simple and having mainly entertainment value. For the sake of planetary survival, non-Indians should be investing far more effort into learning from Native people, and far less in trying to export our worldview and consumptive lifestyle to the rest of the world.

A second contemporary social problem is the erosion of family and community, resulting in growing alienation of youth. Daily one hears laments about family breakdown, with fingers of blame pointed in various directions—toward the church, the women's movement, the schools, television, social policies, and children themselves. For the most part, the dominant society appears to be at a loss as to where to turn for answers, looking most commonly to a "golden era" of family in the past. Paradoxically, while many EuroAmericans admire Asian and Latino family values, few have drawn on the wisdom of non-European groups to construct alternative forms of family and community, and forms of family support systems. African American, Native American, and Latino families and communities have exhibited a degree of strength and resilience over the past 500 years that suggest considerable insight about human social relationships from which all of us can profit. As Brendtro, Brokenleg and Van Bockern (1990) put it, "Refined over 15,000 years of civilization. . . . Native peoples possessed profound child psychology wisdom which might well have been adopted by the immigrants to North America" (p. 34). What are some insights non-European groups have about family?

While no group adheres to a single family structure, African American, Latino, Asian American, and Native American communities all regard a family unit that is larger than the nuclear family as a valuable resource. Whether that larger unit is the tribe (Brendtro, Brokenleg & Van Bockern, 1990), extended family, system of fictive kin (Stack, 1974), or "la familia" (Carrasquillo, 1991; Mirande & Enriquez, 1979), it offers a wider network of support than a one- or two-parent family can usually provide. African American, Latino, Asian American, and Native American families historically have taught family members to assume responsibility for the family as a collective, placing collective responsibility, cooperation, and mutual aid alongside or above individual achievement. Systems of mutual responsibility are built into some languages such as Japanese, in which interpersonal relations are affirmed through choice of pronouns and verb endings. Within such systems, people of both sexes and all ages—including those who are elderly—have distinct and valued roles to play. From an early age children assume meaningful tasks, and grow to adulthood viewing their contribution to the family as valuable and essential to its survival. At the same time, however, individuals are expected to vary in rate of development and personal characteristics, in contrast to middle-class Anglo society's belief in a standardized "normal" child (Brendtro, Brokenleg & Van Bockern, 1990; Gibbs & Huang, 1989; Harry, 1992; Hill, 1972; Mirande & Enriquez, 1979).

Cross-culturally, families vary in gender roles; while Latino families tend to be patriarchal and divide responsibilities by sex (an institution Anglos usually misrepresent through their own experience with patriarchy [Mirande & Enriquez, 1979, pp. 241–242]), African American families tend to have an egalitarian authority structure and flexible sex roles (Billingsly, 1968), and families in some Indian tribes are woman-centered (P. G. Allen, 1986). But a common thread is interdependence among diverse family members, and collective responsibility. In Anglo society, with its stress on mobility and individual acquisition, family support systems have been replaced increasingly by impersonal government agencies, which many Americans of color regard as contributing to social pathology. The discourse on family would be considerably enriched if it were opened to an examination of how to structure extended or fictive kin systems on a much wider basis, and what kinds of policy and cultural changes would be needed in order to do this, drawing on the wisdom and insights that all American cultural groups have to offer.

There are many, many more examples of areas for which multiple funds of knowledge and wisdom have great value. Western scientists have thoroughly studied only about 1,100 of the earth's 265,000 species of plants, but many species known to tribal healers, but not Western science, have medicinal value (Linden, 1991, p. 52). The Quechua Indians of South America grow over 50 strains of potatoes; "if these natives switched to modern crops, the global potato industry would lose a crucial line of defense against the threat of insects and disease" (p. 54). Hundreds of languages are spoken within the United States, which could be a valuable resource for international communication if we cultivated that resource rather than trying to assimilate everyone into "English Only." Western and Asian cultures developed print as a communication vehicle; many others, such as African cultures, developed orature to a high degree of sophistication (Asante, 1987), thus providing two different language forms which both have value.

As it is, American culture is already a synthesis of widely diverse cultural inputs to a far greater degree than most Americans recognize. For example, Weatherford (1988) discusses many areas of American life that draw on Indian culture, including American democracy, road systems, pharmaceuticals, and food products. People of African descent have contributed, for example, to the development of American music forms, speech and language patterns (Sutcliffe, 1992), and art and literature (Morrison, 1992; Winkler, 1992). People of Spanish, Mexican, Puerto Rican, and other Latino ethnic backgrounds have influenced American urban planning (Weatherford, 1988), cuisine, music, language and literature (Saldivar, 1990). In other words, American culture has always benefitted from the inputs of diverse people. By not acknowledging or teaching these diverse bases of American culture, however, schools perpetuate the idea that non-European groups have little to contribute in the future. Rather than trying to diminish the cultural resources that are within and entering our borders, we would do well to acknowledge and value diverse perspectives from which we all can learn.

Many people initially regard this position as an attack on Western culture. My position does attack the notion that Western people have the best answers for every significant problem, as well as the practice of privileging EuroAmerican people and ideas. Advocates of multicultural education do not, however, wish to throw out Western culture and replace it with something else (Banks, 1991/1992). Clearly, European and EuroAmerican cultures also contribute a rich repertoire of wisdom. Henry Louis Gates (1991) talks about nurturing a "conversation among different voices" and cultural traditions, including EuroAmericans. To a degree, such a conversation has been occurring for 500 years, but without being widely embraced or legitimated, and without teaching young Americans the skills and knowledge for engaging productively in such conversations and cross-cultural sharings as they grow up. We greatly limit our ability to fashion a better world when we draw only on the wisdom of European and EuroAmerican people; it is in everyone's best interest that we open ourselves to possibilities and perspectives in a much wider range of cultural traditions, and reverse the trend toward standardizing the curriculum in such a way that only one version of human wisdom remains.

Multicultural Democracy and Social Justice

To what extent has the United States achieved its ideals of equality, freedom, and justice for all? Every schoolchild learns to verbalize these ideals, and many textbooks suggest that they have been fairly well achieved (e.g., Armento et al., 1991), proclaiming consensus about not just the ideals themselves but also the degree to which the ideals reflect reality. Multicultural education critiques U.S. society for its inequalities and persistent injustices, envisioning a better future that has yet to be constructed. But while critics of multicultural education lamented its presumed effect of "disuniting" a supposed American consensus (Schlesinger, 1991), Los Angeles went up in flames precisely because thousands of people faced "a perception of a future already looted" of opportunity, freedom, and justice (M. Davis, 1992, p. 743).

A multicultural, multilingual education for all Americans ought to mean an education that teaches us to listen to and dialog with voices of dissension, so that we can actually create a social system based on the freedom, justice, and equality we advocate. Right now these ideals simply do not translate into reality for growing numbers of Americans, and to claim consensus about how to interpret U.S. society is to ignore very real frustration. For example, the wealthiest 1 percent of the population currently earn more than the poorest 40 percent, and the distribution of wealth is becoming progressively less rather than more equal (Hacker, 1992; Reeves, 1990). Institutional racism means that about one-third of African Americans and over one-fourth of Latino and Native Americans live persistently below the poverty line, while only about one-tenth of Whites do so (U.S. Bureau of the Census, 1991, p. 462). Employment opportunities, decent housing, health care, and longevity are more accessible to Whites than to Americans of color. Freedom is somewhat illusory to people in ghettos that are patrolled regularly by police, to Americans who are penalized for fluency in a language other than English, and to Native Americans who cannot legally engage in some Native religious practices. Women and children increasingly find themselves in the ranks of the impoverished, partly due to the gross underpayment of women's work, lack of childcare options, and penalizing welfare policies (Sidel, 1986).

Benevolent helping relationships are the model for social reform most of us are most familiar with, placing "experts" with power and knowledge in the position of helping those who presumably lack knowledge (Brickman, et al., 1982). For example, legislative bodies composed primarily of wealthy White men debate policies supposedly aimed to promote economic independence among current welfare recipients. Many community social service agencies are controlled by the state and directed primarily by well-educated White middle-class people whose intentions are altruistic, but who regard their own "expertise" as superior to the knowledge of people they are trying to help. The problem with benevolent helping relationships is that those with the greatest vested interest in change, and the most direct knowledge of the realities of life "on the bottom," are not in a position of directing change. Consequently real, substantive changes tend not to happen; the same problems persist.

Those who have the greatest vested interest in addressing racism, sexism, and institutionalized poverty, as well as the best sense of the barriers created by them, are those who currently experience the brunt of inequality. For example, people of color frequently remark that Whites describe racism, while non-Whites look for strategies to eliminate it. Based on an analysis of reform movements, R. Allen (1974) noted that, "White reformers, themselves largely unaffected by racism, generally fail to perceive its full ramifications and subtleties" (p. 279), and are therefore satisfied with far less than leaders of color. Over the twentieth century, White racism has been one of the main barriers to Black economic progress, while Black self-help efforts have been crucial to Black advancement (Swinton, 1989). Yet Whites very often refuse to work *WITH* minority leadership to change racist institutions, assuming that those with the greatest economic and political resources also have the best expertise.

Similarly, Americans whose native language is not English know quite a bit about second-language learning and push actively for bilingual policies. Monolingual English-speakers, however, who usually control policy-making, base policies on their own poorly-informed myths about language.

> Bilingual education arouses opposition because it contradicts peculiarly American notions about language. As a people we have relatively limited experience with bilingualism on the one hand, and strongly held myths about it on the other. Monolinguals in this country seldom appreciate the time and effort involved in acquiring a second language (although they may not feel up to the task themselves). (Crawford, 1989, p. 14)

Nor do monolinguals or White economically privileged individuals direct attention very consistently to the root causes of oppression that people of color and poor people experience. In her critique of language programming for Black English speakers, Smitherman (1981) remarked:

> Note that it is not high unemployment, or the shifting balance in world economic power, or the crises caused by a highly advanced, technological capitalist society in the United States but "linguistic separation," mind you, that will keep black children and youth from making it in the United States. (p. 53)

The United States has a long history of social movements directed toward equality, the recent Civil Rights Movement being one example. Movements for equality and justice often fall short of their goals, however, partly because they fracture along racial, cultural, class, and sometimes gender lines, thus losing power (see for example, R. Allen, 1974; A. Y. Davis, 1981; Hewitt, 1984; Marable, 1992). In his analysis of contemporary social movements, Boggs (1986) predicted an increasingly vibrant kaleidoscope of democratic agendas and advocacy groups "linked to the demands of antinuclear activists, ecologists, urban communities, women, minorities, and youth" (p. 222). Marable (1992), too, discussed connected agendas of the Black freedom movement, movements of indigenous people, the women's movement, the growth of Latino power, disenfranchised poor Whites, and the gay-rights movement. However, both echoed concern about their ability to form coalitions that would effectively address central problems related to inequality and democracy.

For the sake of a multicultural democracy, we must learn to build bridges across very real differences in experience and perspective in order to reconstruct social institutions around the ideals of equality and justice. For example, "equality" can be defined as "one person, one vote." But it can be conceptualized in many other ways as well, such as groups equally sharing power, or equality of wealth, or equal access to a decent living standard. To those without a job, decent housing, or adequate health care, "the system uses the rhetoric and myth of equality to hide the process of oppression" (Marable, 1992, p. 17). Rebellion is the result, as the recent rebellion in Los Angeles illustrates.

A multicultural education for all Americans should help young people learn to forge coalitions for social improvement, involving a broad spectrum of groups that include members of the dominant society, working collaboratively and sharing power with members of oppressed groups. For middle class (especially male) Anglo children, this means learning to communicate and listen effectively, and to recognize and value expertise of people who are poor, female and/or not Anglo. It means building personal as well as intellectual relationships, in the context of empowerment rather than benevolent helping relationships. For minority children, this means full appropriation of both the language and culture of the dominant group, as well as their own group's primary language and intellectual traditions (e.g., Delpit, 1988; King & Wilson, 1990; Macedo, 1991). Collaboration also means learning to listen to, and work with other minority groups, since prejudice and competition is often very strong between oppressed groups.

For all children, a multicultural education focused on social justice means engaging in substantive discussion about what our national ideals actually mean, and examining the roots of very real inequalities and injustices—including the class structure, which is usually "out of bounds" for critique—in addition to celebrating social achievements (such as relative freedom of speech) that the United States has developed. A just society should promote justice for everyone. Multicultural education does not mean substituting the belittling of one group for another, although it must entail criticism of unjust practices and policies. But coming to grips with historic as well as contemporary injustices should aim directly toward forging a more just multicultural society for us all.

Cultivation of All Students' Talents and Minds

About 35 years ago in New York, a Puerto Rican boy who had not yet learned much English was referred for special education, his teacher believing him to be retarded. His parents fought this classification, successfully. He continued through the regular education system, eventually obtained a Ph.D., and is now an assistant superintendent for a school district. He has a reputation as being innovative, an advocate for children, and a very bright and articulate speaker; he is now sought after by several school districts. This is a true story. What is unusual about it is that this person successfully resisted the low expectations that had been imposed on him, and went on to contribute to an important profession. What is not unusual is the imposition of depressed learning expectations on children who do not fit the "norm" in this society.

It is common knowledge that some categories of students generally do better in schools that others. Students from upper-middle class backgrounds, and those who are EuroAmerican and native English-speakers achieve on the average at higher levels than students from low-income backgrounds, students of color, and students whose native language is not English; and in some important areas boys fare better than do girls. Why do such patterns exist, to what degree can schools change them, and to whose detriment do they persist?

Probably the most common but least helpful perspective holds that differences in student achievement persist because of the differences in learning capabilities and resources that students bring to school with them, which correspond to socioeconomic status, ethnicity, and, to some degree, gender. And, many would argue, low-achievers do not have much to contribute to the rest of society because if they did, they would not have been identified as low-achievers.

A sizable body of research demonstrates, however, that schools themselves contribute to, exacerbate, and sometimes create differences in student achievement. I will provide examples, arguing that not only do the students themselves suffer, but the wider society also pays a price. As the United Negro College Fund proclaims, "A mind is a terrible thing to waste"; but many schools habitually waste many young minds that could otherwise contribute to society. Schools structure education around a fairly standardized version of what the "good student" should be like; students who fit that image are taught well, and students who do not are deemed "low ability," and may even be punished for their lack of conformity. By subscribing to the view that schools are simply identifying natural differences among students, however, most educators regard this process as fair. This standardization of the "good student" and subsequent "miseducation" (Woodson, 1969) of students of color, language minority students, students from low-income backgrounds, and girls is challenged by multicultural education.

Based on a synthesis of ethnographic studies of classroom teaching, elsewhere I described what takes place in most classrooms:

> [A] main order of business in U.S. schools is to fill students' minds with a predetermined body of knowledge, and at the same time, to keep order. The most efficient ways of conveying information are telling it to students orally so they can write it down, and having them read it. Order is maintained by keeping them busy, allowing them few decisions, and requiring that they either work alone or listen to the teacher as a whole group. Students are invited to think creatively and make classroom decisions mainly when they have mastered the expected material, and when the teacher feels reasonably comfortable that they will not seriously challenge what the school expects them to do. (Sleeter, 1987, p. 76)

The ideal "good student" is competent with, and can relate to, that predetermined body of knowledge and the language in which it is encoded; can work well alone; learns well through print; and complies with the behavior, interpersonal manner, and thinking the teacher expects. Standardized tests, then, slot "children according to prior assumptions about the races and classes they belong to," justifying dominant notions about who has intellectual ability and who does not (Mensh & Mensh, 1991, p. 158). An array of differentiated programs institutionalize very different levels of expectations and very different degrees of academic development (Oakes, 1985). What happens to students who do not comply—or comply "too well"?

One group of students who comply but in ways that are often to their detriment are girls, especially bright girls. Girls still face conflicting future roles: wife and mother, on one hand, and worker and achiever, on the other. Many girls, especially academically capable girls, experience pressure to subordinate their academic ability to social success and attractiveness to boys. Although girls earn higher grades than boys, they are less likely to be identified as gifted than boys and less likely to be awarded scholarships (Sadker, Sadker, & Long, 1989). By the time they are making the transition to adulthood, many (probably most) follow "the traditional female patterns of involvement in romantic relationships and disengagement from work" (Holland & Eisenhart, 1988, p. 297). Girls disproportionately elect not to persist in higher-level math and science courses (Fennema & Leder, 1990), questioning their competence more than do boys (McDade, 1988), and many gradually compromise career ambitions in order to prepare themselves for marriage (Grant & Sleeter, 1988). Over the past decade the broader society has sold the "beauty myth" to women, succeeding to the point where a *Glamour* magazine poll found that "thirty-three thousand American women . . . would rather lose ten to fifteen pounds than achieve any other goal" (Wolf, 1991, p. 10).

By failing to scrutinize the perpetuation of gender roles and gender inequality, by viewing schools as "gender-neutral" and taking for granted gendered behavior of students as "natural," educators allow many young women to submerge a wide range of talents, abilities, and ideas (Cushner, McClelland, & Safford, 1992; Sadker, Sadker, & Long, 1989). This does prepare a broad spectrum of the population to agree to work for low wages or no pay at all (Weis, 1990; Wolf, 1991). However, it also robs the broader society of a large pool of intelligence and creativity.

Students of color—including those who are exceptionally bright—are another category who fare poorly in many schools, and whose abilities often subsequently do not become developed and put to their best use. For example, although they are 16 percent of the students in public schools, African American students are only 8 percent of those in programs for the gifted, but 35 percent of those labeled "educable mentally retarded," 27 percent of the "trainable mentally retarded," and 27 percent of the "severely emotionally disturbed" (Harry, 1992, p. 22). In a publication aptly titled *Engaging the Battle for African American Minds*, Shade (1990) argued that while bright African American students exhibit behaviors that are like those of bright White students, educators interpret the behavior of African American students through a "deficiency" framework, and penalize them rather than capitalize on their attempts to learn. Bright African American students often move about while working, talk and contribute ideas freely, engage in multiple activities simultaneously, draw relationships between a wide range of ideas rather than focusing on one idea at a time, and act as if they are "on stage." Teachers interpret their behavior as hyperactive rather than energetic, defiant rather than enthusiastic; and view their responses as wrong rather than novel, disorganized and confused rather than holistic. Shade concludes that,

> Unfortunately, because of these oppositional approaches to ideas, events and people, African American children are labeled as deficient and treated as though they are unable to learn. So, although these students arrive at school with hope and high expectations, by third grade they have fully accepted the level of expectations attributed to them. Hope and curiosity turn to frustration; belief that they can succeed becomes fear of failure, and bright and curious minds become dormant. They wait only for some excitement which might occur because someone verbally or physically defies this alien system. (no page number)

By secondary school a large proportion of them have been placed into special education (Harry, 1992) or tracked into vocational rather than college preparatory programs (Oakes, 1985). Because relatively few African American students are regarded by schools as high achievers, bright students perceive having to choose between being Black versus being academically successful (Fordham, 1991).

By adulthood, in 1990, 609,000 African American men were in the penal system, while only 436,000 were in college (Mauer, 1990). Bright African American students particularly, whose capabilities are not recognized and developed in the schools, become bored with school and often channel their energies and talents into street life, which appears to offer more opportunities and rewards than school (Kunjufu, n.d., pp. 51–52). The failure to teach African American students costs the Black community considerably. But it also costs non-African Americans, who end up paying for police protection and prisons, and who do not benefit from what African Americans could offer as doctors, scientists, architects, business developers, and so forth.

Language-minority students also frequently are dealt with from a "deficiency" orientation. Trueba (1989), for example, has documented processes by which language minority children come to be classified as "learning disabled." When educators fail to connect meaningfully with language minority families, they damage families' attempts to prepare their children for productive adulthood (Harry, 1992). For example, a local administrator commented to some Spanish-speaking parents that their children may need "special education"; the parents, not realizing that he was referring to a particular kind of program that houses the lowest achievers, replied that this was exactly what they wanted for their children: an education that is special (enriched). As a result of inadequate language programs, cultural ethnocentrism, and low expectations, language minority students become concentrated in remedial and lower-track programs in school and drop out at considerably higher rates than native English-speaking students (Medina, 1988; Rumberger, 1987).

These kinds of social wastes can be prevented. Some schools do cultivate the academic potentials of minority students very well. For example, Lucas, Henze and Donato (1990) identified six high schools in which Latino language minority students were achieving relatively well, then investigated features of the schools that promoted success. They found that the successful schools actively valued students' languages and cultures, encouraging these to be a part of the curricular program. The staffs maintained high academic expectations for students, and translated those expectations into active teaching. The schools instituted courses and programs to develop students' language competence in both Spanish and English; they made active use of research on second language learning and effective teaching strategies for Latino ESL students. In other words, the human waste that happens when young minds are not developed very effectively was prevented by those schools that engaged in the kinds of teaching strategies recommended in this volume.

Artist Linda Nochlin (1971) has often been asked to explain why there are so few great women artists. She explains that a first reaction is to refute the claim that there are few, and dig up as many as one can. A next reaction is to critique the prevailing standards for "greatness" as male rather than female. While both reactions do help address the question, the main problem is that,

> things as they are and as they have been in the arts, as in a hundred other areas, are stultifying, oppressive, and discour-

aging to all who did not have the good fortune to be born white, preferably middle-class or above, males. (p. 483)

Institutional reform is required so that everyone may develop fully their artistic talents; anything short of reforming institutions that deny full education and access to everyone means settling for less than we should.

We might ask today: Why does the United States have so few statespersons, and who will they be in the next few decades? Who will develop a cure for AIDS? Who will produce excellent American literature in the twenty-first century? Who will develop food distribution processes that eliminate hunger? And who will take care of me when I am elderly? The talent and intellect for doing these things is in schools right now. That talent and intellect resides in children of varied skin colors, cultural backgrounds, language backgrounds, socioeconomic statuses, and of both sexes. Nurturing that talent and intellect as it appears in this wide diversity of children is to the benefit of us all.

Conclusion

The United States is in the process of becoming the most racially and culturally diverse nation in human history, drawing significant portions of its population from all over the globe. Many Americans regard this diversity as a problem, pointing to the fragility of other nations such as the former Soviet Union and Yugoslavia, wondering how the United States will survive. One can, however, view diversity as a tremendous resource, providing Americans with a rich repository of cultural resources. Whether our diversity strengthens us or tears us apart depends on how seriously we delve into its strengths, support the potentials and dreams of all our citizens, and significantly reduce or even eliminate the glaring inequalities among groups. The knowledge for how to accomplish this exists within our borders; the desire to do so depends on us.

REFERENCES

Acuna, R. (1988). *Occupied America: A history of Chicanos*, 3rd ed. New York: Harper & Row.

Allen, J. L. (Ed.) (1992). *Environment 92/93*. Guilford, CT: The Dushkin Publishing Group.

Allen, P. G. (1986). *The sacred hoop*. Boston: Beacon Press.

Allen, R. (1974). *Reluctant reformers: The impact of racism on American social reform movements*. Washington, DC: Howard University Press.

Armento, B. J., Nash, G. G., Salter, C. L., & Wixson, K. K. (1991). *America will be*. Boston: Houghton-Mifflin.

Asante, M. K. (1987). *The Afrocentric idea*. Philadelphia: Temple University Press.

Banks, J. A. (1991/1992). Multicultural education: For freedom's sake. *Educational Leadership, 49* (4): 32–36.

Billingsly, A. (1968). *Black families in White America*. Englewood Cliffs, NY: Prentice-Hall.

Boggs, C. (1986). *Social movements and political power*. Philadelphia: Temple University Press.

Brendtro, L. K., Brokenleg, M., & Van Bockern, S. (1990). *Reclaiming youth at risk: Our hope for the future*. Bloomington, IN: National Educational Service.

Brickman, P., Rabinowitz, V., Kazura, J., Coates, D., Cohn, E., & Kidder, L. (1982). Models of helping and coping. *American Psychologist, 37*, 368–384.

Carrasquillo, A. L. (1991). *Hispanic children & youth in the United States*. New York: Garland Publishing Inc.

Crawford, J. (1989). *Bilingual education: History, politics, theory and practice*. Trenton, NJ: Crane Pub. Co.

Cushner, K., McClelland, A., & Safford, P. (1992). *Human diversity in education: An integrative approach*. New York: McGraw-Hill.

Davis, A. Y. (1981). *Women, race, and class*. New York: Random House.

Davis, M. (1991). In L.A., burning all illusions. *The Nation, 254* (21): 743–746.

Delpit, L. D. (1988). The silenced dialogue: Power and pedagogy in educating other people's children. *Harvard Educational Review, 58* (3): 280–299.

Fennema, E., & Leder, G. C. (Eds.) (1990). *Mathematics and gender*. New York: Teachers College Press.

Fordham, S. (1991). Peer-proofing academic competition among Black adolescents: "Acting White" Black American style. In C. E. Sleeter (Ed.), *Empowerment through multicultural education.* Albany, NY: State University of New York Press, 69–94.

Gates, H. L., Jr. (1991). Multiculturalism: A conversation among different voices. *Rethinking Schools, 6* (1): 1+.

Gibbs, J. T., & Huang, L. N., Eds. (1989). *Children of color.* San Francisco: Jossey-Bass.

Grant, C. A., & Sleeter, C. E. (1988). Race, class, gender and abandoned dreams. *Teachers College Record, 90* (1): 19–40.

Hacker, A. (1992). *Two nations: Black and White, separate, hostile, and unequal.* New York: Charles Scribner's Sons.

Harry, B. (1992). *Cultural diversity, families, and the special education system.* New York: Teachers College Press.

Hau de no sau nee (1977). *A basic call to consciousness.* Mohawk Nation: Akwesasne Notes.

Hawkins, B. D. (1992). Journalism diversity standard hampers HBCU accreditation. *Black Issues in Higher Education, 9* (15): 24–25.

Hewitt, N. A. (1984). *Women's activism and social change.* Ithaca, NY: Cornell University Press.

Hill, R. (1972). *The strengths of Black families.* New York: Emerson Hall.

Holland, D. C., & Eisenhart, M. A. (1988). Women's ways of going to school: Cultural reproduction of women's identities as workers. In L. Weis (Ed.), *Class, race & gender in American education.* Albany, NY: State University of New York Press, 266–301.

King, J. E., & Wilson, T. L. (1990). Being the soul-freeing substance: A legacy of hope in Afro humanity. *Journal of Education, 172* (2): 9–28.

Kunjufu, J. (n.d.). *Countering the conspiracy to destroy Black boys, Vol. III.* Chicago: African American Images.

Linden, E. (1991). Lost tribes, lost knowledge. *Time, 138* (12): 46–56.

Lucas, T., Henze, R., & Donato, R. (1990). Promoting the success of Latino language-minority students: An exploratory study of six high schools. *Harvard Educational Review, 60* (3): 315–340.

Macedo, D. (1991). English-only: The tongue-tying of America. *Journal of Education, 173* (2): 9–20.

Mann, E. (1991). *L.A.'s lethal air*. Los Angeles: A Labor/Community Strategy Center Book.

Marable, M. (1992). *The crisis of color and democracy*. Monroe, ME: Common Courage Press.

Mauer, M. (1990). Young black men and the criminal justice system. *Chicago Tribune*, March 4, Section 4, p. 3.

McDade, L. A. (1988). Knowing the "right stuff": Attrition, gender, and scientific literacy. *Anthropology and Education Quarterly, 19* (2): 93–114.

Medina, M. (1988). Hispanic apartheid in American education. *Educational Administration Quarterly, 24*, 336–349.

Mensh, E., & Mensh, H. (1991). *The IQ mythology*. Carbondale, IL: Southern Illinois University Press.

Minority Trendsletter (1991). Special issue on "Toxics and communities of color," Vol. 4, No. 4.

Mirande, A., & Enriquez, E. (1979). *La chicana*. Chicago: The University of Chicago Press.

Morrison, T. (1992). *Playing in the dark: Whiteness and the literary imagination*. Cambridge: Harvard University Press.

Nochlin, L. (1971). Why are there no great women artists? In V. Gornick & B. K. Moran (Eds.) *Woman in sexist society*. New York: Basic Books, 480–510.

Oakes, J. (1985). *Keeping track*. Princeton: Yale University Press.

Philips, S. U. (1983). *The invisible culture*. New York: Longman.

Reeves, R. (1990). Who got what in the 1990s? *Kenosha News*. August 30, p. 10.

Riche, M. F. (1991). We're all minorities now. *American Demographics, 13* (10): 26–34.

Rosaldo, R. (1989). *Culture and truth*. Boston: Beacon Press.

Rumberger, R. W. (1987). High school dropouts: A review of issues and evidence. *Review of Educational Research, 57*, 101–121.

Sadker, M., Sadker, D., & Long, L. (1989). Gender and educational equality. In J. A. Banks & C. M. Banks (Eds.), *Multicultural education: Issues and perspectives*. Needham Heights: Allyn & Bacon, 106–123.

Saldivar, R. (1990). *Chicano narrative*. Madison, WI: University of Wisconsin Press.

Schlesinger, A. M. (1991). The disuniting of America. *American Educator, 15* (3): 14+.

Shade, B. J. (1990). *Engaging the battle for African American minds*. Washington, DC: National Alliance of Black School Educators, Inc.

Sidel, R. (1986). *Women and children last*. New York: Viking.

Sleeter, C. E. (1987). Literacy, definitions of learning disabilities and social control. In B. M. Franklin (Ed.), *Learning disability: Dissenting essays*. London: The Falmer Press, 67–87.

Sleeter, C. E. (1992). *Keepers of the American dream*. London: The Falmer Press.

Smitherman, G. (1981). What go round come round: King in perspective. *Harvard Educational Review, 51* (1): 40–56.

Stack, C. (1974). *All our kin: Strategies for survival in a Black community*. New York: Harper & Row.

Sutcliffe, D. M. (1992). *System in Black language*. Clevedon, PA: Multilingual Matters.

Swinton, D. H. (1989). Racial parity under laissez-faire: An impossible dream. In W. A Van Horne & T. V. Tonnesen (Eds.), *Race: Twentieth century dilemmas—twenty-first century prognoses*. Milwaukee, WI: The University of Wisconsin System Institute on Race and Ethnicity, pp. 206–254.

Trueba, H. T. (1989). English literacy acquisition: From cultural trauma to learning disabilities in minority students. In B. J. R. Shade (Ed.), *Culture, style, and the educative process*. Springfield, IL: Charles C. Thomas, 49–70.

U.S. Bureau of the Census. (1991). *Statistical abstract of the United States: 1991* (111th ed.). Washington, DC: U.S. Government Printing Office.

Weatherford, J. (1988). *Indian givers*. New York: Crown Publishers.

Weis, L. (1990). *Working class without work*. New York: Routledge.

Winkler, K. J. (1992). A scholar's provocative inquiry: Was Huckleberry Finn Black? *Chronicle of Higher Education, 38* (44): A6–A8.

Wolf, N. (1991). *The beauty myth*. New York: Wm. Morrow & Co.

Woodson, C. G. (1969). *The miseducation of the Negro*. Washington, DC: The Associated Publishers.

✧ Chapter 5

Research Knowledge and Policy Issues in Cultural Diversity and Education

Roland G. Tharp

The increasing diversity of cultural and ethnic groups in American schools has led to a parallel increase in concern for the implications of this demographic shift for education. Research on cultural issues in education is by no means complete. But fortunately, pertinent literature from other disciplines, notably anthropology and linguistics, is available and to some degree we can invoke the parallel concerns of child-service delivery programs in mental health, social service, public health, and community development. There is more scatter than focus in the national research agenda, but there are also indications for a more coherent program of inquiry. Altogether, there may be sufficient evidence to indicate some basic policy directions for effective education of a diverse population. The purpose of this paper is to consider these issues at a broad level, in the hope of pointing in profitable directions, both for policy and the research that can continue to guide policy.

The Basic Questions

The implications of cultural membership for the education of children can be phrased as four basic questions:

(1) Can we account for important current student features in terms of the historical forces operating on his or her ancestors in a time frame of hundreds to thousands of years? That is, can the *ethnogenetic* level of analysis provide guidance for the design of effective educational programs?

(2) Are culture members privileged in the capacity to teach, administer or investigate the education of their children?

(3) Are there forms of education that are specifically or uniquely suited for the treatment of children of different cultures?

(4) Are there general or universal forms of schooling and teaching that will equally and adequately address students of diverse cultures?

Each of these questions will be addressed in turn.

Can Ethnogenetic Analysis Contribute to the Design of Effective Educational Programs?

What is a culture? Even more fundamentally, what is an ethnic group? Ethnic boundaries are not fixed; they are dynamic, evolving, and responsive to political and economic forces (Dominguez, 1985). As a critical current example, for certain purposes—whether political, policy, or language research—all Spanish-speaking groups consider themselves, and are considered by outsiders, as a single "Hispanic" ethnic or cultural group. For other purposes, Hispanics differentiate among themselves: Cuban-, Mexican-, and Puerto Rican Americans celebrate their distinctions as well as their common causes.

While there is little in educational research that addresses important differences within broad ethnic groups, there is considerable attention paid to the issue in clinical services research. For example, Everett, Proctor, and Cartmell (1983) point out the vast intertribal, interclan, urban-traditional, and individual differences among American Indian clients. Isomura, Fine, & Lin (1987) discuss the differences in offering services to Japanese immigrant families of the first, second and third generations. While people expect respect and understanding of their culture and values, they resent being seen merely as a representative of a cultural central tendency.

Perhaps even more critical is the issue of intra-cultural variability. Within all cultures, there are variations of considerable magnitude. How are these differences to be addressed? For example, within any cultural group, motivation, social organization, and ways of speaking and thinking vary with education, income, and class status. Broad educational prescriptions for "Hawaiians" or "African Americans" or "Native Indians" are often resented by culture members who are not well described by these generalizations. Culture and education research has tended to focus on those members of cultural groups who do less well in school, whereas there are major subcultural groups of Black, Indian or Hawaiian people who do not fit these descriptions in the social science and education literature. None of this invalidates the cultural level of explanation, but it behooves us to develop a more differentiated grid for study than has yet been achieved.

A part of the research agenda must therefore be to unpack the cultural variable (Whiting, 1976) so that differentiating characteristics within culture can be understood for clinical implications for individuals. In this way culture can be analyzed for its variable influence on individuals, in contrast to approaches which assign an equal value to culture for all members of a group (e.g.,Weisner, Gallimore & Jordan, 1988). Gallimore et al. (1991), investigating the correlates of academic success for children of Mexican immigrants, found that the domestic variable with the strongest relationship to a child's school success is whether the father uses skills of literacy/numeracy in his employment (not the level of father's education). This kind of finer-grained analysis of cultural and community life allows us accurately to perceive the dynamics of the daily cultural life of the individual child.

Figure 5.1 presents a conceptual scheme that places ethnogenetic analysis within a comprehensive framework of four levels of developmental processes which contribute to every human event, which are interactive, and all of which are potent in present time (Tharp, in press).

The phylogenetic level of causation operates through processes that we term "evolutionary," and, in human development, in spans of time between aeons and millennia. In clinical work, detailed phylogenetic analysis is not often employed, but is present in the background as a set of limitations, such as the processes of maturation

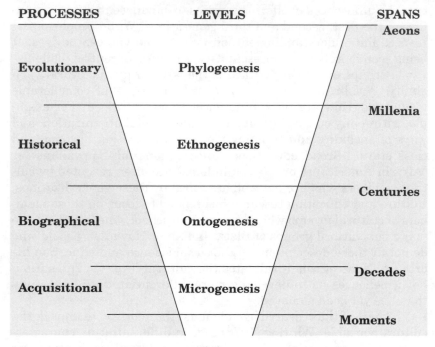

Figure 5.1   The Funnel and Filters of Development

that produce predictable changes in psychomotor coordination, language capacities, or the sexual drives of adolescence. The effects of phylogenetic processes may be altered, disguised, or emphasized by historical or biographical or acquisitional events, but all other levels of genetic process are conditioned by the phylogenetic.

The ontogenetic level of causation operates through processes that we describe as "biographical," in timespans roughly between a century and decades. Ontogenetic analysis is foundational to traditional psychology, in the sense of accounting for present conditions by reference to life history. In most human services, ontogenetic processes are systematically invoked: family dynamics are treated in an effort to alter major continuing influences on children's lives; or major new socialization figures may be introduced through removal from the home, in the knowledge that the parents, teachers, and heroes of childhood exercise great force in creating life history.

In education we are more accustomed to considering microgenetic processes—which operate through the agents of mentors, teachers and other adults who teach children particulars. The microgenetic level operates through acquisitional processes (of learning, imitation, and the like), and in time periods that vary from decades to moments.

Each of these factors are potent in present time and operate simultaneously; each conditions the processes below it.

Seldom considered, however, is the level of causation that operates in processes that we call historical, and in time periods between millennia and centuries. In Figure 5.1 that level is labelled ethnogenetic, meaning the process whereby a people (that is, an ethnic group) comes into being and modifies the terms of its existence.

This "funnel and filter" concept is the latest revision (see, e.g., Tharp & Burns, 1989) of my efforts to schematize this layering of genetic levels. The concept itself derives from L. S. Vygotsky, and many of his interpreters have made similar efforts (e.g., Engstrom, 1990). Versions of this conception are beginning to impact American academic developmental psychology, but ethnogenesis as an explanatory level has been historically and peculiarly absent from major theoretical systems of western psychology. This is in spite of the obvious: conditions of human life, present in every significant transaction, flow from historical processes that have matured for hundreds of years, and that operate causatively in present time.

By introducing this model, I hope to suggest a way that we may consider cognitive and educational issues and policies at the ethnogenetic level, that is by taking into account the historical processes of culture of origin, but considering them as they are filtered by events and forces in individual life history, learning experiences, and current conditions. Ethnogenetic analysis does not, *per se*, discount more contemporary and individual developmental events; to consider less than the entire layered funnel of developmental processes would indeed result in stereotypy, and deny the richness of the individual differences in accommodation characteristic of the members of each ethnic group.

Can the *ethnogenetic* level of analysis provide guidance for the design of effective educational programs? Yes, within a balance, and within limits.

Are Culture Members Privileged in the Capacity to Contribute to the Education of Their Children?

Can children be best educated by teachers who are members of the same culture as their students? The question can be expanded to include administrators and researchers. Is there a privilege attached to insider status, deriving from a deeper and more appropriate knowledge?

There is surprisingly little research evidence on this issue. However, we can take some guidance from clinical/counseling psychology, where the issue has been discussed for some time. For example, do social attitudes, particularly racism, affect the delivery of psychological services? It is easy to transpose the setting in the following reports from the consulting room to the classroom. Greene (1985), following Kupers (1981), articulates four general stances which are expressions of racism, and for which white therapists are enjoined to self-examination. They are (1) bigotry—"a conscious or unconscious belief in white supremacy, and as a consequence, the feeling that the black patient's problems are an outgrowth of the patient's inferiority"; (2) color blindness, which "may represent the therapist's resistance to confronting the meaning of the color difference"; (3) paternalism, which "involves the attribution of all of the patient's problems to society and the effects of racism. To do this will fail to help patients to understand any role they may have in their dilemma"; and (4) "often a result of the therapist's racial guilt, is the unquestioning compliance with the rhetoric of black power . . . (which) can result in a failure or reluctance to set appropriate limits or interpret acting-out." The black patient may consciously or unconsciously put the white therapist to a series of "tests" to determine the acceptance as an individual. "It remains, however, the therapist's responsibility to be familiar with the black patient's culture to some extent, and with his/her own personal feelings and motivations for and about working with black patients" (Greene, 1985, all quotations from pages 392–393).

Is there any acceptable stance? Or are same-ethnicity therapists (or educators) privileged in knowledge and attitude, and thus in power of effectiveness?

Another line of inquiry derives from psychological services in educational settings. College youth have clear preferences for counselors that are like themselves—counselors who are well educated, of the same ethnicity, the same gender, and who share their attitudes and values. By and large students report themselves more likely to use counseling services when their preferences are met (Haviland, Horswill, O'Connell, & Dynneson, 1983; Atkinson, Furlong, & Poston, 1986; Ponterotto, Alexander, & Hinkston, 1988; Atkinson, Furlong, Poston & Mercado, 1989).

The effectiveness of counseling, however, may or may not follow preferences. Both sides of that issue are presented by DeBlassie (1976), who insists that a therapist need not be Hispanic to be effective with young Mexican American clients; instead, he argues, common humanity, counseling skills, and generous attitudes are the critical issues for counselor effectiveness. However, he goes on to report many areas of values and beliefs that are arguably specific to Mexican American youth, and he appears to argue that knowledge of these is necessary for empathy to develop (DeBlassie, 1976).

Stanley Sue has devoted a long and distinguished career to the field of culture and psychological treatment. In his review of the literature on ethnic matching of therapist and client in psychotherapy (Sue, 1988), he finds contradictory and inconclusive evidence as to whether matching produces more effective treatment. A major contribution of this article is in distinguishing between ethnic membership (which emphasizes national or geographic origin of ancestors) and cultural membership (which emphasizes current identifications with the group(s), and their commonalties of values, attitudes, motives, etc.). Sue concludes that ethnic matching is irrelevant, whereas he finds cultural matching to be an authentic distal variable affecting outcome.

Sue urges researchers to consider more proximal variables, such as how cultural knowledge is translated into particular therapeutic behaviors and decisions. This position emphasizes the therapist's capacity for correct understanding, and for comfortable communication. "The issue is not whether patients are treated more effectively by same-race, same-class, or same-sex therapists, but whether the therapists' interpretation of the clients' cultural experience creates the ambience that is necessary to establish rapport and an empathic bond which facilitates the therapeutic process" (Juarez, 1985, p. 441).

This resolution is similar to that espoused for cultural research by the Cuban American anthropologist Dominguez (1985; 1986), who has worked both as "member" and "outsider" in cultural research. Her position is that "native" members' accounts of their own situation may well be privileged, because of their intimate, subjective, and empathic knowledge. This does not excuse "native" anthropologists' accounts from the disciplines of their scholarship and profession, and does not invalidate the "outsider" anthropologist's account, over which in terms of objectivity the "native" account is not *ipso facto* privileged (Tharp, 1991).

By analogy, it appears that teaching, relying so heavily on both subjective and objective accuracy of perception, must attempt to maximize that accuracy in a variety of ways. Ethnic matching may contribute, cultural matching may also contribute.

But as a matter of practicality, is cultural matching an available strategy? At the present time, it is clearly not so, since cultural groups are not proportionately represented in the educational professions. Even were that proportionality to be achieved, is matching socially desirable? If matching were to be achieved, then all teachers would teach only their own kind, and children would be limited in the educational advantages of learning from and about other peoples.

Are culture members privileged in the capacity to teach, administer or investigate the education of their children? Yes, in that empathy may be fostered by a shared subjectivity; but that privilege does not extend to objective description nor substitute for professional competence.

Are There Forms of Education That Are Specifically Suited for the Education of Different Cultures?

The hypothesis of cultural compatibility (Tharp 1989b) suggests that education is more effective when compatible with culture patterns. The hypothesis has an extensive and growing research base in child education (Tharp, 1989a), a modest one in child mental health (Tharp, 1991), and a beginning in child-community psychology (O'Donnell & Tharp, 1990). In all these fields, the issues are present in substantially the same terms. Three forms of the compatibility hypothesis exist. The strong form, or culturally specific version, suggests that the most effective interventions for different cultures will be different and specific (if not unique) to cultures. Proponents are associated with the effort to derive culturally based modalities or variations of education.

A weaker form is the two-type hypothesis, which suggests that there are two types of cultures, and therefore two types of most-effective clinical interventions. The first type is the majority, or EuroAmerican, culture; the second type includes those cultures whose students typically experience problems in schools, who are by-and-large "children of color," less industrialized, or urbanized, or western acculturated, and who thus share crucial incompatibilities with standard education and service-delivery practices. In this position, effective treatment strategies for "children of color" would not be critically different from one another. This position is more salient in social work (e.g., Lum, 1986) than in education.

The null form of the cultural-compatibility hypothesis is the universalistic argument that effective pedagogy will follow the same course for members of all cultures. This is the default hypothesis of education, in that the unreflective proceed as though there are no significant differences. A universalist position in education is entirely consistent with universalist theories of psychology, which, of course, have been predominant since the inception of the discipline. While the evidence for differential effects of standard education on members of different cultures intrudes more and more into consciousness, the default action is to continue to do the same, but harder, or longer, or more sincerely. Thus, in terms of action, the universalist hypothesis is associated with the status quo, or with widely accepted reform movements such as "restructuring." That is no logical necessity, and as we will see, there is good evidence that if a universalism is to be discovered for pedagogy, it will be of a different kind than is now conventional.

The Nature of the Evidence

A few years ago (Tharp, 1989a), I wrote that the most energy of those interested in African American educational improvement has been channelled into desegregation, and into equal treatment for all students; and that most Hispanic attempts at education reform have been directed toward issues in bilingualism, particularly toward issues of English acquisition, Spanish use and/or preservation, and improvement both of ESL pedagogy and of school attitudes toward bilingualism. Further, most inquiries into the schooling experiences of Asian American students have concentrated on parent-child relationships.

The intervening years have produced some changes, though not so many as might have been hoped. There has been an increase in the level of activity in the study of home-school relationships in Hispanic communities, in which the variables and processes present in the home are analyzed for their effects on school success. Notable in this work are Gallimore and his associates (e.g., 1991), Delgado-Gaitan (1987), and emerging studies such as Gibson and her associates (personal communication). Some few studies of the particularities of African American children in classrooms have been added (e.g., Allen & Boykin, 1991), but this rich research-and-development opportunity (outlined by Shade in 1982) remains largely unexplored, apparently due to the belief by the majority of Afro-American educators that standard education is the only assurance of fair education.

Thus, the preponderance of evidence for cultural issues in

education came from classrooms of Native Americans in the Western United States, Alaska, Hawaii, and Canada. A major source of theory, research and demonstration was the Kamehameha Early Education Program (KEEP), which over a 20-year period developed and studied a culturally compatible K–6 language arts program for children of Hawaiian ancestry (Tharp, Jordan, Speidel, Au, Klein, Sloat, Calkins, & Gallimore, 1984). Effectiveness data have been reported both by the program operators (Tharp & Gallimore, 1988; Klein, 1988; Tharp, 1982; Gallimore, Tharp, Sloat, Klein, & Troy, 1982), and by external experts (e.g., Calfee, Cazden, Duran, Griffin, Martus, & Willis, 1981). The KEEP group also operated a research and development site on the Navajo reservation of northern Arizona for six years. Selected because of the sharp contrast in ecocultural setting between the two cultures, Navajo and Hawaiian versions of the KEEP program emerged with clear differences.

In addition, there is a broad base of evaluation and program development literature coming from Native American schooling, both in the United States and Canada, which seeks to find ways of teaching and schooling that are compatible with traditional cultures and the current community. A recent review of that material is available (Tharp & Yamauchi, 1991).

The Evidence for the Compatibility Hypothesis

One line of argument for the compatibility hypothesis lies in discovering a minority group whose culturally based teaching-learning proclivities match well with standard schooling practices. The compatibility hypothesis would predict school success for such a group. Chinese children, as described by Wu (1982), would appear to be an example. Wu emphasizes that, on the basis of traditional culture, Chinese children are highly respectful of writing and written text, are respectful of the teacher as authority, are accustomed to individual, competitive effort, and rely on repetition and practice. These qualities are probably more pronounced in Chinese children than in majority-culture children, for whom (presumably) the standard school was designed. These qualities, nevertheless, are virtually defining expectations for standard American schooling, which emphasizes assignment of text, individual assessment, and repetitive practice activities. The high comparative success in schooling of Chinese American students is consistent with the compatibility hypothesis. Of course, this argument is based on logical analysis; I know of no empirical evidence that bears directly on the issue.

The evidential case for cultural compatibility can be discussed under the headings of the four classes of variables that have been most studied in the conscious tailoring of classrooms to children of different cultures: (1) social organization, (2) sociolinguistics, (3) cognition, and (4) motivation.

Social Organization

The typical North American classroom uses primarily whole-class organization, with rank-and-file seating and a teacher-leader who assigns text, instructs or demonstrates to the whole group, followed by some form of individual practice, and then teacher-organized individual assessment. This system is not the most effective for the students from all cultures. For many it produces a low level of child attention to teachers and classwork, which is disturbing to teachers, who attribute the problem to low academic motivation , rather than to an alien social organization (Tharp & Gallimore, 1976).

In the natal Hawaiian culture, collaboration, cooperation and assisted performance are commonplace. Sibling caretaking is common in Hawaiian socialization, and the sibling group and companion band are ubiquitous social organizations which tend to create their own activities (Gallimore, Boggs, & Jordan, 1974; Boggs, 1985). In the culturally compatible KEEP program, a small-group classroom organization was designed for Hawaiian children. The teacher engaged in an intense instructional conversation with a small group of students, while the majority of mixed-sex and mixed-ability students worked in independent groups of 4 to 5. A peer teaching-learning interaction occurred there every 3 minutes per child in kindergarten; in the first grade, once every 2.5 minutes (Jordan, 1977; 1983; 1984). The KEEP group, in its comparison study, introduced this identical pattern of classroom organization into a Northern Arizona Navajo classroom, as a modest test of the "two-type" compatibility hypothesis.

Navajo children also worked diligently in the independent work groups (centers). However, they worked much more independently, with few instances of offering or requesting peer assistance. Individuality and self-sufficiency of children is not surprising in the Navajo pastoralist culture, where six-year olds begin to herd sheep far from home, alone. Sibling and peer groups are present in Navajo culture, whenever brothers, sisters or cousins live together, and certainly in ceremonial and other community gatherings, but most are single-sex groups. In adult Navajo society, male and female roles are clearly defined and separated. Around the age of eight, boys and girls are cautioned against playing with each other. In the Navajo classroom, only when the groups were reorganized as same-sex did peer assistance become frequent (Vogt, Jordan, & Tharp, 1987).

Minority children all have social skills and problem solving abilities, though they may take several forms depending on culture. These skills can be brought into play by creating compatible social organizations of the classroom. Ethnographic work in urban Black ghetto schools described students' intense and sensitive peer relationships, physical expressiveness, and their skillful manipulations of the behavioral dynamics of their classrooms. The staging of impromptu "dramas," designed to tease, test, and sometimes to intimidate teachers, was a frequent technique (Williams, 1981).

> These skills are not developed in ghetto schools but are suppressed and interpreted as delinquency. . . . Left undeveloped, these skills get more disruptive . . . and can reach a level where they appear to be violent rebellions (Williams, 1981, p. 214).

By creating settings using group interaction and competitions, these tendencies can be brought into instructional use. Front-of-the-class performances related to instructional goals, with the balance of the class attentive to discovering errors that will allow them to replace the performers, were highly motivating for individual "performers" and "audience" alike (Williams, 1981).

To activate Indian student strengths, small-group problem-solving structures and individual assignments are preferred (Leith & Slentz, 1984). In the effective Athabaskan Indian classrooms studied by Barnhardt (1982), the majority of each school day was spent in individual or small group activities. The teachers moved from student to student, kneeling or squatting down on the floor for lengthy quiet individual discussions. When the teacher raised her voice again it signaled that the larger group was once again part of the audience (Barnhardt, 1982).

Sociolinguistics

The courtesies and conventions of conversation are among the most powerful differentiating elements of culture. Critical differences exist across cultures, and between many cultural groups and the classrooms in which their children are educated. When violations of the expectations of either teacher or children occur, it results in anger, alienation, or withdrawal. The result is often a school diagnosis of "low verbal ability," even for children who in other settings are highly verbal. Some variables studied by sociolinguistics can seem esoteric and inconsequential. But the weight of all those courtesies and conventions of discourse is enormous in determining relationship, learning, and satisfaction in the classroom.

Narrative Style

Michaels (1984) has shown that children of different cultures tell stories in different ways, with startling audience effects. In her study, White children were topic-centered in their narratives, with thematic cohesion and a temporal reference. Black children used a topic-associating style, consisting of a series of implicitly associated anecdotal segments with no explicit statement of an overall theme or point. White adults (including teachers) criticized the topic-associating style as incoherent, but Black adults found it interesting with lots of detail and description. It is apparent that this cultural difference in basic language structure can lead to quite different judgments and predictions in the classroom, with consequences often bewildering to both teachers and children.

Wait Time

Wait-time I is the amount of time given by teachers for students to respond to questioning; wait-time II is the amount of time following a student response before the teacher again speaks (Rowe, 1974).

Wait-times are to some degree culture-dependent. White and Tharp (1988) investigated differences in wait-time between an Anglo and a Navajo teacher of the same Navajo third-grade students; the Navajo teacher had considerably longer wait-time II than did the Anglo. What was perceived by the Anglo teacher as a completed response was often intended by the child only as a pause, which the Anglo teacher interrupted. Pueblo Indian children in experimental science classes participated spontaneously twice as frequently in longer wait-time classes than in shorter wait-time classes (Winterton, 1976). Even in college, Indian students report that short wait-time in seminar interactions is still a difficulty for them (Leacock, 1976).

On the other hand, Native Hawaiian children have a characteristic negative wait-time in informal settings, a pattern which produces overlapping speech, and which demonstrates involvement and relationship (White & Tharp, 1988). In classrooms, this is interpreted by other-culture teachers as rude interruption. Schools' attempts to curtail this overlapping speech only results in inhibiting participation of Hawaiian children in instructional activities.

Rhythm

Pioneering work in the sociolinguistic consequences of teacher/child interaction was done by Erickson and Mohatt (1977), in their classic report of an Indian teacher/student classroom that followed a slow, fluid, rhythmic tempo in the presentation of materials, in the voice inflections and vocalization tempo on the parts of both teacher and students, and even in the pace of movement in the classroom. The homes of some of those students revealed similar patterns. When this rhythm went unnoticed and was disrupted by an Anglo teacher, a more disorganized and less efficient pattern of interaction, as well as a lower level of rapport between teacher and students, resulted.

Barnhardt (1982) discovered Athabascan Alaskan classrooms in which Native children were eager to participate, volunteered answers, spoke and read well, and asked questions. She analyzed these classrooms in terms of rhythm patterns of event emphasis (beat), rate (density), and silence (pauses), and found them to be similar to interaction rhythms of the home and community. She argues that the disruptive effects of alien rhythmic structures on children in the classroom may be compared to the distress of listening to music with incomprehensible rhythmic structures.

For Afro-American classrooms, a quite different rhythmic structure has been proposed for promoting teacher-student rapport (Hale, 1982). Hale suggests that effective speech rhythms during instruction by teachers of Black children would be much like the rhythmic pattern of mother-child interaction, a "contest" style in which mother and child volley rhythmically. The child is encouraged to be assertive and to develop an individual style. Many Afro-American mothers give directions for household tasks to their children in a rhythm that approximates the call and response patterns found in Black music (Young, 1970). Hale (1982) and Wharton-Boyd (1983) both suggest that classroom teaching patterns could be based on these call-and-response children's singing games.

Participation Structures

The KEEP "talk-story" pattern of classroom discourse was developed to counter the phenomenon in which, in ordinary classrooms, Hawaiian children are "nonverbal," and seldom ask questions. In out-of-school situations, though, there is a social organization that facilitates children's narrative production: a number of children, together with an encouraging, participating, but non-directing adult, in an informal setting. Identified, facilitated, and described by Watson-Gegeo and Boggs (1977), these activity settings found children taking turns as principal speaker, but all the children "co-narrated," with overlapping speech and frequent references to shared experiences. Watson-Gegeo and Boggs (1977) discussed this activity setting in terms of a frequently enjoyed speech event in adult Hawaiian culture, called "talk-story." They also observed that children cannot manage a talk-story session alone until adolescence; in earlier years, an assisting adult is needed.

In an effort to create comparable classroom participation structures that would also produce child fluency and participation, KEEP developed the instructional-conversation format they call Center One. Each day, each child meets in a small group with the teacher for a 20-minute discussion of some text. The participation structures of the KEEP Center One lesson resemble those in the Watson-Gegeo narratives and in adult talk-story (Au, 1980; Au & Jordan, 1981). There is rapid-fire response, liveliness, mutual participation, interruption, overlapping volunteered speech, and joint narration. Au and Mason (1981) found higher rates of academically productive student behavior in these talk-story-like participation structures.

A sharper contrast could hardly be found than that between the Hawaiian pattern and that of the Navajo culture. Whereas Hawaiian children speak vigorously in shorter bursts of overlapping speech, and the teacher must often be "assertive" in getting the floor, long, patient turn-taking has been the standard description of Native American meetings, from the earliest pow-wows reported by Europeans. In the Navajo version of KEEP instructional conversations, each student speaks for longer periods while other students wait courteously. Ideas are developed with greater leisure, and are often individualistic rather than tied to statements of previous speakers. Navajo children volunteer both questions to the teacher and comments to the group at large.

When school sociolinguistic patterns are incompatible with natal culture patterns—for example, when the teachers use the "switchboard" pattern of interaction—many Indian culture children develop patterns of short answers, interruptions, and silence, which by high school, have calcified into a controlling and resentful repertoire of hostility (Greenbaum & Greenbaum, 1983).

When sociolinguistic school/home compatibilities are present, children are more comfortable, participate, and display their abilities appropriately. Another instance is Lein's study of Black migrant children. Teachers found them below grade level and unresponsive. But at home and in the community these same children speak and act in complex and competent ways. At home and at church, the expectations are similar; therefore, at church they exhibit full competence and full participation. This can offer an example to schools of how formal institutions can engage their young by compatibilities of expectations with child repertoires (Lein, 1975).

Cognition

North American schools expect, and instructional practices presume, a certain pattern of cognitive functioning in students: for example, a tendency toward verbal-analytic thought rather than visual/wholistic. When children correspond to that pattern, they are more likely to succeed in school, and that is the apparent pattern for Japanese- and Chinese Americans. The available evidence is inferential, but Stevenson, Stigler, Lee, Lucker, Kitamura, & Hsu (1985) studied a cross-national comparative sample of Japanese, Chinese, and White American first and fifth grade children. They concluded that children in each culture "have strengths and weaknesses, but by the time they are enrolled in the fifth grade of elementary school, the most notable feature of their performance is the similarity in level, variability, and structure of their scores on the cognitive tasks" (p. 734). From the cultural-compatibility point of view, this helps to explain why Japanese American and Chinese American students typically hold their own (or better) even as minorities in American schools: the levels and patterns of cognitive skills fit school expectations. Do students from other minorities, those who do not prosper in the schools, have different patterns of cognitive functioning from those expected by schools? The evidence is scattered, and again largely restricted to Native Americans, but differences appear.

Specific Cognitive Abilities

Internationally, typical school instruction appears to depend more heavily on verbal and sequencing skills than on performance and spatial skills. Native Americans consistently score in the opposite patterns, that is, higher in performance than in verbal abilities, and higher in spatial than in sequencing skills (e.g., Browne, 1984; Kaulback, 1984; McShane & Plas, 1982; Gallimore et al., 1982). However, Native children have improved significantly in sequential memory tasks (Krywaniuk & Das, 1976; More, 1985), and have demonstrated satisfactory progress in text-dominated courses (John-Steiner & Osterreich, 1975), when culturally compatible instructional features are present . The explanation for differential achievement lies in some interaction of instructional procedures with cognitive proclivities.

Wholistic/Visual vs. Verbal/Analytic Thought

Is the explanation in patterning of abilities, or in some system for organizing learning and thought? "Cognitive style" has been a loose construct that various writers have used to refer to such diverse variables as representational structures, sensory modality strengths, processing sequences, incentive valences, attributional probabilities, and implicit judgments of virtue, often bundled together without regard to any theoretical justification (Cazden & Leggett, 1981). Two aspects of cognitive style have suggested some cultural differences. One, *field dependence/independence* has generated much research on cross-cultural cognition (Witkin, 1967), but has contributed little to educational research and development (Cazden & Leggett, op.cit.).

Another "cognitive-style" variable that may make a difference is a visual, as opposed to a verbal, emphasis in perception and representational structures (for reviews see Berry, 1976; Kaulback, 1984; More, 1985; Tharp, in press). A visual emphasis is closely related to wholistic (vs. analytic) thought processes. In wholistic thought, the pieces derive their meaning from the pattern of the whole. In analytic thought, the whole is revealed through the unfolding of the sections. Wholistic comprehension proceeds by incorporating phenomena into ever-expanding circles of context, rather than by reducing phenomena to their disassembled parts (Tharp, in press).

Rather than through analytic and linear means, the concept of wholism may be communicated best by a wholistic device: a "teaching story." Joan Gentles, a Chilcotin Indian educator, has told me how, as a girl, she learned to prepare salmon. After watching her mother, she was allowed to gradually take on portions of the task, and to ask questions only if they were important. Once she told her mother that she didn't under-stand how to do "the backbone part." So her mother took another entire fish, and repeated the de-boning. It is not possi-ble to fully comprehend the backbone part except in the con-text of the whole fish. (Tharp, 1989, p. xx)

An entire "observation-learning complex" is involved in the kinds of cultural socialization that produce wholistic thinking. The complex includes: observing first, and thus gaining competence before performance; learning-by-doing, rather than through verbal instructions; a centrality of visual cognitive representational struc-tures; and a sociological pattern of children's involvement with adult activities (Cazden & John, 1971; Rogoff, 1986; Tharp, 1989a).

Lipka (1991) provides an analysis of Eskimo teachers' lesson transcripts; they reflect observational learning strategies. Lipka describes the lessons thus:

Activities begin without the customary lengthy verbal intro-duction Anglos expect. . . . The students seem quite comfort-able following the modeled behavior. The teacher's instruc-tional style also includes modeling (doing his "own work"), joining in with the students (seated on the floor with the stu-dents as he blends into the class), and reinforcing peer-group solidarity and deep respect for individuals.

There is intentionality in his style. For example, there are a few times during the lesson when students will say *nutmen* (where), and the teacher intentionally ignores the students. He does not want to reinforce dependence on verbal instruc-tion during activities that call for observation. (Lipka, 1991, pp. 213–214)

Wholism in the Classroom

Even for basic skill literacy and numeracy lessons, it is possible to systematically favor wholistic and visual teaching strategies, by emphasizing whole-story discussions, overarching themes, and by using visual diagrams and metaphors. KEEP has reported that Navajo children often demanded to hear or read a story through to the end before starting discussion (Vogt, Jordan, & Tharp, 1987). In community story-telling, children are not asked to recite details of the story or to dissect it, but are expected to listen quietly to the long telling of stories. Teachers of Indian children who frequently interrupt narrative events with assessment questions produce a sharp cultural discongruity (Philips, 1972, 1983; Wyatt, 1978–79).

John-Steiner & Oesterreich (1975) discuss this same phenomenon among Pueblo children, and provide a link from this interpersonal event to a cognitive style:

> Children listening to the many legends of their people learn to represent these visually . . . because they are not allowed to ask questions or verbally reflect on what they hear. They are to say only *aeh hae* to acknowledge auditory attention. As a result, while the verbal representations of some of these legends are fairly simple nursery tales, the inner representations of the same legends, for older children and adults, are replete with highly abstract visual and symbolic articulations of cultural values. (John-Steiner & Oesterreich, 1975, p. 192)

Every advisor and researcher familiar with Native American education urges the use of wholistic presentations and visual representations during teaching of Native children. These strategies are often advocated by educational reformers for majority culture students, too, though for different reasons. White and Asian children may well need such "training," whereas Native children may require wholistic and verbal contexts in order to frame the development of analytic and verbal skills. When reading programs are congruent with the "simultaneous" (wholistic) style of Indian children, as opposed to the "successive" style of non-Natives, they can strengthen "successive," or linear, abilities (More, 1985). For example, reading and mathematics instruction, when presented in a visual, wholistic manner, strengthens the students' abilities to read and calculate in a linear, verbal mode.

The more general issue raised by the visual/verbal representations is that of learning through participation of the several sensory modalities. Allen & Boykin (1991) demonstrated that Afro-American primary children, as opposed to Euro-American counterparts, learned a picture-pairing task best in a "High Movement Expressive" context—that is, with an opportunity to move to music during acquisition trials. This study continues Boykin's (1978) interest in

Afro-American children's "verve"—a preference for a variety of rapid paced and varied stimulation. Allen & Boykin's important analog study is evidence for cultural differences in school-learning tasks, attributable to differential involvement of sensory modalities.

This is at the heart of Vera John-Steiner's concept of "cognitive diversity":

> In proposing a pluralistic approach to thinking, I have argued that while an individual may have a dominant mode of representation (or internal code), there is no single universal language of thought . . . there are wide variations among individuals in the extent to which their internal, symbolic codes are based on verbal language, abstract visual schemata, musical representations, or kinesthetic images (see Gardner {1987}) . . . the coordinated use of two differing codes can assist a thinker in successfully solving a demanding task. (John-Steiner, 1991, p. 73)

Motivation, Trait and State

"Trait" Motivation

Some motivations are relatively consistent, persistent, and supported by parental, community, and cultural reinforcement—these can be considered "trait" motivations. An example that has powerful effects on school outcome can be drawn from the remarkable success and satisfaction with school achieved by recent immigrant Hmong, Vietnamese, and Korean groups—in spite of the fact that 80 percent of these children report language conflicts, prejudice, and teasing from other children. The families, however, tend toward strong beliefs in education, high expectations for school performance, and constant admonitions to study (Hirayama, 1985).

This is reminiscent of Punjabi immigrant families in the California community of "Valleyside," whose children are highly successful students. They know that failure puts them at risk for being withdrawn from school and put to work in the fields. They are clearly and often told by their families that they bear the responsibility for school success themselves; they must study hard, respect their teachers, stay out of fights with their peers, finish their homework, and generally succeed for the honor of themselves, their families, and the entire Punjabi community (Gibson, 1986).

In many immigrant groups, there is parental emphasis on the welfare of the family as a whole, and the assumption by the student of the moral burden of succeeding for the whole family, if not the whole community. These factors are both characteristic and predictive of success within the Asian groups studied by Hirayama (1985). Suarez-Orozco (1987) discussed the Mexican child's responsibility for the honor of the entire family, and has also described the burden of guilt and responsibility of Central American refugee students in Los Angeles schools, many of whose families have suffered extreme misfortune, and even death, in bringing them to America. Now they must succeed, through education. This is motivation indeed.

While many immigrant groups do succeed in American schools, immigrant status *per se* does not produce school success. In Hawaii, both Samoan and Filipino immigrant students are at-risk groups for school failure. And school-relevant motivations change as immigrant children learn different motivations in schools themselves, such as competition and individualism (Trueba & Delgado-Gaitan, 1985).

As for more conventional psychological measures of trait motivation, the "Need for Achievement" (NAch) is, among majority culture students, generally associated with school success. Although Black, Hispanic, and Hawaiian children's tests often show less need for achievement and more need for affiliation, they do not lack motivation for accomplishment, recognition, and reward. But achievement is more often sought in a context and for the purpose of family and peer-group solidarity and identification, rather than for individual and independent attainment (Gallimore, Boggs & Jordan, 1974; Ramirez & Price-Williams, 1976).

"State" Motivation

State motivation refers here to those motivational and incentive variables existing in the classroom itself, and which are manipulable by teachers and program designers. Motivation by interest-level of materials, by contingent reinforcement and punishment, and by teacher relationships may not be crucial for children whose school-motivation is inculcated and continually supported by their own families and community; but these features are often imperative for engaging and managing disaffected, underachieving children. For example, the introduction of supplementary incentives for frequency of reading was more effective for Chicano children than for Anglos (Hosford & Bowles, 1974).

KEEP researchers report on-task rates for their Hawaiian classrooms of 80 percent plus (Tharp, 1982), which they attribute both to a manipulation of school-based incentives, and to a system of teacher-child relationship developed by close study of Hawaiian children at home and at school (Gallimore, Boggs, & Jordan, 1974). For example, Hawaiian children are highly peer oriented, and are taught not to approach adults except on invitation (Gallimore, Boggs, & Jordan, op.cit.). Therefore, every teacher in every class in every year must reestablish her legitimate claim to authority by establishing a warm, firm, but personal and affective link with students.

Among the Navajo, punishment, contingent reward, or any openly manipulative effort to control the behavior of others—including children—is a violation of cultural values. Navajo adults are more reserved in their affectionate displays, but are highly respectful of children's individuality and their rights for self-determination. This is notable in comparing the atmosphere of the two classrooms. The teachers in both KEEP programs maintain high on-task rates, orderly rotations, and excellent compliance. But the Navajo teachers accomplish this while moving through the classroom in what seems, by Hawaiian comparison, virtual silence.

Thus for Navajos, the reinforcing and punishing value of identical teacher behaviors are often reversed from those for Hawaiians. The reinforcing valence of particular classroom conditions and events may also be quite different for Navajo and Hawaiian children. For example, "time-out" from the social interactions of recess or in-class activities is a painful punishment for Hawaiian children. In Navajo classrooms, children are quite content to be alone, and often have to be escorted from one area of school to another to prevent their running away to spend the balance of the school day playing alone.

In summary, there is evidence that cultural differences in social organization, sociolinguistics, cognition, and motivation, when reflected in compatibilities in classroom practices, make for classrooms that are endorsed by culture members and other students of those cultures, are associated with greater child participation and enjoyment, are associated with better school achievement, and produce classrooms that are discernibly different for students of different cultures.

Now let us consider the apparent limitations on the development of specific-culture educational programs. It must be noted that comparatively few have been designed to survive the practicalities of schools. In the culture and education movement, most compatibilities have been established through choosing established modalities which *per se* allow for greater influence of the child's culture, or at least do not demand incompatible child behavior.

The majority of mental health programs for minority children appear to be using that same tactic: Few specific treatment modalities have been invented (for an exception, see Costantino, Malgady, & Rogler, 1986). Certain modalities, however, are overwhelmingly preferred by therapists knowledgeable of certain cultures; and each instantiation is recommended to be conditioned by the culture. Thus, family therapy is repeatedly recommended for Hispanic children, but the recommendation is equally strong that the family must be treated in ways that reflect that family's composition, values, and language (e.g., Inclan, 1984; Vazquez-Nuttal, Avila-Vivas, & Morales-Barreto, 1984). By electing modalities that naturally include family and community members and/or settings, some compatibility is assured by the objective introduction of the cultural context.

Likewise, the cultural-compatibility movement in education appears to have settled on the "least-change" principle (Tharp, et al., 1984) which calls not for inventing entire new pedagogies or teaching modalities, but the careful selection of modalities of demonstrated effectiveness in real schools and by working teachers. The selection and mix of such modalities may be quite different for children of different cultures, and it is certain that the instantiation of the modalities will be modified by contextualizing them in the experience and language of the children's daily lives.

We may now return to the original question. Are there forms of education that are specifically suited for the treatment of children of different cultures? Yes.

Are there Universal Forms of Teaching That Will Equally and Adequately Address Classrooms of Students of Diverse Cultures?

Having reviewed the evidence for cultural differences that impact teaching, learning and schooling, we are in a much better position to consider another problem of the highest social import, that of the multicultural classroom. Critics of the cultural compatibility movement too often leap to a dismissive conclusion that classrooms cannot possibly be compatible with more than one, and often a great many cultures and therefore, cultural dimensions of teaching/

learning are irrelevant. This is, in my view, a grave error. Awareness of the variables in which cultural incompatibilities interfere with teaching/learning alerts us to possibilities for correction and rearrangement. Even more important, this awareness allows us to devise conditions of instruction in which the variables (sociolinguistic, motivational, cognitive, and social organizational) *are least likely to be divisive.*

In more conventional phrasing, the question is: Under what conditions will effective education for classrooms of diverse students be most likely to occur? While cultural differences can never be completely abrogated, and will always require some accommodation and special attention, we do know major conditions, which, if achieved, will reduce the divisive impact of cultural differences. To many policy makers it may be a surprise, but the answer is well enough known, and is sufficiently consensual, for us to proceed with confidence.

Prescriptions for Improvement: The Four Principles[1]

Although the cultural compatibility research base has been developed by examination of monocultural classrooms, it is possible to look at these studies of minority cultures in another way. That is, are there any uniformities among the recommendations of those researchers who have studied African American, American Indian, Eskimo, Hawaiian, Puerto Rican and all the other culture-school relationships? Indeed there are. In fact, remarkable similarities are present in the recommendations. Another way of phrasing this is: The four variables discussed previously are those which, if incompatible, can divide and interfere with progress among members of the learning community. The four principles discussed in this section are educational processes that can unite the members of the community, or at least minimize the impact of their cultural differences. The list has been developed by examining the existing literature, and assembling the recommendations, research results, and advice of experts, and by case study implications that are now available to scholarship.

All the principles are stated as descriptors of schooling in which the distilled recommendations are operating.

Principle I. Developing competence in the language of instruction is a metagoal of all instructional activities of the school day. Mastery of the language of instruction, whether in bilingual or monolingual programs, will continue to be the *sine qua non* for academic achievement to the extent that verbal means of instruction continue to dominate, and to the extent that literacy continues as the core goal of education.

Cultural groups that do not emphasize verbal analytic problem solving are handicapped in schools because teachers are so heavily reliant on verbal analytic methods and the use of verbal forms of instruction. For such children, cultural compatibility educators have repeatedly advocated the use of visual and wholistic methods for the teaching of literacy, numeracy, and science. However, they also advocate the inclusion in educational programs of activities specifically designed to produce language development (e.g., Kaulback, 1984; Speidel, 1987b).

The current literacy movement in cognitive and educational research is revealing the deep ties among language, thinking, values and culture. Language development at all levels—vocabulary through syntax—is advocated as a self-conscious and ubiquitous goal for the entire school day. Evidence is also strong that language development of this kind should be fostered through use, and through purposive conversation between teacher and students, rather than through drill and decontextualized rules (Speidel, 1987a; 1987b). The methods appropriate to language development in the multicultural classroom will be discussed under two other principles below; however it is done, the first principle for the multicultural classroom is that development of the language of instruction should be a metagoal of all instruction, and should be pursued throughout the day and across the curriculum.

Principle II: Teaching, curriculum and the school itself are contextualized in the experiences, skills and values of the community. The second constant recommendation of the culture and education field, and indeed of developmental theorists and educational reformers, is for an increase in contextualized instruction. Schools teach rules, abstractions, and verbal descriptions. They teach by means of rules, abstractions, and verbal descriptions. Many cultural communities do not. Schools must assist such students by providing experiences of how rules, abstractions, and verbal descriptions are drawn from the everyday world, and how they are applied to it.

In an unusual culture and education study, Hvitfeldt (1986) studied the classroom behavior of Hmongs in an adult education English class, who had enough influence over their classroom and instructor to persist in their preferred sociolinguistic and role-relationships. No matter how hard the instructor would try to use abstract and decontextualized examples, the Hmong would themselves contextualize the instruction by promoting a warm, personal relationship with the instructor, by asking him personal questions, teasing, laughing, and joking with him. When the instructor would not specify context, the students themselves would relate it to a known, personal context. When the instructor used fictional Hmong names in drills, the students invariably stopped the lesson to check with one another about who this person might be in the Hmong community. These adults forced contextualization on the instructor. Child students can seldom do so. Contextualization must therefore be provided by the teacher and school.

Three levels of contextualization are discussed in the culture and education literature. At the first, or pedagogical level, is the necessity to invoke children's existing schema as they relate to material being instructed (Au, 1979). That is, the content of instruction should be drawn from, or carefully related to, the child's own environment and experience (Garcia, 1991).

At the second, or curriculum level, there is uniform advocacy for instructional use of cultural materials and skills as the media in which goals of literacy, numeracy, and science are contextualized, drawing on personal, community-based experiences as the foundation for developing school skills (e.g., Wyatt, op. cit.), and thus affording students opportunities to apply skills acquired in home and school contexts (Garcia, 1991).

At the third, or policy level, there are advocates for contextualization of the school itself. School-learning is a social process that affects and is affected by the entire community. "More long-lasting progress has been achieved with children whose learning has been explored, modified, and shaped in collaboration with their parents and communities" (John-Steiner & Smith, 1978, p. 26).

All levels of contextualization by anchoring in personal, community, and cultural meanings appear to have this same felicitous, if paradoxical, effect. The high-literacy goals of schools—verbal, analytic, and abstract knowledge and cognition—are better achieved in everyday, culturally meaningful contexts. This contextualization utilizes child experiences and skills as a sound foundation for appropriating new knowledge. This approach fosters pride and confidence, as well as greater school achievement.

The first two principles that we have discussed are entirely consistent with all available research and theory. And Garcia (1991) is pointed and accurate in urging these conditions all the more for culturally diverse classrooms. This introduces an apparent paradox: the greater the need for contextuality, the greater the apparent difficulty of producing it. How is the teacher to provide for contextualization in the experienced life of the student when the students vary so widely in their life contexts? And how can teachers know that context for each diverse child?

Principle III: Teaching and learning occurs in contexts of joint productive activity with peers and teacher. The basic strategy for maximizing the contextuality for students of diverse cultural origins, is *to create a common context of experience in the school itself.* Contemporary sociocultural theory emphasizes that learning takes place best in joint productive activity, that is, when experts and novices work together for a common product or goal, and have ample opportunity to converse about the activity while it is ongoing (Wertsch, 1985; Tharp & Gallimore, 1988; Rogoff, 1991).

In natural (non-formal) settings even the youngest children, as well as mature adult learners, develop their competencies in the context of joint activity. Shared ways of understanding the world are created through the development of language systems and word meanings that are used during shared activity. Schools typically do not do it this way; there is little joint activity from which common experiences emerge, and therefore, there is no common context that allows students to develop a common understanding with the teacher and with each other.

The well-understood, formal task of schools is to promote the development of discourse competencies, word meaning, and conceptual structures in a variety of content areas. How are those competencies developed? Schools do not yet understand that it requires everyday, shared experiences in which the concepts take on meaning, activities that provide an interface of the content area systems with those of everyday concepts. It is on that interface that the highest order of meaning is achieved, insuring that tools of verbal thought can be manipulated for the solution of practical problems of the experienced world. "Effective instruction with young children involves a continuous integration of language and action" (Wood, 1980, p. 290).

This system is used consistently in the highest reaches of scientific and philosophical thought. Theoretical thought and discussion requires a continual freshening by example, and a testing against sensory data. This constant connecting of schooled concepts and everyday concepts is the basic process of understanding the world used by mature, schooled thinkers.

Joint productive activity is also motivating. For example, we know that the discourse of science occurs in a particular register, with its distinct rules and formalities. In the teaching of science, however, these conventions are frequently violated by the interpolation of everyday discourse. These variations stimulate student interest. These alternations are marked by tone of voice, laughter, asides, etc. *During these times, the attention of students is at its highest* (Cazden, 1987).

One final characteristic of joint productive activity as the basic context of instruction for culturally diverse classrooms: the activities should be shared both by students and teacher. Only if the teacher is also involved in the experiences can the kind of discourse take place that builds basic schooled competencies.

This principle of joint productive activity has been summarized by Garcia (1991) as a set of teaching principles for Hispanic students. The conclusions are no different for any classroom in which a shared children-teacher cultural and community context is lacking. In such classrooms there should be (1) activity settings for joint work with peers and teacher; (2) learning through active rather than passive endeavors; (3) in an integrated curriculum, providing opportunities to study a topic in depth, and applying skills acquired in home and school contexts; and (4) opportunities for applying concepts to a meaningful context (paraphrased from Garcia, 1991).

Principle IV: The basic form of teaching is through dialogue between teacher and learners—through the Instructional Conversation. For so long as the basic goal and process of school is verbal knowledge and verbal analysis, then the royal road to educational attainment, which can provide the cognitive and experiential basis for allowing teachers to relate emerging knowledge to the individual, community and family knowledge of the student, is the instructional conversation. The development of thinking skills, the abilities to form, express, and exchange ideas in speech and writing: for all these basic processes, the critical form of assisting learners is through dialogue, through the questioning and sharing of ideas and knowledge that happens in the instructional conversation.

The concept appears to be a paradox: "instruction" and "conversation" appear contradictory, the one implying authority and planning, the other equality and responsiveness. The task of teaching is to resolve this paradox. To most truly teach, one must converse; to truly converse is to teach.

In the instructional conversation, there is a fundamentally different assumption from that of traditional lessons. Teachers who engage in conversation, like parents in their natural teaching, are assuming that the child may have something to say beyond the "known answers" in the head of the adult. They occasionally extract from the child a "correct" answer, but to grasp the communicative intent of the child requires the adult to listen carefully, to make guesses about the meaning of the intended communication (based on the context, and on knowledge of the child's interests and experiences), and to adjust their responses to assist the child's efforts—in other words, to engage in conversation.

Through this conversation, the culture of the learner is clearly revealed. The assumptions, perceptions, values, beliefs, experiences—all the subjective and cognitive components of cultural membership will be revealed through genuine conversation, thus allowing the teacher to be responsive, to contextualize teaching in the experience base of the learner, and actually to individualize instruction, in the same way that each learner is individualized within culture.

Teaching through dialogue is (in one way) already present in the cultural repertoire of most teachers, and in another way is an exquisite skill that requires much work to perfect. While good instructional conversations often appear to be "spontaneous," they are not—even though young students may never realize it. The instructional conversation is pointed toward a learning objective by the teacher's intention, and even the most sophisticated learners may lose consciousness of the guiding goal as they become absorbed in joint activity with the mentor.

In American schools the instructional conversation is rare indeed. More often our teaching is through the "recitation script," in which the teacher repeatedly assigns and assesses, assigns and assesses. But when true dialogic teaching occurs, classrooms and schools are transformed into "the community of learners" that schools can become "when teachers reduce the distance between themselves and their students by constructing lessons from common understandings of each others' experience and ideas" and make teaching a "warm, interpersonal and collaborative activity" (Dalton, 1989).

These four principles are related, and form one wholistic view of education for classrooms of diversity. That is, the *instructional conversation* is the best method for *development of the language* of instruction, which occurs best when *contextualized* in experience, the ideal form of which is by creating *joint productive activity,* which becomes the setting for the *instructional conversation.* These principles distill the uniform research and experience of those who have worked in schooling of monocultural minority and of multicultural and linguistically diverse classrooms.

Are these principles valid only for minority students? Far from it! Indeed, the principles are entirely consistent with natural teaching and learning, as practiced by homo sapiens traditionally, in all informal community, cultural, productive and familial settings since the dawn of time and on every continent. The principles may also be used to describe most effective education for majority-culture students also. Traditional North American education, however, has not practiced such education, because the schools have relied on the family and community experiences of majority-culture adults to provide the activity, the conversation, the language development and the shared context upon which the schools could depend.

This is no longer true, in culturally and linguistically diverse nations. The schools must now provide the common experience, activity, language and conversation that learners require, both for individual development and the development of a common, shared and mutually endorsed community.

Therefore, we may confidently summarize the implications of research and development for policy:

- To the extent that cultural diversity is present, it is all the more critical that developing competence in the language of instruction is a metagoal of all instructional activities of the school day.

- To the extent that cultural diversity is present, it is all the more critical that teaching, curriculum, and the school itself are contextualized in the experiences, skills and values of the community.

- To the extent that cultural diversity is present, it is all the more critical that teaching and learning occurs in contexts of joint productive activity with peers and teacher.

- To the extent that cultural diversity is present, it is all the more critical that the basic form of teaching is through dialogue between teacher and learners—through the instructional conversation.

Adherence to these four principles will not remove the cultural differences that divide teachers and students. But classrooms so organized will provide for the common understanding and shared experiences upon which unity can be expanded. Adherence to these four principles will not change the wisdom of teacher sensitivity to differences among children in the courtesies and conventions of conversation that make them most comfortable, but it will provide common experiences upon which a new classroom convention and courtesy can be built. In short, these principles do not dissolve childrens' cultures; rather, they describe the best known available means of creating a new culture of the school which will move toward unity through a new, created microculture of the school.

That these guidelines are the best now known must be emphasized. These conclusions derive from widely available published sources, and, as such, reflect the (surprisingly) consensual conclusions of active researchers, developers and theoreticians at this time. Much remains to be known, and there is no doubt that richer, wiser, and more inclusive knowledge can be developed. Additional knowledge, however, will now require that we begin the detailed study of classrooms that incorporate these state-of-the-art recommendations, so that the limitations of our current knowledge will be revealed. This should be the next emphasis of educational research and development.

NOTE

1. The four principles do not map onto the four variables discussed in the preceding section; they speak to quite different issues. That each list numbers four is coincidental.

REFERENCES

Allen, B. A., & Boykin, A. W. (1991). The influence of contextual factors on Afro-American and Euro-American children's performance: Effects of movement opportunity and music. *International Journal of Psychology, 26*, 373–387.

Atkinson, D. R., Furlong, M. J., & Poston, W. C. (1986). Afro-American preferences for counselor characteristics. *Journal of Counseling Psychology, 33*, 326–330.

Atkinson, D. R., Furlong, M. J., Poston, W. C., & Mercado, P. (1989). Ethnic group preferences for counselor characteristics. *Journal of Counseling Psychology, 36*, 68–72.

Au, K. H. (1979). Using the experience-text-relationship method with minority children. *The Reading Teacher, 32* (6): 677–679.

Au, K. H. (1980). Participation structures in a reading lesson with Hawaiian children: Analysis of a culturally appropriate instructional event. *Anthropology & Education Quarterly, 11*, 91–115.

Au, K. H., & Jordan, C. (1981). Teaching reading to Hawaiian children: Finding a culturally appropriate solution. In H. T. Trueba, G. P. Guthrie, & K. H. Au (Eds.), *Culture and the bilingual classroom: Studies in classroom ethnography*. Rowley, MA: Newbury House Publishers, Inc., 139–152.

Au, K. H., & Mason, J. M. (1981). Social organizational factors in learning to read: The balance of rights hypothesis. *Reading Research Quarterly, 17* (1): 115–152.

Barnhardt, C. (1982). Tuning-in: Athabaskan teachers and Athabaskan students. In R. Barnhardt (Ed.), *Cross-Cultural issues in Alaskan education. Vol. II*. Fairbanks: University of Alaska, Center for Cross-Cultural Studies. (ERIC Document Reproduction Service No. ED 232 814).

Berry, J. W. (1976). *Human ecology and cognitive style*. New York: Sage Halsted, Inc.

Boggs, S. T. (1985). *Speaking, relating, and learning: A study of Hawaiian children at home and at school*. Norwood, NJ: Ablex Publishing Co.

Boykin, A. W. (1978). Psychological/behavioral verve in academic/task performance: Pre-theoretical considerations. *The Journal of Negro Education, 68*, 343–354.

Browne, D. A. (1984). WISC-R scoring patterns among Native Americans of the northern plains. *White Cloud Journal, 3*, 3–16.

Calfee, R. C., Cazden, C. B., Duran, R. P., Griffin, M. P., Martus, M., & Willis, H. D. (1981). *Designing reading instruction for cultural minorities: The case of the Kamehameha Early Education Program*. Cambridge, MA: Harvard Graduate School of Education.

Cazden, C. B. (1987, January). Text and context in education. Paper presented at the Third International Conference on Thinking, Honolulu.

Cazden, C. B., & John, V. P. (1971). Learning in American Indian children. In M. L. Wax, S. Diamond, & F. O. Gearing (Eds.), *Anthropological perspectives on education*. New York: Basic Books, 252–272.

Cazden, C. B., & Leggett, E. L. (1981). Culturally responsive education: Recommendations for achieving Lau remedies. In H. T. Trueba, G. P. Guthrie, & K. H. Au (Eds.), *Culture and the bilingual classroom: Stud-*

ies in classroom ethnography. Rowley, MA: Newbury House Publishers, Inc., 69–86.

Costantino, G., Malgady, R. G., & Rogler, L. H.. (1986). Cuento therapy: A culturally sensitive modality for Puerto Rican children. *Journal of Consulting and Clinical Psychology, 54,* 639–645.

Dalton, S. (1989). *Teachers as assessors and assistors: Institutional constraints on interpersonal relationships.* Paper delivered at the meetings of the American Educational Research Association, San Francisco.

DeBlassie, R. R. (1976). *Counseling with Mexican American youth: Preconceptions and processes.* Austin, TX: Learning Concepts, Inc.

Delgado-Gaitan, C. (1987). *Literacy for empowerment: The role of parents in children's education.* London: Falmer Press.

Dominguez, V. (1985). *White by definition.* Baton Rouge: Louisiana State University Press.

Engstrom, Y. (1990). *Learning, working and imagining: Twelve studies in activity theory.* Helsinki: Orienta-Konsultit Oy.

Erickson, F., & Mohatt, G. (1977). *The social organization of participation structures in two classrooms of Indian students.* Report to the Department of Indian Affairs and Northern Development, Ottawa (Ontario). (ERIC # ED 192 935).

Everett, F., Proctor, N., & Cartmell, B. (1983). Providing psychological services to American Indian children and families. *Professional Psychology: Research and Practice, 14,* 588–603.

Gallimore, R., Boggs, J. W., & Jordan, C. (1974). *Culture, behavior and education: A study of Hawaiian-Americans.* Beverly Hills, CA: Sage Publications.

Gallimore, R., Reese, L. J., Balzano, S., Benson, C., & Goldenberg, C. (1991). *Ecocultural sources of early literacy experiences: Job-required literacy, home literacy environments, and school reading.* Paper read at the Annual Meetings of the American Educational Research Association, Chicago.

Gallimore, R., Tharp, R. G., Sloat, K., Klein, T., & Troy, M. E. (1982). *Analysis of reading achievement test results for the Kamehameha Early Education Project: 1972–1979* (Tech. Report No. 102). Honolulu: Kamehameha Schools/Bishop Estate.

Garcia, E. E. (1991). "Hispanic" children: Theoretical, empirical and related policy issues. *Educational Psychology Review.*

Gardner, H. (1987). *The mind's new science: A history of the cognitive revolution.* New York: Basic Books.

Gibson, M. A. (1986, December). *Parental support for schooling.* Paper presented at the Annual meeting of the American Anthropological Association, Philadelphia.

Greenbaum, P., & Greenbaum, S. C. (1983). Cultural differences, non verbal regulation, and classroom interaction: Sociolinguistic interference in American Indian education. *Peabody Journal of Education, 61,* 16–33.

Greene, B. A. (1985). Considerations in the treatment of Black patients by White therapists. *Psychotherapy, 22,* 389–393.

Hale, J. (1982). *Black children: Their roots, culture, and learning styles.* Provo, Utah: Brigham Young University Press.

Haviland, M. G., Horswill, R. K., O'Connell, J. J., & Dynneson, V. V. (1983). Native American college students' preference for counselor race and sex and the likelihood of their use of a counseling center. *Journal of Counseling Psychology, 30,* 267–270.

Hirayama, K. K. (1985). Asian children's adaptation to public schools. *Social Work in Education, 7,* 213–230.

Hosford, R. E., & Bowles, S. A. (1974). Determining culturally appropriate reinforcers for Anglo and Chicano students. *Elementary School Guidance and Counseling, 8,* 290–300.

Hvitfeldt, C. (1986). Traditional culture, perceptual style, and learning: The classroom behavior of Hmong adults. *Adult Education Quarterly, 36,* 65–77.

Inclan, J. (1985). Variations in value orientation in mental health work with Puerto Ricans. *Psychotherapy, 22,* 324–334.

Isomura, T., Fine, S., & Lin, T. (1987). Two Japanese families: A cultural perspective. *Canadian Journal of Psychiatry, 32,* 282–286.

John-Steiner, V. (1991). Cognitive pluralism: A Whorfian analysis. In R. L. Cooper & B. Spolsky (Eds.), *The influence of language on culture and thought: Essays in honor of Joshua A. Fishman's sixty-fifth birthday.* Berlin; New York: Mouton de Gruyter.

John-Steiner, V. P., & Osterreich, H. (1975). *Learning styles among Pueblo children: Final report to National Institute of Education.* Albuquerque: College of Education, University of New Mexico.

John-Steiner, V., & Smith, L. (1978). *The educational promise of cultural pluralism: What do we know about teaching and learning in urban schools? Vol. 8.* St. Louis, MO: CEMREL, Inc.

Jordan, C. (1977). *Maternal teaching modes and school adaptations in an urban Hawaiian population* (Tech. Report No. 67). Honolulu: The Kamehameha Schools/Bishop Estate.

Jordan, C. (1983). Cultural differences in communication patterns: Classroom adaptations and translated strategies. In M. Clark & J. J. Handscombe (Eds.), *TESOL '82: Pacific perspectives on language, learning and teaching.* Washington, DC: Teachers of English to Speakers of Other Languages, 285–294.

Jordan, C. (1984). Cultural compatibility and the education of ethnic minority children. *Educational Research Quarterly, 8* (4): 59–71.

Juarez, R. (1985) Core issues in psychotherapy with the Hispanic child. *Psychotherapy, 22,* 441–448.

Kaulback, B. (1984). Styles of learning among Native children: A review of the research. *Canadian Journal of Native Education, ll,* 27–37.

Klein, T. W. (1988). *Program evaluation of the Kamehameha Elementary Education Program's reading curriculum in Hawaii public schools: The cohort analysis 1978–1986.* Honolulu: Kamehameha Schools/ Bishop Estate.

Krywaniuk, L. W., & Das, J. P. (1976). Cognitive strategies in native children: Analysis and intervention. *Alberta Journal of Educational Research, 22,* 271–280.

Kupers, T. (1981). *Public therapy: The practice of psychotherapy in the public mental health clinic.* New York: Macmillan.

Leacock, E. (1976). The concept of culture and its significance for school counselors. In J. I. Roberts & S. K. Akinsanya (Eds.), *Schooling in the cultural context.* New York: David McKay.

Lein, L. (1975). "You were talkin' though, oh yes, you was". Black American migrant children: Their speech at home and school. *Council on Anthropology and Education Quarterly, 6* (4): 1–11.

Leith, S., & Slentz, K. (1984). Successful teaching strategies in selected Northern Manitoba schools. *Canadian Journal of Native Education, 12,* 24–30.

Lipka, J. (1991). Toward a culturally based pedagogy: A case study of one Yup'ik Eskimo teacher. *Anthropology & Education Quarterly, 22,* 203–223.

Lum, D. (1986). *Social work practice and people of color: A process-stage approach.* Monterey, CA: Brooks/Cole.

McShane, D. A., & Plas, J. M. (1982). Wechsler Scale performance patterns of American Indian children. *Psychology in the Schools, 19,* 8-17.

Michaels, S. (1984). Listening and responding: Hearing the logic in children's classroom narratives. *Theory into Practice, 23,* 218–244.

More, A. J. (1985, November). *Indian students and their learning styles: Research results and classroom applications.* Paper read at the meetings of the National Indian Education Association, Spokane.

O'Donnell, C. R., & Tharp, R. G. (1990). Community intervention guided by theoretical development. In A. S. Bellack, M. Hersen, & A. E. Kazdin (Eds.), *International handbook of behavior modification and therapy,* 2nd ed. New York: Plenum Press, 251–266.

Philips, S. U. (1972). Participant structures and communicative competence: Warm Springs children in community and classroom. In C. B. Cazden, V. John, & D. Hymes (Eds.), *Functions of language in the classroom.* New York: Teachers College Press, 370–394.

Philips, S. U. (1983). *The Invisible culture: Communication in classroom and community on the Warm Springs Indian Reservation.* New York: Longman, Inc.

Ponterotto, J. G., Alexander, C., & Hinkston, J. (1988). Afro-American preferences for counselor characteristics: A replication and extension. *Journal of Counseling Psychology, 35,* 175–182.

Ramirez, M. & Price-Williams, D. R. (1976). Achievement motivation in children of three ethnic groups in the United States. *Journal of Cross-Cultural Psychology, 7,* 49–60.

Rogoff, B. (1986). Adult assistance of children's learning. In T. E. Raphael (Ed.), *The contexts of school-based literacy.* New York: Random House, 27–40.

Rogoff, B. (1991). *Apprenticeships of the mind.* Cambridge University Press.

Rowe, M. B. (1974). Wait-Time and rewards as instructional variables: Their influence on language, logic, and fate control, Part One: Wait-Time. *Journal of Research in Science Teaching, 11* (2): 81–97.

Shade, B. J. (1982). Afro-American cognitive style: A variable in school success? *Review of Educational Research, 52,* 219–244.

Speidel, G. E. (1987a). Conversation and language learning in the classroom. In K. E. Nelson & A. van Kleeck (Eds.), *Child Language Vol. 6.* Hillsdale, NJ: Lawrence Erlbaum.

Speidel, G. E. (1987b). Language differences in the classroom: Two approaches for developing language skills in dialect-speaking children. In E. Oksaar (Ed.), *Sociocultural perpectives of language acquisition and multilingualism.* Tubingen: Gunter Narr Verlag.

Stevenson, H. W., Stigler, J. W., Lee, S., Lucker, G. W., Kitamura, S., & Hsu, C. (1985). Cognitive performance and academic achievement of Japanese, Chinese, and American children. *Child Development, 56,* 718–734.

Suarez-Orozco, M. M. (1987). Becoming somebody: Central American immigrants in U.S. inner-city schools. *Anthropology & Education Quarterly, 18,* 287–298.

Sue, S. (1988) Psychotherapeutic services for ethnic minorities. *American Psychologist, 43,* 301–308.

Tharp, R. G. (1982). The effective instruction of comprehension: Results and description of the Kamehameha Early Education Program. *Reading Research Quarterly, 17* (4): 503–527.

Tharp, R. G. (1989a). Psychocultural variables and constants: Effects on teaching and learning in schools. *American Psychologist, 44,* 349–359.

Tharp, R. G. (1989b). Culturally compatible education: A formula for designing effective classrooms. In H. T. Trueba, G. Spindler, & L. Spindler (Eds.). *What do anthropologists have to say about dropouts?* New York: The Falmer Press, 51–66.

Tharp, R. G. (1991). Cultural diversity and treatment of children. *Journal of Consulting and Clinical Psychology, 59,* 799–812.

Tharp, R. G. (in press). *Intergroup differences among Native Americans in socialization and child cognition: Native Hawaiians and native Navajos.* In: P. Greenfield & R. Cocking, Eds., *The development of the minority child: Culture in and out of context.* Hillsdale, NJ: Lawrence Erlbaum Associates.

Tharp, R. G., & Burns, C. E. B. (1989). Phylogenetic processes in verbal language imitation. In G. E. Speidel & K. Nelson (Eds.). *The many faces of imitation in language learning.* New York: Springer-Verlag, 231–250.

Tharp, R. G., & Gallimore, R. (1976). *The uses and limits of social reinforcement and industriousness for learning to read* (Tech. Rep. No. 60). Honolulu: Kamehameha Schools/Bishop Estate (ERIC Document ED 158 861).

Tharp, R. G., & Gallimore, R. (1988). *Rousing minds to life: Teaching and learning in social context.* New York: Cambridge University Press.

Tharp, R. G., Jordan, C., Speidel, G. E., Au, K. H., Klein, T. W., Calkins, R. P., Sloat, K. C. M., & Gallimore, R. (1984). Product and process in applied developmental research: Education and the children of a minority. In M. E. Lamb, A. L. Brown, & B. Rogoff (Eds.), *Advances in developmental psychology*, Vol. III. Hillsdale, NJ: Lawrence Erlbaum & Associates, Inc.

Tharp, R. G., and Yamauchi, L. (1991). *Effective instructional conversation in Native American classrooms.* Paper read at the meeting of the American Anthropological Association, Chicago, November.

Trueba, H. T., & Delgado-Gaitan, C. (1985). Socialization of Mexican children for cooperation and competition: Sharing and copying. *Journal of Educational Equity and Leadership, 5,* 189–204.

Vazquez-Nuttal, E., Avila-Vivas, Z., & Morales-Barreto, G. (1984). Working with Latin American families. *Family Therapy Collections, 9,* 75–90.

Vogt, L. A., Jordan, C., and Tharp, R. G. (1987). Explaining school failure, producing school success: Two cases. *Anthropology & Education Quarterly, 18,* 276–286.

Watson-Gegeo, K. A., & Boggs, S. T. (1977). From verbal play to talk story: The role of routines in speech events among Hawaiian children. In S. Ervin-Tripp & C. Mitchell-Kernan (Eds.), *Child discourse.* New York: Academic Press, 67–90.

Weisner, T. S., Gallimore, R., & Jordan, C. (1988). Unpackaging cultural effects on classroom learning: Hawaiian peer assistance and child-generated activity. *Anthropology and Education Quarterly 19,* 327–353.

Wertsch, J. V. (1985). *Vygotsky and the social formation of mind.* Cambridge, MA: Harvard University Press.

Wharton-Boyd, L. F. (1983). The significance of Black American children's singing games in an educational setting. *Journal of Negro Education, 52,* 46–56.

White, S., & Tharp, R. G. (1988, April). *Questioning and Wait-Time: A cross-cultural analysis.* Paper presented at the annual meeting of the American Educational Research Association, New Orleans.

Whiting, B. B. (1976). The problem of the packaged variable. In K. Riegel &

J. A. Meacham (Eds.), *The developing individual in a changing world: Historical and cultural issues: Vol. 1*. Chicago: Aldine, 303–309.

Williams, M. D. (1981). Observations in Pittsburgh ghetto schools. *Anthropology & Education Quarterly, 12*, 211–220.

Winterton, W. A. (1976). *The effect of extended wait-time on selected verbal response characeristics of some Pueblo Indian children.* Unpublished Doctoral Dissertation, University of New Mexico. Dissertation Abstracts International, 38, 620–A. University Microfilms 77–16, 130.

Witkin, H. A. (1967). A cognitive-style approach to cross-cultural research. *International Journal of Psychology, 2*, 233–250.

Wood, D. J. (1980). Teaching the young child: Some relationships between social interaction, language, and thought. In R. Olson (Ed.) *The social foundations of language and thought.* New York: W. W. Norton & Co., 280–296.

Wu, H. T. (1982). Learning styles of Chinese children. In: J. Young & J. Lum, Asian bilingual education teacher handbook. Cambridge, Massachusetts: Evaluation, Dissemination and Assessment Center for Bilingual Education, 121–127.

Wyatt, J. D. (1978–1979). Native involvement in curriculum development: The native teacher as cultural broker. *Interchange, 9*, 17–28.

Young, V. H. (1970). Family and childhood in a Southern Georgia community. *American Anthropologist, 72*, 269–288.

Part III

Language and Literacy

INTRODUCTION

This section focuses on the traditional educational concern for students from non-English language backgrounds—language. Such students have been categorized by their lack of English language skills, and much of the controversy in this field has revolved around the appropriate language of instruction for these students.

The two chapters in this section represent different perspectives on these issues. Barry McLaughlin summarizes research from the cognitive psychological tradition on learning to read and write in a second language. Lilia Bartolomé's chapter questions the emphasis on language, arguing that the more fundamental issue is status. Catherine Snow (1992) describes these two approaches as follows:

> When psychologists and linguists think about language acquisition, they emphasize cognition—the problems faced by the learner acquiring a complex system that has more or less overlap with complex systems already acquired. Anthropologists, social psychologists, and sociolinguists, on the other hand, think about the societal context of bilingualism. . . . Sociocultural approaches are particularly helpful in understanding the social and cultural pressures affecting learners in situa-

171

tions where different social value is attached to their two languages. (pp. 17 & 18)

Joseph Murphy (1991) notes a similar dichotomy between the assumptions embodied in traditional schooling for minority populations and contemporary reform trends:

A fundamental shift in the underlying model of learning is occurring in schools engaged in restructuring for equity. There is movement away from a psychologically based model of learning that emphasizes the innate capacity of the student to a sociological framework that underscores the importance of the conditions of learning. (p. 60)

The new attention to sociological factors has been necessitated by the recognition of cultural differences among American schoolchildren, and it has been championed particularly by educators who themselves come from non-English language backgrounds. Are we witnessing a paradigm shift, or are the two camps examining different parts of the elephant? Certainly the two approaches ask different questions, focus on different issues, and define the situation differently, in an attempt to understand the low academic achievement of students from non-English language backgrounds.

The two approaches agree about the general educational goal for students from non-English language backgrounds—parity of achievement with students who are native English speakers. But they disagree about the operationalization of this goal. The traditional approach assumes that parity will be achieved by similarity, that students will have an equal chance to succeed once they learn English, either through bilingual or through English-only programs. The approach is to change the child—from a non-English speaker to an English speaker—to make him or her acceptable in mainstream society.

The sociological approach argues that parity should be achieved without sacrificing diversity, and that the denigration of groups with subordinate status, not language, is the major obstacle to their academic success. This approach seeks to change society—to accept the non-English speaker into the mainstream as he or she is.

Each approach has strengths and blind spots. The traditional approach assumes that the best path to success is to imitate already successful groups, but it carries with it the (intended or unintended) consequence of devaluing groups that are different from the mainstream. It places heavy emphasis on research into the processes of second language learning. But less attention is paid to the application of this research in the classroom. If, as Bartolomé notes, students in transitional bilingual programs are instructed in English more than three-quarters of the time, then bilingual programs are bilingual in name only, and have not benefitted from the insights of cognitive research. By focusing on cognitive processes, the traditional approach also ignores the emotional and identificational aspects of second language learning, well documented by Wallace Lambert and others.

While the traditional approach emphasizes ends, the sociological approach focuses on means, on the way non-English language background students are treated day to day in the classroom and in the society. This approach assumes that if the means are just and fair, the ends will take care of themselves. This stand is similar to Sarason's (1990) contention that education reform should be first and foremost *for* teachers, and that empowering teachers should be seen as an end in itself and not merely as a means to improved student achievement.

The sociological approach is shaped by the impetus of reversing the deficit model, a noble goal, but advocates of this approach may not pay sufficient attention to ultimate ends or to the question of *how* to translate improved relations among groups of different status into improved achievement for non-English language background students.

The chapters in this section reflect the different emphases of the two approaches: McLaughlin focuses on methodological concerns—*how* humans learn language and *how* we can improve second language teaching and learning, while Bartolomé poses philosophical questions—*why* educators are so preoccupied with language issues, and *why* they neglect the influence of status.

But the two approaches share an emphasis on the importance of explicitly teaching metacognitive strategies. McLaughlin describes "reciprocal teaching," a method of helping students improve their reading by teaching them how to generate questions, summarize, and predict about written text with others in a group. Bartolomé discusses "strategic teaching" as an approach that equips students with learning strategies to become independent and self-monitoring learners by asking questions and making predictions. In both methods, teachers draw upon and build on students' previous knowledge, apprentice students by first modeling new cognitive skills and gradually turning over that role to the students, use "scaffolding" to help students reach beyond their unassisted capabilities, and promote discussion with and among students as a critical aspect of the learning process.

It is interesting that both the cognitive and the sociological approach converge in a new model of teaching, a model that embodies an implicit recognition of the importance of both cognitive and socio-emotional factors in the learning process. Perhaps they are seeing the same elephant after all.

But some parts of this elephant remain hazy. For example, are reciprocal teaching and strategic teaching essentially the same, or do they contain significant differences in approach and philosophy? By developing *models*, educators often obscure the *principles* underlying the teaching strategies advocated and make it difficult to compare models.

Looking at the broader picture, the material presented by McLaughlin and Bartolomé raises questions that affect our perspective on language arts instruction for students from non-English language backgrounds, some of which can only be answered by international comparisons:

- Why is so much emphasis placed on language arts in U.S. schools, relative to other subjects? Stigler and Baranes (1988–89, p. 296) note that fifth-grade teachers in Japan and Taiwan spend an equal number of instructional hours on language arts and mathematics, while American teachers spend nearly two-and-a-half times more hours on language arts than on math. (Looked at another way, American teachers spend roughly the same amount of time as Japanese and Taiwanese teachers on language arts, but much less time on math.)

- Are some languages inherently more difficult to read, or learn to read, than others? How much of the widely varying literacy rates among countries can be accounted for by differences among languages? Stigler and Baranes (1988–89) make the argument that the logicality and regularity of number words in Chinese gives Chinese children an advantage over English speakers in learning numbers and understanding the number system. Are there comparable differences among languages that impact learning to read and write?

- On the other hand, some languages, like Chinese and Japanese, are extremely challenging orthographically, and the written language takes many years to master. How is

Japan able to achieve a high literacy rate, while the United States, with a simple alphabet-based written language, has significant literacy gaps among its population?

- Since writing styles differ in different languages, and since languages are orthographically and grammatically different, do optimal reading strategies also differ? Is the cognitive process of reading Chinese text similar to or different from the process of reading English text?

- The cultural basis of writing (Kaplan, 1966; Farr, 1986) means that the characteristics of poor quality writing in one language tradition may be the same as good writing in another. If there are no universally accepted attributes for good writing, are there universal processes or stages of development in learning to write?

- Much has been learned about the cultural effects of language from studies demonstrating that bilinguals assume different cultural "personalities" when speaking different languages (Ervin-Tripp, 1964). Comparable investigations of reading and writing by biliterate people could yield insights useful for teaching these skills in a second language.

- How do cognitive and socio-emotional factors actually interact to affect the process of learning to read and write in a first or second language? Exactly how do motivation and confidence facilitate or impede learning and performance?

- How are students taught, and how do they learn, to read and write in non-native languages in countries where bilingualism is the norm?

- To determine the relative importance of language (cognitive psychological) vs. social status (sociological) factors in language arts achievement, we need an analysis of educational outcomes in countries that regularly instruct students in non-native languages. Most importantly, we need to compare the situation in which *all* students are taught in a second language with situations in which *minority* students or students from *subordinate status* groups are taught in a non-native language—the language of the majority group or socially dominant group.

- Does subordinate status always result in low achievement? If so, is this due primarily to motivational factors or to substandard education? What about students educated in colonial systems—students in Indochina and Africa taught a French curriculum in French, students in British colonies taught a British curriculum in English? Do students in this situation fail to achieve in the same manner, for the same reasons, as Hispanic and African American students in the United States? Is colonial education inferior to the education offered French children in France or British children in Britain?

- Whether English fluency is considered the primary goal of education for non-English language background students, or one of several goals, are we going about it the right way? At the turn of the century, educators saw English as vitally important for new immigrants, but, as Brumberg (1986) reports, the linguistic fare offered Jewish immigrants in New York schools makes today's educational diet seem sparse:

Public school education was saturated with reading English, memorizing and reciting English prose and poetry, participating in plays and assemblies, arguing in debates, writing stories and essays, reading the English language classics, improving one's diction, [and] taking compulsory speech classes. (p.219)

What is the most powerful influence on the achievement of students being schooled in a non-native language—the inherent difficulty of the cognitive task, the poor quality of schooling they receive, or the discouragement that results from negative social comparisons? The chapters in this section cannot answer this question, but they offer perspectives that delineate the complexity of the issue. Despite their differing approaches, they also offer similar prescriptions for change, prescriptions that include elements of both approaches.

REFERENCES

Brumberg, S. F. (1986). *Going to America, going to school: The Jewish immigrant public school encounter in turn-of-the-century New York City*. New York: Praeger.

Ervin-Tripp, S. (1964). Interaction of language, topic, and listener. *American Anthropologist, 66* (2): 86–102.

Farr, M. (1986). Language, culture, and writing: Sociolinguistic foundations of research on writing. *Review of Research in Education, 13,* 195–223.

Kaplan, R. B. (1966). Cultural thought patterns in inter-cultural education. *Language Learning, 16,* 1–20.

Murphy, J. (1991). *Restructuring schools: Capturing and assessing the phenomena.* New York: Teachers College Press.

Sarason, S. B. (1990). *The predictable failure of educational reform: Can we change course before it's too late?* San Francisco: Jossey-Bass.

Snow, C. E. (1992). Perspectives on second-language development: Implications for bilingual education. *Educational Researcher, 21* (2): 16–19.

Stigler, J. W., & Baranes, R. (1988–89). Culture and mathematics learning. *Review of Research in Education, 15,* 253–306.

✧ Chapter 6

First and Second Language Literacy in the Late Elementary Grades

Barry McLaughlin

Several years ago, the National Assessment of Educational Progress (NAEP) issued a report called, "Learning to be Literate in America." That report begins:

> The recent Nation's Report Cards based on NAEP assessments of reading, writing, and literacy indicate that most children and young adults can understand what they read and can express their thoughts in writing at a surface level. Only a small percentage, however, can reason effectively about what they are reading or writing. The NAEP data also suggest that there are serious disparities in literacy learning among American schoolchildren. Black children, Hispanic children, children living in disadvantaged urban communities, and those whose parents have low levels of education are particularly at risk for

future educational failure. In spite of gains during the past decade, the performance of these groups remains far below national averages. (Applebee, Langer, & Mullis, 1987, p. 5)

Children for whom reading in English is reading in a second language constitute a particularly high risk group. In a study of high-school dropouts among minority-language children, Steinberg, Lin Blinde, and Chan (1984) noted that individuals from homes where English is not spoken are almost twice as likely to drop out before graduating from high school as are individuals from homes where English is the primary language.

The same study also indicated that if, in addition, the child does not use English as the primary language, the likelihood of prematurely dropping out of school increases to four times that of English monolingual speakers (40 percent vs. 10 percent). In California, 45 percent of Hispanic students leave high school between the ninth and twelfth grades (California Office of Research, 1985). Fifty percent more Hispanic students fail district twelfth grade proficiency tests than do Anglo students (ibid.).

These statistics underscore the importance of research on second-language learning. The dimensions of the problem are enormous in this country, where it is estimated that 4.5 million children come to school from families where the home language is other than English. The second-language literature suggests that—contrary to conventional wisdom—second-language learning is not easy and automatic for children. For a child to acquire a second language requires a great deal of trial-and-error, creative hypothesis-testing, and awkward experimentation. Especially in the classroom context, second-language learning is a difficult and frustrating enterprise for many children. One area of critical importance is learning to read in a second language. For many minority-language children, reading is the beginning of school failure.

The Reading Process

Cognitive Skills

Reading can be viewed as a cognitive skill; indeed, as the most complex and difficult of all the cognitive skills that the child must master in school. The child who accurately and efficiently translates a string of printed letters into meaningful communication may appear to be accomplishing that task with little mental effort. In fact, however, the child is engaging in complex interactive processes that are dependent on multiple subskills and an enormous amount of coded information. The fluent reader must have automated language skills, intact visual and auditory memory, the ability to associate and integrate intra- and intermodal stimuli, and the ability to abstract and generalize patterned or rule-generated information (Vellutino & Scanlon, 1982).

More specifically, to become an accomplished reader, the child must have mastered three important tasks. These are shown in Figure 6.1. These three tasks are developmentally linked to each other. Only after the child has automated word-decoding operations, is it possible to acquire more sophisticated reading and comprehension skills. Similarly, the automation of word-decoding skills is dependent on mastery of symbol-sound correspondence rules.

Figure 6.1 Developmental Progression of Reading Tasks

(1) First, the child must master the rules governing symbol-sound correspondences in English.

(2) The child must be able to use those rules in learning words and must progressively refine and automate word-decoding operations.

(3) Building on automated decoding skills, the child must acquire and perfect a complex set of processing skills that allows for rapid processing of incoming material and the extraction of meaning.

Research with children learning to read in their first language has shown that good readers differ from poor readers in their ability to capitalize on automated decoding skills, to acquire and perfect a complex set of processing skills that allows for rapid processing of incoming material and the extraction of meaning. In addition, the research literature indicates that good readers are able to utilize short-term memory, to exploit orthographic regularities, to use orthographic cues and to attend to material selectively, to identify syntactic relations among words, and to use syntactic and semantic context as an aid to recognizing words currently under perceptual scrutiny (LaBerge & Samuels, 1974).

Research indicates that the causes of individual differences in reading ability in children are multiply determined and highly interactive (Perfetti & Hogaboam, 1975). From an information-processing point of view, when skill is low, there is competition for limited processing resources. For the skilled reader, on the other hand, component processes are highly automatic and integrated. Furthermore, expertise in one processing component may alter the character of processing for some other component, so that the mechanisms for process interaction may differ for expert and nonexpert readers. Figure 6.2 provides a summary of the components identified as distinguishing good readers from poor readers.

Figure 6.2 Componential Analysis: Research on Good and Poor Readers

Good readers are distinguished from poor readers by:

Bottom-up skills:

(1) superior ability to store information in short-term memory.
(2) superiority in visual discrimination.
(3) superior phonological analysis skills.
(4) superior attentional abilities.

Top-down skills:

(1) superior ability to use syntactic knowledge.
(2) superior semantic knowledge and ability to use context.
(3) superior ability to go beyond the single sentence in drawing inferences about the story line.

Metacognition Skills

A great deal of recent research on the comprehension process in reading focuses on metacognitive skill (e.g., Brown, 1978, Brown, Armbruster & Baker, 1986; Paris, 1986; Paris & Oka, 1986; Paris & Wixson, 1986). These researchers and others use the insights of contemporary cognitive psychology and argue that children need to learn specific strategies for becoming fluent readers. These strategies are rarely taught explicitly. For example, skilled readers in high school and beyond often scan a text quickly to judge its difficulty before reading it thoroughly, pause while reading to check understanding, re-read thorny passages and mentally summarize the text. Poorer readers lack many or all of these strategies, but when they learn such strategies, they come to understand more clearly that the purpose of reading is to get information and insight, not just to decode the words on a page.

This point has been made by Ann Brown, a leading reading researcher. She uses the concept "metacognition" (which literally means transcending knowledge) to refer to one's understanding of any cognitive process. She argues that understanding in the context of reading can be revealed in two ways: first in one's knowledge of strategies for learning from texts, different demands of various reading chores, textual structures, and one's own strengths and weaknesses as a learner; second, in the control readers have of their own actions while reading for different purposes. Successful readers monitor their state of learning; they plan strategies, adjust effort appropriately, and evaluate the success of their on-going efforts to understand (Palincsar & Brown, 1984).

Brown advocates a "reciprocal teaching" method, in which students and teacher begin by discussing why students have problems understanding what they read. After some discussion, students are informed that they are about to learn four activities (i.e., question generating, summarizing, predicting, and clarification) that will help them keep their attention on what they are reading, as well as enable them to continuously check to ensure that they are comprehending.

It is the combination of comprehension-fostering and monitoring activities that is essential. Neither questioning nor summarizing alone has proven to be as effective as the combination of both. Equally important is the fact that all activities are taught in a "natural setting," where they are immediately applied to a reading context, making them more concrete than activities taught in isolation. All of these factors work together to make explicit to the poor comprehender that which the good comprehender intuitively knows.

Reading in a Second Language

It seems reasonable to argue that the cognitive and metacognitive skills described above are difficult tasks for many children to master and often lead to frustration and school failure. A critical period is the late elementary grades. It is at this time that children typically read reasonably smoothly in units larger than individual words, but are not yet fully mature and skilled readers (Gibson & Levin, 1975). The jump to mastery in reading requires that the child learn how to extract meaning quickly from text—a task that assumes that words are decoded quickly enough to allow space in working memory for retaining the evolving meanings (LaBerge & Samuels, 1974; Perfetti & Hogaboam, 1975). Hence, poor readers may be hampered in achieving comprehension by their inability to achieve automatic word-decoding or even by non-automatic symbol-sound matching.

Reading in a second language requires all these "bottom-up" skills. Furthermore, children who are learning to read in a second language may have more problems than monolingual children because of their lack of familiarity with the semantic and syntactic constraints of the target language. If children are not able spontaneously to identify and exploit syntactic relations and are not flexible in their use of semantic context as a guide to prediction, their reading comprehension and speed decline (Carr, 1981).

In addition, children who are learning to read in English as a second language may receive instruction in their second language that focuses on the mechanical process of reading—even when their skills in "going for meaning" are fairly advanced in their first language. Teachers may assume that because a child cannot pronounce English correctly, more time has to be spent on symbol-sound correspondences, when in fact the child has automated decoding skills and needs more skill at extracting meaning from text. Often these children receive a sparse literacy diet, one that is excessively weighted toward lower level phonics and decoding skills, when they are in fact capable of more advanced work.

Assuming that children are dealing with literary texts that are appropriate for their age and abilities, second language readers may also need special help in three areas: (1) vocabulary development, (2) syntactic development, and (3) cultural knowledge.

Failure to comprehend text may often be the result of lack of appropriate *vocabulary knowledge*. Studies have shown that a strong relationship exists between knowledge of word meaning and ability to comprehend passages containing those words. The more difficult the words of a passage are for a reader, the more difficulty the reader will have in making sense of the text. Research has also shown that student comprehension of the gist of a text is increased by teaching the meanings of a few key words during each lesson, and explicitly drawing the semantic and topical relations of the words to students' background knowledge. Such training has also been shown to enhance their inferencing abilities.

Children for whom English is a second language can benefit from such intense training, as the emphasis is not upon rote knowledge of the words, but rather on the integration and association of previous words and knowledge acquired in their first language with new words and concepts presented in English. It is important that the vocabulary knowledge be assimilated and that students learn to use target words in novel sentences.

Research also shows that a strong relation exists between knowledge of *syntax* and reading comprehension. The better a reader is at understanding how syntax can constrain meaning, the more able that reader will be to predict the information contained in on-coming text. Being able to predict and verify the prediction with continued reading is a crucial part of the reading process. Because poor readers often misunderstand the gist of a text, bolstering their syntactic knowledge may greatly enhance their comprehension. This is especially important for poor readers for whom English is a second language, as it provides the explicit information that often is implicitly known by the native English speaker.

Sentence combining and sentence reduction have been found to be effective in providing syntactic training. Involvement in such activities has also been shown to increase poor readers' awareness of semantic variance, by demonstrating changes that occur in meaning as groups of words are combined or deleted from a variety of sentences. Reading by phrase is another strategy that poor readers often cannot use. Phrases can be considered the primary elements of meaning into which a sentence can be divided. As poor readers come to understand the structure of phrases in the text, and the nuance of meaning that a phrase can convey by its position in a sentence, their comprehension should increase.

Strong evidence has been found for the existence of a causal relationship between *background knowledge* and reading comprehension. Intervention techniques that improve children's background knowledge have been found to lead to significant improvements in reading. Inadequacies in background knowledge have been thought to play a large role in producing comprehension difficulties for children from linguistic minority backgrounds. After determining the level of background information through questioning, teachers can expose poor readers from linguistic minorities to an appropriate level of cultural information by use of analogy and indirect, inductive techniques. Analogy allows these readers to compare sets of familiar information developed through their native culture to new, less familiar information sets they are attempting to learn.

Indirect, inductive techniques are also useful methods of conveying cultural information at various levels to linguistic minority poor readers. The teacher or dialogue leader can discuss concrete examples of cultural information necessary for the comprehension of a text, and then explain specific examples when they appear in the text. Initially, however, it may be helpful to have the children read stories that have a direct relationship to their own family and social circumstances. Texts based on the child's own experiences can be especially helpful during this early phase.

The Writing Process

Research on writing has been heavily influenced by the notion that the development of writing involves changing one's communicative competence (Hymes, 1971). Becoming literate is thought to affect how people use language and how they think (Goody & Watt, 1963). Initially, researchers explored the difference between oral and spoken language. Olson (1977), for example, argued that in written language meaning resides mainly in the text itself, whereas in oral language much of the meaning is communicated in the context in which the language is used. Written language was thought to be more decontextualized than oral language.

This work has been criticized as not taking into account the full range of different types of oral and written language. Researchers such as Tannen (1984), Heath (1984), and Scollon and Scollon (1981) have argued that all language, whether spoken or written, is embedded in a social context that affects both its form and its function. In a literate society, oral and written modes often overlap and draw on each other.

This argument is supported by research on the development of children's early writing, which indicates that there is a strong relationship in development among all language processes—speaking, listening, reading, and writing (Farr, 1986). Preschoolers use all their language capacities to perform reading and writing tasks before they can perform these tasks in adult, conventional ways (Sulzby, 1985). There are also parallels between how language is used in play and how it is used in writing (Gundlach, McLane, Stott, & McNamee, 1985).

The focus on the social uses of language has led to sociolinguistic studies that indicate that writing is not a single entity that occurs in different contexts, but that it is a social practice that varies according to the particular use to which it is put in context (Heath, 1984). For example, in a study of reading and writing among the Vai in Liberia, Scribner and Cole (1981) reported that literate individuals demonstrated superior performance over non-literates on various cognitive tasks. However, the specific tasks on which each group of literates showed superior performance were closely related to how these groups used reading and writing. Thus, the practice of letter-writing improved the writer's cognitive skill in taking the view of another.

Researchers have also examined cultural variables in writing. Erickson (1984) studied Black adolescents informally discussing politics and found that shifts from one topic to another were not explicitly stated, but depended for understanding on a shared cultural discourse style. This style depends on audience-speaker interaction and is at odds with the linear, sequential style assumed in school literacy in this country. This is one of a number of issues involved in learning to write in a second language.

Writing in a Second Language

Writing is an important "gate-keeper" in the American educational system. It functions as a means of determining who has access to college-preparatory curricula, and as a means of tracking students (Oakes, 1985). Students for whom English is a second language perform markedly worse than native speakers in English writing skills. For example, NAEP writing assessment data showed that one-half of all Latino students tested could not produce a minimally competent written response to assessment tasks designed to measure their informative, persuasive, or narrative English writing skills. This figure contrasts to a 75 percent minimally competent level for non-Hispanic White students (Applebee, Langer, Jenkins, Mullis, & Foertsch, 1990).

There have been a number of studies of the nature and effectiveness of writing instruction and a renewed interest in the role of writing in successful instruction (Applebee, 1984), as well as increasing attention to the writing instruction given to ethnic and language minority students (Delpit, 1986; Heath, 1983; Gutierrez, 1992). The National Center for the Study of Writing has recently published an annotated bibliography of research on writing in a non-native language (Schecter & Harklau, 1991), and a comprehensive overview of language issues in writing in a second language has recently appeared (Valdes, 1991).

As Valdes (1991) notes, existing research on writing in a second language has concentrated largely on ESL writers—that is, on students who are enrolled in ESL programs. This research includes such topics as business letter writing in English, the revising and composing strategies used by learners, the development of appropriate discourse organization, the development of temporality, and the development of pragmatic skills.

One area that has received considerable attention is research on the role of first language transfer on second language writing via error analysis, especially in syntax and vocabulary. For example, Cronnell (1985), in one of the few studies with children, examined text errors from third- and sixth-grade Latino students and found that 27 percent of the errors made by the third-graders and 36 percent of the errors made by the sixth-graders could be considered to have been influenced by Spanish, Chicano English, or interlanguage. Third-graders made more errors in Spanish-influenced spelling of English words, and in the influence of Spanish pronunciation on written English. Sixth-graders made more errors in syntax and misuse of English vocabulary. However, because data were not collected in the first language, errors could not be definitively attributed to the influence of Spanish, interlanguage, or Chicano English.

Work in the tradition of "contrastive rhetoric" suggests that there is cultural variation in the emphasis placed on criteria for editing versus planning and drafting. For instance, Purves and Hawisher (1990) argued that there is a relatively low emphasis on organization in Chile and on style and tone in the Netherlands. In New Zealand and Sweden, teachers appear to emphasize process more than in other countries, but in Sweden more of this emphasis concerns choice of topic than in the case of New Zealand. Purves and Purves (1986) saw the need for more information on how and where individuals learn what constitutes good or appropriate writing in a given culture.

Kaplan (1966) has argued that native and non-native writers differ in what they assume to be shared knowledge between writer and reader. He contended, furthermore, that native and non-native writers differ in the strategies they use to develop and keep the focus on a topic. Soter (1988) found that Vietnamese- and Arabic-speaking children in Australian schools drew on different cultural models for story structure and content. The Vietnamese stories appeared less goal-oriented and less focused on the plot than the typical English story. A greater emphasis was placed on the relationship between characters; dialogue between them was frequent. The Arabic students provided more information about the scene of the story.

Work in the contrastive rhetoric tradition assumes that students have learned to write in their first language. For example, Soter's subjects were sixth- and twelfth-grade students. These students may have had experience writing in their first language with teachers who reinforced a specific cultural model. Valdes (1991) maintained that writers who are young or basic writers, in addition to being second language learners, will progress somewhat along the lines that any developing basic writers progress on their way to becoming good writers. She maintains that discourse characteristics that have been interpreted as evidence for cross-linguistic transfer may in fact be the product of beginning writing development. Second language writers display a number of features typical of basic writers that have very little to do with transfer from their first language.

Recent research has led to a growing sense that learning how to write in a second language involves much more than simply learning how to avoid interference from the first language. Rather than looking for influences from the first language or culture, much of current research examines what it means to write in a second language. For instance, Liebman-Kleine (1987) studied the preferences of advanced ESL students for three prewriting techniques to determine how like native writers they were. The three techniques were (1) open-ended exploratory writing, (2) systematic heuristics, and (3) hierarchical treeing. Unlike native speakers, ESL students were found to avoid systematic heuristics because these techniques depend to a large extent on linguistic abilities. Open-ended exploratory writing was only moderately helpful. Hierarchical structuring was preferred because it provides students with more structure than the other methods. The author concluded that more highly developed linguistic abilities in the language in which they are writing allow for more diverse strategies. Less developed linguistic abilities restrict the strategies writers are likely to use.

Research with children supports the notion that transfer from the first language is not a primary issue. For example, Edelsky and her colleagues (1982, 1983; Edelsky & Jilbert, 1985) found that Spanish-English bilingual children used similar segmentation strategies in first- and second-language writing. Personal writing style was applied in both languages (Edelsky, 1982), and learners did not confuse their first- and second-language systems, though they did borrow from one system to augment their capacity to communicate in the other (Edelsky & Jilbert, 1985). Edelsky argued that it is not necessary for children to have total control over spoken English before they learn to read and write in that language.

In similar work with Indochinese children, Urzua (1987) found that children exhibited growth in their ability to manipulate and reshape written language and in their ability to add to their written repertoire. The author argued that both the cognitive and social aspects of literacy develop in similar ways for native and non-native writers. Seda and Abramson (1989) also found that literacy development followed similar patterns in native and non-native children.

A number of developmental studies have been carried out in the context of French-immersion programs in Canada. In these studies children show a progression toward standard French usage

(Pringle, 1986), although the influence of the first language (English) was pervasive. Verb conjugation and subject-verb agreement, misuse of prepositions, incorrect gender, all typify the French writing of immersion students (Swain, 1975).

Elliott (1986) reported that a non-native Australian child showed the same developmental pattern for genres that has been hypothesized for first-language English writers. However, the child seemed to advance in stages rather than in a linear progression. Cohesion in writing moved from a reliance on coordination to use of subordination. Translation was used on occasions when the child needed to access language that was more advanced than he was capable of in English. The child did not produce expository texts or revise, most likely because of linguistic limitations.

Linguistic limitations appear to affect the strategies that students use in their writing. Eversen (1985) described a study tracing the development of written interlanguage, focusing on the use of connectors in eighth- through eleventh-grade Norwegian EFL students. The use of connectors was found to increase steadily as a function of skill level within each grade and across grade levels. However, it was also found that students showed little variety in the choice of connectors. A relatively small number of connector words accounted for a large percentage of the total connectors used in EFL writing.

In short, this research suggests that bilingual children follow a similar pattern of development in writing as is shown by native speakers, though their linguistic limitations cause them to develop various strategies to convey meaning. However, research on the process and development of writing in bilingual students leaves many questions unanswered.

Valdes (1991) notes that most studies of the writing of language minority students focus on interference (negative language or rhetorical transfer) between the first language and English. There are few studies examining the process of writing in relationship to bilingualism, bilingual processing, or second language acquisition. Few investigators assess both the first- and second-language proficiencies of the bilingual students.

Other unresolved questions relate to the relationship between culture and writing. It is sometimes maintained that language minority students encounter difficulties in writing because what they are asked to do in the classroom is not relevant or connected to their cultural background or to their daily lives. As Valdes notes, however, before such statements can be made validly, research on background factors and their influence on writers needs to be carried out on different groups and compared with similar studies of mainstream students. Studies are needed on how writing fits into the lives of both mainstream and minority families and communities. Valdes continues:

> Before we paint a picture of minority families in which the absence of books leads us to the conclusion that members of the family seldom write, we must spend time observing these families closely as they go about their business. We must be aware, however, that seeing exactly how writing is used among specific groups of people may take a very long time. . . . Moreover, the notions that make up the construct of "background factors" are often fuzzy. Almost anything can be attributed to cultural differences. (p. 30)

It may be that a student's perception of what the teacher expects or cultural traditions governing interactions with authority figures play a greater role in how language minority students write than family experiences or a "home-school mismatch."

The Whole Language Movement

During the past decade or so, a reform movement has attempted to change the ways in which reading and writing are taught in the nation's schools. In the reading area, there has been extensive concern that what children read is meaningful to them and involves them personally. The "whole language" movement attempts to make language an essential focus of the entire curriculum. Thematic instruction makes reading an integral part of instruction, not a subject matter of its own.

Whereas the traditional cognitive approach discussed in this paper views the teacher as an expert and the students as apprentices, the whole language approach sees the teacher as a facilitator and the student as defining the task of making meanings. The traditional approach tends to view the skills involved in reading as developmentally sequenced, whereas in the whole language approach a skill is taught when a particular child needs it for something that the child is working on. Literacy skills are seen as interrelated in the whole language approach; oral skills need not be fully developed before reading, nor does reading necessarily precede writing. Table 6.1 summarizes critical differences between the cognitive and the whole language approaches.

Table 6.1 A Comparison of Cognitive Approach and Whole Language Approach

	COGNITIVE APPROACH	WHOLE LANGUAGE
Orientation	Teacher as Expert	Teacher as Facilitator
Students' Role	Apprentice	Define Tasks
Literacy Skills	Separate	Interrelated
Materials	Specially Developed	Authentic
Progress	Oral before Reading	No Sequence
Mistakes	Corrected	Not Corrected
Focus	On Skills	On Functional Literacy

The whole language movement is more than a theory of language learning; it represents a philosophical stance on education and makes a political statement regarding the distribution of power (Edelsky, 1990). It sees education as a socially and culturally shared activity and asks how literacy is socially constructed in the classroom. Students need to be empowered so that they value their own experiences, communities, and cultures.

The whole language movement has impacted more traditional views of literacy instruction. For example, Means and Knapp (1991), in a discussion of how the cognitive approach applies to children from culturally diverse backgrounds, argue that curricular changes need to have a focus on complex, meaningful problems and that connections should be made with students' out-of-school experience and culture. While stressing the importance of modelling powerful thinking strategies and providing scaffolding to enable students to accomplish complex tasks, these authors also note the importance of encouraging multiple approaches and solutions and making dialogue the central medium for teaching and learning. Similarly, in a recent discussion of methods of teaching comprehension strategies, Harris and Graham (1992) noted that such instruction must take place in appropriately meaningful contexts and environments.

In the area of writing, similar efforts have been made to place the construction of meaning at the center of the curriculum and to make writing integral to all instruction. This movement views writing as a process, and has been brought into the classroom by the National Writing Project and the Writing Project of the University of California. The writing process approach is used widely with mainstream children and has been applied in some contexts to language minority children (Gutierrez, 1992).

In a review of the research base of the whole language approach, Pearson and Raphael (1991) noted that several features of the whole language model have been positively associated with successful literacy instruction. For example, there is considerable evidence that reading literature results in better reading comprehension than does isolated skill practice. Similarly, research has indicated that the quality and quantity of children's writing are improved when they are encouraged to participate in wide-ranging, unfettered writing activities from the outset of schooling. In addition, reliance on authentic functional literacy tasks has been shown to develop a more realistic view of the uses of reading and writing.

A number of authors have recently attempted to reconcile whole language and more traditional cognitive approaches (e.g., Garcia & Pearson, 1990; McKenna, Robinson, & Miller, 1990). However, Edelsky (1990) and others have argued that such attempts are futile and that whole language represents a paradigm shift. Attempts, for example, to use traditional assessment instruments as outcome measures to determine instructional effectiveness are regarded by whole language advocates as instances of paradigm blindness. Reliance on test score data is seen by whole language advocates as reinforcing mechanisms for stratifying society—i.e., test score-based tracking.

Whether these conflicting views can be reconciled remains to be seen. However, regardless of whether researchers use the more qualitative methods of the whole language paradigm or more traditional quantitative methods, it is important to determine under what conditions innovative instruction is effective with language minority students. Especially in the late elementary grades, where literacy skills are central to academic success for these children, there few more important educational challenges.

Conclusion

A study conducted by the Council of Chief State School Officers that appeared in 1990 found that many language minority students do not receive the services they need in the educational system, are more likely to be held back, tracked in low academic groupings, or even placed in special education classes, and that their dropout rates are alarmingly high. These children represent a challenge for researchers and practitioners.

A large part of the problem is a cycle of frustration and failure that relates to the acquisition of literacy skills. It is assumed that children in the late elementary grades have gone beyond "learning to read" and are now "reading to learn." But it may be that language minority students are not skilled enough at the basic reading processes—e.g., word-decoding and symbol-sound matching processes—and do not have sufficient syntactic and semantic knowledge in their second language to extract meaning quickly from text. If their instruction has focused on the mechanical process of reading, their skills at "going for meaning" might be less advanced. Indeed, research suggests that much reading instruction for language minority children is focused on phonics and decoding. Similarly, much instruction in writing in a second language has also traditionally been concerned with the mechanics of the writing process, especially with spelling and punctuation.

There is evidence that the whole language approach reduces the cultural mismatch that frequently occurs in classrooms with children from linguistically and culturally diverse backgrounds because the students and not the teacher define the context of the learning situation. However, there are also unanswered questions about the effectiveness of reform efforts in teaching literacy skills to ethnic and language minority children. Delpit (1986) and others have been critical of the effects of writing process instruction on minority children. The concern is that such methods do not allow students to learn and produce the type of discourse upon which assessment is based—i.e., standard academic discourse.

Little is known about whether process-oriented instruction is successful with second-language learners, or how it has been adapted for this population of students. Do language minority students with limited language proficiencies profit from the use of such activities as brainstorming, free writing, peer response groups, prereading and prewriting activities? These are important questions that require answers if educational reform is to impact these children favorably.

REFERENCES

Applebee, A. (1984). *Contexts for learning to write: Studies of secondary school instruction*. Norwood, NJ: Ablex.

Applebee, A., Langer, J., and Mullis, I. (1987). *Learning to write in our nation's schools.* Princeton, NJ: National Assessment of Educational Progress, Educational Testing Service.

Applebee, A., Langer, J., Jenkins, L., Mullis, I., & Foertsch, M. (1990). *Learning to write in our nation's schools: Instruction and achievement in 1988 at grades 4, 8, and 12.* Princeton, NJ: National Assessment of Educational Progress, Educational Testing Service.

Brown, A. L. (1978). Knowing when, where, and how to remember: A problem of metacognition. In R. Glaser (Ed.), *Advances in instructional psychology.* Hillsdale, NJ: Erlbaum.

Brown, A. L., Armbruster, B. B., & Baker, L. (1986). The role of metacognition in reading and studying. In J. Orasanu (Ed.), *Reading comprehension: From research to practice.* Hillsdale, NJ: Erlbaum.

California Office of Research (1985). Reports on the High Schools. Sacramento, CA: California State Department of Education.

Carr, T. (1981). Building theories of reading ability: On the relation between individual differences in cognitive skills and reading. *Cognition, 9,* 73–114.

Cronnell, B. (1985). Language influences in the English writing of third- and sixth-grade Mexican-American students. *Journal of Educational Research, 78,* 168–173.

Delpit, L. (1986). Skills and other dilemmas of a progressive Black educator. *Harvard Educational Review, 56,* 379–385.

Edelsky, C. (1982). Writing in a bilingual program: The relation of L1 and L2 texts. *TESOL Quarterly, 16,* 211–218.

Edelsky, C. (1983). Segmentation and punctuation: Developmental data from young writers in a bilingual program. *Research in the Teaching of English, 17,* 135–156.

Edelsky, C. (1990). Whose agenda is this anyway? Aresponse to Mckenna, Robinson, and Miller. *Educational Researcher, 19* 7–11.

Edelsky, C., & Jilbert, K. (1985). Bilingual children and writing: Lessons for all of us. *The Volta Review, 87,* 57–72.

Elliott, M. (1986). Nasr's development as a writer in his second language development: The first six months. *Australian Review of Applied Linguistics, 9,* 120–153.

Erickson, F. (1984). Rhetoric, anecdote, and rhapsody: Coherence strategies in a conversation among Black American adolescents. In D. Tannen (Ed.), *Coherence in spoken and written discourse.* Norwood, NJ: Ablex.

Eversen, L. S. (1985). Discourse-level interlanguage studies. In N. E. Enkvist (Ed.), *Coherence and composition: A symposium.* Abo, Finland: Research Institute of the Abo Akademi Foundation.

Farr, M. (1986). Language, culture, and writing: Sociolinguistic foundations of research on writing. *Review of Research in Education, 13,* 195–223.

Garcia, G. E., & Pearson, P. D. (1990). Modifying reading instruction to maximize its effectiveness for "disadvantaged" students. In *Better schooling for children of poverty: Alternatives to conventional wisdom.* Washington, DC: U.S. Department of Education, Office of Planning, Budget, and Evaluation.

Gibson, E., & Levin, H. (1975). *The psychology of reading.* Cambridge, MA: MIT Press.

Goody, J., & Watt, I. (1963). The consequences of literacy. *Comparative Studies in Society and History, 5,* 304–345.

Gundlach, R., McLane, J. B., Stott, F. M., & McNamee, G. D. (1985). The social foundations of children's early writing development. In M. Farr (Ed.), *Advances in writing research: Children's early writing development.* Norwood, NJ: Ablex.

Gutierrez, K. (1992). A comparison of instructional contexts in writing process classrooms with Latino children. *Education and Urban Society, 24,* 244–262.

Harris, K. R., & Graham, S. (in press). Self-regulated strategy development: A part of the writing process. In *Promoting academic competence and literacy in schools.* New York: Academic Press.

Heath, S. B. (1983). *Ways with words.* Cambridge: Cambridge University Press.

Hymes, D. (1971). Competence and performance in linguistic theory. In R. Huxley & E. Ingram (Eds.), *Language in acquisition: Models and methods.* London: Academic Press.

Kaplan, R. B. (1966). Cultural thought patterns in intercultural education. *Language learning, 16,* 1–20.

LaBerge, D. & Samuels, S. J. (1974). Towards a theory of automatic information processing in reading. *Cognitive Psychology, 6,* 293–323.

Liebman-Kleine, J. (1987). Teaching and researching invention: Using ethnography in ESL writing classes. *English Language Teaching Journal, 1987, 41,* 104–111.

McKenna, M. C., Robinson,, R. D., & Miller, J. W. (1990). Whole language: A research agenda for the nineties. *Educational Researcher, 19*, 3–6.

Means, B., & Knapp, M. S. (1991). Models for teaching advanced skills to educationally disadvantaged children. In *Teaching advanced skills to educationally disadvantaged children.* Washington, DC: U.S. Department of Education, Office of Planning, Budget, and Evaluation.

Oakes, J. (1985). *Keeping track.* New Haven, CT: Yale University Press.

Olson, D. (1977). From utterance to text: The bias of language in speech and writing. *Harvard Educational Review, 47*, 257–281.

Palincsar, A. S., & Brown, A. L. (1984). Reciprocal teaching of comprehension-fostering and monitoring activities. *Cognition and Instruction, 1*, 117–175.

Paris, S. G. (1986). Teaching children to guide their reading and learning. In T. Raphael (Ed.), *The contexts of school-based literacy.* New York: Random House.

Paris, S., & Oka E. (1986). Self-regulated learning among exceptional children. *Exceptional Children, 23*, 110–135.

Paris, S., & Wixson, K. (1986). The development of literacy: Access, acquisition, and instruction. In D. Bloome (Ed.) *Literacy and schooling.* Norwood, NJ: Ablex.

Pearson, P. D., & Raphael, T. E. (1990). Reading comprehension as a dimension of thinking. In B. F. Jones & L. Idol (Eds.), *Dimensions of thinking and cognitive instruction.* Elmhurst, IL: North Central Regional Educational Laboratory.

Perfetti, C. A., & Hogaboam, T. W. (1975). The relationship between single word decoding and reading comprehension skill. *Journal of Educational Psychology, 67*, 461–469.

Pringle, M. V. (1986). Learning to write in French immersion. *Carleton Papers in Applied Language Studies, 3*, 27–45.

Purves, A., & Hawisher, G. (1990). Writers, judges, and text models. In R. Beach & S. Hynds (Eds.), *Developing discourse practices in adolescence and adulthood.* Norwood, NJ: Ablex.

Purves, A., & Purves, W. C. (1986). Viewpoints: Cultures, text models, and the activity of writing. *Research in the Teaching of English, 20*, 175–197.

Schecter, S. R., & Harklau, L. A. (1991). *Annotated bibliography of research on writing in a non-native language.* Berkeley, CA: National Center for the Study of Writing.

Scollon, R., & Scollon, S. B. (1981). *Narrative, literacy and face in interethnic communication.* Norwood, NJ: Ablex.

Scribner, S., & Cole, M. (1981). *The psychology of literacy.* Cambridge, MA: Harvard University Press.

Seda, I., & Abramson, S. (1989). *English writing development of young, linguistically different learners.* ERIC Document Reproduction Service No. ED 321 882.

Soter, A. O. (1988). The second language learner and cultural transfer in narration. In A. C. Purves (Ed.), *Writing across languages and cultures: Issues in contrastive rhetoric.* Newbury Park, CA: Sage Publications.

Steinberg, L., Lin Blinde, P., & Chan, K. S. (1984). Dropping out among language minority youth. *Review of Educational Research, 54,* 113–132.

Sulzby, E. (1985). Kindergartners as writers and readers. In M. Farr (Ed.), *Advances in writing research: Children's early writing development.* Norwood, NJ: Ablex.

Swain, M. (1975). Writing skills of grade three French immersion pupils. *Working Papers on Bilingualism, 7.* (ERIC Document Reproduction Service No. ED 125 262).

Tannen, D. (Ed.) (1984). *Coherence in spoken and written discourse.* Norwood, NJ: Ablex.

Urzua, C. (1987). "You stopped too soon": Second language children composing and revising. *TESOL Quarterly, 21,* 279–304.

Valdes, G. (1991). *Bilingual minorities and the language issues in writing: Toward profession-wide responses to a new challenge.* Berkeley, CA: National Center for the Study of Writing.

Vellutino, F. R., & Scanlon, D. M. (1980). *Free recall of concrete and abstract words in poor and normal readers.* Paper presented at the conference of Cognitive Processes in Reading, sponsored by the British Psychological Society, Exeter, England, March.

✧ Chapter 7

Teaching Strategies:
Their Possibilities and Limitations

Lilia I. Bartolomé

Much of the current discussion regarding linguistic minority academic achievement in our schools stresses the topic of successful or effective teaching strategies. The term teaching strategies refers to an educational plan or a series of activities/lessons designed to obtain a specific goal or result. Research studies have begun to identify characteristics of teachers, educational programs, approaches and teaching strategies found to be successful in working with linguistic minority student populations (Carter & Chatfield, 1986; Garcia, 1988, 1991; Lucas, Henze & Donato, 1990; Moll, 1988). In addition, there has been specific interest in identifying teaching strategies for more effective transitioning or transferring of students out of learning environments where native language instruction is offered and into mainstream classrooms where instruction is offered solely in English (Chamot, 1983; Escamilla, 1993; Moran,

1993; O'Malley & Chamot, 1990; Tinajero & Huerta-Macias, 1993). Although it is important to identify useful and promising teaching strategies, it is erroneous to assume that teacher mastery of particular teaching strategies or methods will guarantee successful student learning and transition into English-only settings.

While one purpose of this paper is to discuss language arts transitioning teaching strategies identified as potentially effective, this discussion needs to occur taking into account both the possibilities and limitations of teaching strategies. Before we can discuss effective teaching strategies in general and transitioning teaching strategies in particular, it is necessary to discuss their perceived effectiveness within the larger sociocultural context. We must consider why, on the one hand, these strategies are warranted, and, on the other hand, why these strategies are deemed effective in a given sociocultural context.

In his letter to North American educators, Paulo Freire (1987) warns against uncritically importing and exporting strategies and methods with no regard for sociocultural contexts. Freire challenges the belief that teacher mastery of content area and methodology is sufficient to ensure effective instruction of students from subordinate status populations (status that reflects the linguistic minority group's subordinate political and economic status in the larger society). He states that teachers must possess both content area knowledge and political clarity or consciousness to be able to effectively create, adopt, and modify teaching strategies that simultaneously respect and challenge learners from diverse populations and in a variety of learning environments. It is critical that educators become so well versed in the theory of their specializations that they own their knowledge. Under ideal conditions, this ownership imbues the educators with confidence and allows them to simultaneously translate theory into practice *and* consider the population being served and the sociocultural reality in which learning is expected to take place. Let me reiterate, a command of a content area or specialization is necessary but it is not sufficient for effectively working with students from subordinate populations. It is equally critical that teachers comprehend that their role as educators is not politically neutral. In ignoring or negating the political nature of their work with linguistic minority students, teachers maintain the status quo and their students' subordinate status. Conversely, teachers can become conscious of and subsequently challenge the role of educational institutions and their own roles as educators in maintaining a system which often serves to silence students from subordinate groups.

Teachers must remember that schools, similar to other institutions in society, are influenced by perceptions of socioeconomic status (SES), race/ethnicity, language and/or gender. They must begin to question how these perceptions influence classroom dynamics. It is especially important for teachers who work with students from subordinate groups to recognize historical (and current) attributions of low status to members of low SES linguistic minority populations and the subsequent under-servicing of such populations in the schools.

So, while it is certainly important to identify effective instructional strategies, it is not sufficient to restrict our focus to instructional issues solely related to teaching methods and activities. This discussion must be broadened to reveal the deeply entrenched deficit orientation toward "difference" (e.g., social class, race/ethnicity, language, gender) in our schools. We must also ask how this deficit view has affected our perceptions of linguistic minority students and shaped our approaches for teaching them in both English-only and bilingual school settings. It is within this broader and more comprehensive discussion that we can begin to situate and examine potential effective teaching strategies.

In this paper I will argue that by taking this comprehensive approach to analyzing language arts teaching strategies identified as effective within a particular sociocultural reality, we can shift our focus from the strategy itself to more fundamental pedagogical features common across strategies. These student-centered features are known by educators to constitute good teaching for any population. More important, in the case of linguistic minority students, they serve to offset potentially unequal relations and discriminatory structures and practices in the classroom and to humanize the instructional process for both student and teacher. Without underestimating the importance of teachers' knowledge of methodology, such focus is neither sufficient nor a substitute for comprehensive and critical understanding of pedagogy and the teacher's role in its implementation—especially as it relates to students from subordinate populations.

For this reason, I will caution readers against the general tendency to reduce complex educational issues (those that reflect greater social, political, and economic realities) to mere "magical" methods and techniques designed to remediate perceived student cognitive and linguistic deficiencies. I will conclude by proposing what Macedo (in press) calls an

> anti-methods pedagogy that refuses to be enslaved by the rigidity of models and methodological paradigms. An anti-

methods pedagogy should be informed by a critical understanding of the sociocultural context that guides our practices
so as to free us from the beaten path of methodological certain-
ties and specialisms. (p. 8)

This is a pedagogical process that requires both action and reflection. By using it, instead of importing or exporting effective strategies, teachers are required to recreate and reinvent those effective
approaches, taking into consideration the possibilities and limitations of teaching strategies and sociocultural realities.

Our Legacy: A Deficit Orientation and
Unequal Relations in the Classroom

Teaching strategies are neither designed nor implemented in a vacuum. Design, selection, and use of particular teaching approaches
and strategies arise from perceptions about learning and learners.
It is especially important, when discussing learners from subordinate populations, that we deal candidly with our deeply rooted and
traditional deficit orientation toward difference. The most pedagogically advanced strategies prove ineffective in the hands of educators who implicitly or explicitly subscribe to a belief system that
renders linguistic minority students, at best, culturally disadvantaged and in need of fixing (if we could only identify the right
recipe!) or, at worst, culturally or genetically deficient and beyond
fixing. Despite the fact that various models have been proposed to
explain the academic failure of certain linguistic minority groups—
academic failure described as historical, pervasive, and disproportionate—the fact remains that our views of difference are deficit
based and deeply imprinted in our individual and collective psyches
(Flores, 1982; Menchaca & Valencia, 1990; Valencia, 1986, 1991).

The deficit model has the longest history of any model discussed in the education literature. Valencia (1986) traces its evolution over three centuries.

Also known in the literature as the "social pathology" model or
the "cultural deprivation" model, the deficit approach explains
disproportionate academic problems among low status students
as largely being due to pathologies or deficits in their sociocultural background (e.g., cognitive and linguistic deficiencies, low
self-esteem, poor motivation). . . . To improve the educability of

such students, programs such as compensatory education and parent-child intervention have been proposed. (p. 3)

The deficit model of instruction and learning has been critiqued by numerous researchers as ethnocentric and invalid (Boykin, 1983; Diaz, Moll, & Mehan, 1986; Flores, 1982; Sue & Padilla, 1986; Trueba, 1989; Walker, 1987). More recent research offers alternative models that shift the source of school failure away from the characteristics of individual children, their families, or their cultures, and toward the schooling process (Au & Mason, 1983; Heath, 1983; Mehan, 1992; Philips, 1972). Unfortunately, these alternative models often unwittingly give rise to a kinder and liberal, yet more concealed version of the deficit model that views subordinate students as being in need of "specialized" modes of instruction—a type of instructional "coddling" that mainstream students do not require in order to achieve in school. Despite the use of less ethnocentric models to explain the academic standing of linguistic minority students, I believe that our deficit orientation toward difference, especially as it relates to low socioeconomic groups, is very deeply ingrained in the ethos of our most prominent institutions, especially schools, and in compensatory programs such as bilingual education.

Nevertheless, the study of structural factors within the schools has yielded valuable insights with respect to asymmetrical and unequal relations and how they are manifested between teachers and students from subordinate groups. These studies illustrate the link between a deficit orientation and discriminatory practices aimed at students from groups perceived as low status. For example, the number of studies that examine unequal power relations in the classroom have increased in recent years and empirically demonstrate the unequal and discriminatory treatment of students based on their low socioeconomic status, membership in a low status racial/ethnic group, and limited English language use. Findings range from teacher preference for Anglo students, to bilingual teachers' preference for lighter-skinned Latino students, to teachers' negative perceptions of working-class parents compared to middle-class parents, and, finally, to unequal teaching and testing practices in schools serving working-class and more affluent populations (Anyon, 1988; Bloom, 1991; Lareau, 1990; U.S. Commission on Civil Rights, 1973). Especially indicative of our inability to deal honestly with our deficit orientation is the fact that the teachers in these studies—teachers from all ethnic groups—were themselves unaware of the active role they played in the differential and unequal treatment of their students.

Furthermore, many research studies which examined culturally congruent and incongruent teaching approaches actually describe the negotiation of power relations in classrooms where teachers initially imposed participation structures upon students from subordinate linguistic minority groups and later learned to negotiate with them regarding rules for acceptable behavior and language use (Au & Mason, 1983; Erickson & Mohatt, 1982; Heath, 1983; Philips, 1972). These studies, in essence, capture the successful negotiation of power relations which resulted in higher student academic achievement and teacher effectiveness. For example, Au and Mason (1983) explain that "one means of achieving cultural congruence in lessons may be to *seek a balance between the interactional rights of teachers and students* [emphasis added], so that the children can participate in ways comfortable to them" (p. 145). Their study compared two teachers and showed that the teacher who was willing to negotiate with students either about the topic of discussion or the appropriate participation structure was better able to implement her lesson. Conversely, the teacher who attempted to impose both discussion topic and appropriate interactional rules was frequently diverted because of conflicts over topics and rules.

Unfortunately, interpretations and practical applications of this body of research have focused on the cultural congruence of the approaches. I emphasize the term *cultural* because in these studies the term is used in a restricted sense devoid of its dynamic, ideological, and political dimensions. "Culture is the representation of lived experiences, material artifacts and practices *forged within the unequal and dialectical relations* [emphasis added] that different groups establish in a given society at a particular point in historical time" (Giroux, 1985: p. xxi). I utilize this definition of culture because, without identifying the political dimensions of culture and subsequent unequal status attributed to members of different cultural groups, the reader may conclude that teaching methods simply need to be culturally congruent to be effective—without recognizing that not all cultures are viewed and treated as equally legitimate in classrooms.

Given the sociocultural realities in the above studies, the specific teaching strategies may not be what made the difference. It could well be that the teacher's effort to "share the power," treating students as equal participants in their own learning and, in the process, discarding (consciously or unconsciously held) deficit views of the students, made the difference. Utilizing a variety of strategies and techniques, students were allowed to interact with teachers in egalitarian and meaningful ways. Teachers also learned to recognize, value, utilize, and build upon students' previously acquired knowledge and skills. In essence, these strategies succeeded in creating a comfort zone so students could exhibit their knowledge and skills and ultimately empower themselves to succeed in an academic setting. McDermott's (1977) classic research reminds us that numerous teaching approaches and strategies can be effective so long as trusting relations between teacher and students are established and power relations are mutually set and agreed upon.

It is against this backdrop that teachers can begin to interrogate the unspoken yet prevalent deficit orientation used to hide SES, race/ethnicity, linguistic, and gender inequities present in American classrooms. And it is against this backdrop that we turn our discussion to bilingual education and its mirroring of a deficit view of linguistic minority students.

Bilingual Education, the Deficit Model, and the Practice of Transitioning

Despite the fact that current bilingual education models emerged from an enrichment two-way bilingual program designed to serve Cuban refugees in Dade County, Florida, in 1963, government intervention changed the program's focus when it was applied to low SES Mexican American and Puerto Rican student populations. Crawford (1989) explains that the focus shifted

> from an enrichment model aimed at developing fluency in two languages to a remedial effort designed to help "disadvantaged" children overcome the "handicap" of not speaking English. From its outset, federal aid to bilingual education was regarded as a "poverty program," rather than an innovative approach to language instruction. (p. 29)

The belief that students from subordinate linguistic minority groups have language problems is very much present in the origins of bilingual education. Flores, Cousin, and Diaz (1991) point out:

> One of the most pervasive and pernicious myths about [language minority] children is that they have a language deficit. This myth is not reserved just for bilingual and non-English speaking students; it is also commonly held about African American and other minority students [as well as English dominant linguistic minority students]. (p. 9)

In addition, these students are perceived as lacking valuable life experiences necessary for academic success and in need of educational programs that will fill them with academic knowledge and language skills perceived as inherently superior to that which the students may already possess and bring to school. The consequent belief is that these deficits, in turn, cause learning problems. Bilingual education is then viewed as a compensatory program designed to remediate the students' language problems, referring to their limited English proficiency. The deficit model may constitute the real problem to the extent that it disconfirms rather than confirms linguistic minority native language experiences.

Currently, the Federal government identifies two needs of limited-English-proficient students: (a) to develop their English proficiency so that they can fully benefit from instruction in English, and (b) to enhance their academic progress in all subject areas (U.S. Department of Education, 1991). The U.S. Department of Education lists three general program types for teaching limited-English-proficient students English language skills necessary for success in school: transitional bilingual education, two-way or developmental bilingual education, and special alternative instructional programs. Only the first two programs utilize the student's native language for academic and instructional purposes. Special alternative instructional programs are "designed to provide structured English-language instruction and special instructional services that will allow a limited-English-proficient child to achieve competence in the English language and to meet grade promotion and graduation standards" (p. 17). Of the three programs, transitional bilingual programs represent the largest percentage of programs currently funded by the Federal government (U.S. Department of Education, 1991).

Broadly defined, transitional bilingual education programs allow the use of limited-English-proficient students' native language in academic settings while they acquire the English-language proficiency necessary to transition into English-only settings. Crawford (1989) criticizes the ambiguity of transitional bilingual education as it relates to native language use:

> The definition of transitional bilingual education is broad, requiring only that some amount of native language and culture be used, along with ESL instruction. Programs may stress native-language development, including initial literacy, or they may provide students with nothing more than the translation services of bilingual aides. Contrary to public per-

ceptions, studies have shown that English is the medium of instruction from 72 to 92 percent of the time in transitional bilingual education programs. (p. 175)

Spener (1988) adds that transitional bilingual education programs too often "provide only a limited period of native-language instruction and do not guarantee English mastery. Thus, these programs often prevent children from attaining fluency in either their native language or in English" (p. 133).

Nevertheless, the common assumption is that students exiting bilingual classrooms and entering "regular" or English-only classrooms necessarily possess native language literacy skills and will therefore transfer or apply these (presumed) skills to their English academic work. The problem is not so much with the assumption that skills transfer from one language to another. A number of recent studies suggest that cross-lingual transfer does occur (Avelar La Salle,1991; Clarke, 1988; Faltis, 1983; Hernandez, 1991; Reyes, 1987; Zhang, 1990). The difficulty lies in the assumption that students are indeed being taught native language literacy skills.

In addition, we need to question the hidden objective embedded in the transitioning model which requires that limited-English-proficient students discontinue the use of their native language as they increase their fluency in English. Again, this subtractive view of bilingualism mirrors our deeply rooted deficit and assimilative orientation that often devalues students' native language. In other words, Freire's (1987) requirement that teachers possess political clarity regarding the sociocultural conditions within which transition takes place will enable them to see the inherent contradiction of the educational language policy. We can accept the native language as long as it is used only minimally and temporarily, that is, until it is replaced with English. Is it not ironic that while we discourage the maintenance of linguistic minority students' native language throughout their education, we require mainstream English-speaking students to study a foreign language as a prerequisite for college—where many continue their foreign language studies for some years?

Even if we accept the underlying deficit notion of transitional bilingual education, we need to question how it is possible to expect students to transfer or apply native language literacy skills to English literacy tasks when, in reality, they have had little opportunity to develop these skills in their native language in school. All too often, students are held accountable and penalized for not possessing the very native language literacy skills that the school has failed to develop in the first place. In situations such as these, we must call into question the assumption that students are helped to develop native language literacy skills so that the transfer of skills really *can* occur. Does shuttling students from so-called bilingual classrooms where English is the medium of instruction from 72 to 92 percent of the time to classrooms where it is the sole medium of instruction constitute transitioning or does it constitute receiving more of the same English-only instruction?

To discuss effective transitioning strategies, it is necessary to contextualize them within the ideal model of bilingual education. That model promotes the development of native language literacy skills beyond basic decoding and encoding skills and teaches English as a second language literacy skills in an additive fashion with native language literacy skills. Building on the assumption that the ideal model is possible, we can then discuss teaching strategies identified as effective for preparing students to learn literacy skills in both the native language and English.

Student-centered Teaching and Equalization of Power Relations

Numerous teaching strategies and approaches promise to facilitate transfer of native language literacy skills to an English as a second language context. However, it is important to reiterate that the effectiveness of the strategy is not inherent to the strategy but rather in the informed manner in which the teacher implements it. Well-known approaches and strategies such as cooperative learning, language experience, process writing, reciprocal teaching and whole language activities can be used to create learning environments where students cease to be treated as objects and yet receive academically rigorous instruction (Cohen, 1986; Edelsky, Altwerger & Flores, 1991; Palincsar and Brown, 1984; Pérez & Torres-Guzmán, 1992; Zamel, 1982). In successful applications of these approaches and strategies, deficit views of students from subordinate groups are discarded and students are treated with respect and viewed as active and capable subjects in their own learning.

Academically rigorous student-centered teaching strategies can take many forms. One may well ask, is it not merely common sense to promote approaches and strategies that recognize, utilize, and build on students' existing knowledge bases? Yes, it is. However, it is important to recognize, as part of our effort to increase our political clarity, that these practices have *not* typified classroom instruction for students from subordinate populations. The practice of learning from and valuing student language and life experiences often occurs in classrooms where students speak a language variety and possess cultural capital that more closely matches the mainstream (Anyon, 1988; Lareau, 1990).

Anyon's research (1988) suggests that teachers of affluent students are more likely than teachers of working class students to utilize and incorporate student life experiences and knowledge into the curriculum. For example, in Anyon's study teachers of affluent students often designed creative and innovative lessons that tapped students' existing knowledge bases; one math lesson asked them to fill out a possession survey that asked about the number of cars, television sets, refrigerators, and games owned at home so as to teach students to average. Unfortunately, this practice of tapping on students' already existing knowledge and language bases is not a given with student populations traditionally perceived as deficient. Anyon reports that teachers of working class students viewed them as lacking the necessary "cultural capital" and therefore imposed content and behavioral standards with little consideration for student input. Student-centered teaching strategies in contexts where teachers work with subordinate populations require teachers to consciously discard deficit notions and genuinely value and utilize students' existing knowledge bases in their teaching. Furthermore, teachers must remain open to the fact that they will also learn from their students. Learning is not a one-way undertaking.

We recognize that no language variety or set of life experiences is inherently superior, yet our social values reflect our preferences for certain language varieties and life experiences over others. Student-centered teaching strategies such as cooperative learning, language experience, process writing, reciprocal teaching and whole language activities (if practiced consciously and critically) can help to offset or neutralize our deficit-based failure to recognize subordinate student strengths. Our tendency to discount these strengths occurs whenever we forget that learning only occurs when prior knowledge is accessed and linked to new information.

Jones, Palincsar, Ogle, and Carr (1987) explain that learning is linking new information to prior knowledge. Prior knowledge is stored in memory in the form of knowledge frameworks. New information is understood and stored by calling up the appropriate knowledge framework and integrating the new information. Acknowledging and utilizing existing student language and knowledge makes good pedagogical sense and it also constitutes a humanizing experience for students traditionally *de*humanized and disempowered in the schools. I believe that strategies identified as effective in the literature have the potential to offset reductive education in which "the educator as 'the one who knows' transfers existing knowledge to the learner as 'the one who does not know'" (Freire, 1985, p. 114).

Creating learning environments which incorporate student language and life experiences in no way negates teachers' responsibility for providing students with particular academic content knowledge and skills. It is important not to link teacher respect and use of student knowledge and language bases with a laissez-faire attitude toward teaching. It is equally necessary not to confuse academic rigor with rigidity that stifles and silences students. The teacher is the authority, with all the resulting responsibilities that entails; however, it is not necessary for the teacher to become authoritarian in order to challenge students intellectually. Education can be a process in which teacher and students mutually participate in the intellectually exciting undertaking we call learning. Students can become active subjects in their own learning instead of passive objects waiting to be filled with facts and figures by the teacher.

As mentioned earlier, a number of student-centered teaching strategies (i.e., cooperative learning, language experience, process writing, reciprocal teaching and whole language) possess the *potential* to transform students into active subjects and participants in their own learning. I emphasize "potential" because teaching strategies in and of themselves are not panaceas. Even the most pedagogically sound strategy can be rendered useless by teachers who do not master their areas of specialization and/or who do not view their students as capable learners who bring valuable life experiences and language skills into the classroom. Again, let me reiterate my belief that teachers who work with subordinate populations have the responsibility to assist them in appropriating knowledge bases and discourse styles deemed desirable by the greater society. However, this process of appropriation must be additive; that is, the new concepts and new discourse skills must be added to, not subtracted from, the students' existing repertoire. In order to assume this additive stance, teachers must discard deficit views so they can utilize and build on life experiences and language styles too often viewed and labelled as "low class" and undesirable. Again, there are numerous teaching strategies and methods which can be utilized in this additive manner.

For the purposes of illustration, I will briefly discuss one approach currently identified as promising for both English-speaking "mainstream" students and linguistic minority students in upper elementary grades. I will highlight some key features of the strategy and explain its potential to humanize the educational process and to create learning contexts in which students empower themselves while acquiring new academic knowledge and skills. The approach is referred to in the literature as "strategic teaching."

Strategic Teaching and the Potential for Student Empowerment

Strategic teaching refers to an instructional model that explicitly teaches students learning strategies which enable them consciously to monitor their own learning; this is accomplished through the development of reflective cognitive monitoring and metacognitive skills (Jones et al., 1987). The goal is to prepare independent and metacognitively aware students. This teaching strategy makes explicit for students the structures of various text types utilized in academic settings and assists students in identifying various strategies for effectively comprehending the various genres. Although text structures and strategies for dissecting the particular structures are presented by the teacher, a key component of these lessons is the elicitation of students' knowledge about text types as well as their own strategies for making meaning before presenting them with more conventional academic strategies.

It is important, however, to point out that mere implementation of strategic teaching does not automatically result in teachers questioning and disowning their deficit orientation. This teaching strategy, like others, can be misappropriated by teachers lacking political clarity and implemented in ways that disconfirm and treat students as incapable in participating in their own learning. Therefore, for the purpose of my discussion, we must keep in mind that one key ingredient for the success of strategic teaching is a teacher who is both well versed in his or her content area and politically conscious and aware of how a group's subordinate social status in the greater society may or may not get played out in the classroom setting. It is this type of teacher who can most effectively create democratic learning environments in which to teach students learning strategies.

Examples of learning strategies include teaching various text structures (i.e., stories and reports) through frames and graphic organizers. *Frames* are sets of questions that help students understand a given topic. Readers monitor their understanding of a text by asking questions, making predictions, and testing their predictions as they read. Before reading, frames serve as an advance organizer to activate prior knowledge and facilitate understanding. Frames can also be utilized during the reading process by the reader to monitor self-learning. Finally, frames can be used after a reading lesson to summarize and integrate newly acquired information.

Graphic organizers are visual maps that represent text structures and organizational patterns used in texts and in student writing. Ideally, graphic organizers reflect both the content and text structure. Graphic organizers include semantic maps, chains, and concept hierarchies and assist the student to visualize the rhetorical structure of the text. Jones et al. (1987) explain that frames and graphic organizers can be "powerful tools to help the student locate, select, sequence, integrate and restructure information—both from the perspective of understanding and from the perspective of producing information in written responses" (p. 38).

Although much of the research on strategic teaching focuses on English monolingual mainstream students, recent efforts to study bilingual and limited-English-proficient linguistic minority students' use of these strategies show similar success. This literature shows that strategic teaching improved the students' reading comprehension and conscious use of effective learning strategies in the native language (Avelar La Salle, 1991; Chamot, 1983; Hernandez, 1991; O'Malley & Chamot, 1990; Reyes, 1987). Furthermore, these studies show that students, despite limited English proficiency, are able to transfer or apply their knowledge of specific learning strategies and text structure to English reading texts. For example, Hernandez (1991) reports that sixth-grade limited-English-proficient students learned, in the native language (Spanish) to generate hypotheses, summarize, and make predictions about readings. He reports:

> Students were able to demonstrate use of comprehension strategies even when they could not decode the English text aloud. When asked in Spanish about English texts, the students were able to generate questions, summarize stories, and predict future events in Spanish. (p. 101)

Avelar La Salle's (1991) study of third- and fourth-grade bilingual students shows that strategic teaching in the native language of three expository text structures commonly found in elementary social studies and science texts (topical net, matrix, and hierarchy) improved comprehension of these types of texts in both Spanish and English.

Such explicit and strategic teaching is most important in the upper elementary grades, when bilingual students are expected to focus on English literacy skills development. Beginning at about third grade, students also face literacy demands distinct from those encountered in earlier grades. Chall (1983) describes the change in literacy demands in terms of stages of readings. She explains that at a stage three of reading, students cease to "learn to read" and begin "reading to learn." Students in third and fourth grade are introduced to content area subjects such as social studies, science, and health. In addition, students are introduced to expository texts (reports). This change in texts, text structures and in the functions of reading (reading for information) calls for teaching strategies that will prepare students to comprehend various expository texts (e.g., cause/effect, compare/contrast) utilized across the curriculum.

Strategic teaching holds great promise for preparing linguistic minority students to face the new literacy challenges in the upper grades. As mentioned earlier, the primary goal of strategic instruction is to foster learner independence. This goal in and of itself is laudable. However, the characteristics of strategic instruction that I find most promising grow out of the premise that teachers and students must actively interact and negotiate meaning as equals in order to reach a goal. To assist students in becoming independent, reflective, and empowered learners, Jones et al. (1987) recommend that teachers follow this instructional sequence:

1. Teachers access and assess current student knowledge about pertinent content and learning strategies via think-aloud and other prereading brainstorming activities. During this phase of instruction, teachers learn about their students' existing knowledge bases as well as students' questions and concerns regarding their own learning.

2. As a result of the above informal assessment, teachers explicitly explain the new content and strategies to the students. After considering the students' existing knowledge bases and questions, the teacher and student link the new content and strategies with prior knowledge and skills. The teacher and students identify and discuss the target strategy or strategies (declarative knowledge), how they should

employ the strategy or strategies (procedural information); and in what context they should employ the strategy (conditional information).

3. Teachers model the new strategy or strategies so that students have the opportunity to witness the thought processes and behaviors involved in the employment of the strategy. For example, similar to reciprocal teaching, teachers initially model for students the process of formulating questions that will assist students to monitor their own learning during reading.

4. Teachers scaffold the instruction and provide students the time to practice and demonstrate their use of the strategy or strategies. Scaffolding is "a process that enables a child or novice to solve a problem, carry out a task, or achieve a goal which is beyond his unassisted efforts" (Wood, Bruner & Ross in Jones et al., 1987).

5. The teacher apprentices the students and provides extensive support of their efforts. This support is temporary; teachers gradually reduce their support so that students assume sole responsibility and become independent learners.

6. Teachers relate strategy instruction to motivation so students recognize the significant role they play in their own learning and academic success. By providing students with experiences in which they see the successful results of strategic learning, it is possible to change students' expectations for success and failure and help them sustain strategy use (modified from Jones et al., 1987).

Ideally, throughout the strategic learning process, students empower themselves in learning contexts where they are permitted to speak from their own vantage points. Before teachers attempt to instruct students in new content or learning strategies, efforts are made to access prior knowledge so as to link it with new information. In allowing students to present and discuss their prior knowledge and experiences, the teacher legitimizes and treats as valuable student language and cultural experiences usually ignored in classrooms. If students are allowed to speak on what they know best, then they are, in a sense, treated as experts—experts who are expected to refine their knowledge bases with the additional new content and strategy information presented by the teacher.

Teachers play a significant role in creating learning contexts in which students are able to empower themselves. Teachers act as cultural brokers of sorts when they introduce students not only to the culture of the classroom but to particular subjects and discourse styles and, in the process, assist students in appropriating the skills (in an additive fashion) for themselves so as to enable them behave as "insiders" in the particular subject or discipline. Gee (1989) reminds us of the social nature of teaching and learning. He contends that for students to do well in school, they must undergo an apprenticeship into the subject's or discipline's discourse. That apprenticeship includes acquisition of particular content matter, ways of organizing content, and ways of using language (oral and written). Gee adds that these discourses are not mastered solely through teacher-centered and directed instruction but by "apprenticeship into social practices through scaffolded and supported interaction with people who have already mastered the discourse" (p. 7).

Models of instruction such as strategic teaching can promote such an apprenticeship. In the process of apprenticing linguistic minority students, teachers must interact in meaningful ways with students. This human interaction often familiarizes individuals from different SES and race/ethnic groups and creates mutual respect instead of the antagonism that so frequently occurs between teachers and their students from subordinate groups. In this learning environment, teachers and students learn from each other. The strategies serve, then, not to fix the student, but to equalize power relations and to humanize the learning environment. Ideally, teachers are forced to challenge implicitly or explicitly held deficit attitudes and beliefs about their students and the cultural groups to which they belong.

A Humanizing Pedagogy: Going Beyond Teaching Strategies

As discussed earlier, numerous teaching strategies possess the potential to humanize the learning process. It is urgent that teachers break free from lock-step methodologies so that they may utilize any number of strategies or features of strategies to serve their students more effectively. I am reminded of the humanizing effects of teaching strategies that, similar to strategic teaching, allow teachers to listen and learn from their students, when I recall a Special Education teacher's experience related in a bilingualism and literacy course I taught. This teacher, for most of her career, had been required to assess her students through a variety of close-ended instruments and then to remediate their diagnosed "weaknesses" with discrete skills instruction. The assessment instruments provided little information to explain why the student answered a question correctly or incorrectly, and they often confirmed perceived student academic and cognitive weaknesses. The fragmented discrete skills approach to instruction restricts the teacher's access to existing student knowledge and experiences not specifically elicited by the academic tasks. Needless to say, this teacher knew very little about her students other than her deficit descriptions of them.

As a requirement for my course, she was asked to focus on one limited-English-proficient special education student over the semester. She observed the student in a number of formal and informal contexts, and she engaged him in a number of open-ended tasks. The tasks included allowing him to write entire texts such as stories and poems (despite diagnosed limited English proficiency) and to engage in "think-alouds" during reading. Through these open-ended activities, the teacher learned about her student's English writing ability (strengths and weaknesses), his life experiences and world views, and his meaning-making strategies for reading. Consequently, the teacher not only constructed an instructional plan much better suited to her student's academic needs and interests; even more important, she underwent a humanizing process which allowed her to recognize the varied and valuable life experiences and knowledge her student brought into the classroom.

This teacher was admirably candid when she shared her initial negative and stereotypic views of the student and their radical transformation. Despite this teacher's mastery of content area, her lack of political clarity blinded her to the oppressive and dehumanizing nature of instruction offered to linguistic minority students. Initially, she had formed an erroneous notion of her student's personality, world view, academic ability, motivation, and academic potential on the basis on his Puerto Rican ethnicity, low-SES background, limited English proficiency, and moderately learning-disabled label. Because of the restricted and closed nature of earlier assessment and instruction, the teacher had never received information about her student that challenged her negative perceptions. Listening to her student and reading his poetry and stories, she discovered his loving and sunny personality, learned his personal history and identified academic strengths and weaknesses. In the process, she discovered and challenged her deficit orientation. The following excerpt exemplifies the power of the student voice for humanizing teachers.

My Father

I love my father very much. I will never forget what my father has done for me and my brothers and sisters. When we first came from Puerto Rico we didn't have food to eat and we were very poor. My father had to work three jobs to put food and milk on the table. Those were hard times and my father worked so hard that we hardly saw him. But even when I didn't see him, I always knew he loved me very much. I will always be grateful to my father. We are not so poor now and so he works only one job. But I will never forget what my father did for me. I will also work to help my father have a better life when I grow up. I love my father very much.

The process of learning about her student's rich and multifaceted background enabled this teacher to move beyond the rigid methodology which required her to distance herself from the student and confirm the deficit model she unconsciously adhered to. In this case, the meaningful teacher-student interaction equalized teacher-student power relations and humanized instruction by expanding horizons through which the student demonstrated human qualities, dreams, desires, and capacities that close-ended tests and instruction never capture. The specific teaching strategies utilized, in and of themselves, may not be the significant factors. The actual strengths of strategies depend, first and foremost, on the degree to which they embrace a humanizing pedagogy that values the students' background knowledge, culture, and life experiences and create learning contexts where power is shared by students and teachers. Teaching strategies are means to an end; that is, humanizing education to promote academic success for students historically under-serviced by the schools. A teaching strategy is a vehicle to a greater goal. A number of vehicles exist which may or may not lead to a humanizing pedagogy depending on the sociocultural reality in which teachers and students operate. Teachers need to examine critically these promising teaching strategies and appropriate the aspects of those strategies which work best in their particular learning environments. Too often, teachers uncritically adopt "the latest in methodology" and blame the students (once again) when the method proves ineffective.

Methods, teaching strategies, and techniques are not panaceas. The answer lies not in methodology but in the humanity with which it is applied. For this reason, I believe that we cannot reduce transitioning success to a specific strategy or methodological paradigm.

More important than strategies are the teacher's political clarity and critical understanding of the need to create pedagogical structures that eliminate the asymmetrical power relations which subordinate linguistic minority students (Freire & Macedo, 1987). As the strategic teaching approach demonstrates, features that lead to a process in which students are treated with dignity and respect make all the difference. In other words, these teaching strategies provide conditions which enable subordinate students to move from their usual object position to subject positions. I am convinced that *transitioning the student from object to subject position* produces more far-reaching effects than *transitioning the student from the native language to English*. In fact, if the former transitioning occurs, the latter should present little difficulty.

I believe that educators, particularly bilingual teachers, would be far more effective if they critically understood the complex interrelationship of sociocultural factors shaping the educational context within which they are expected to transition students. The teachers' high level of critical awareness would enable them to develop the necessary pedagogical structures that cease to view and treat limited-English-proficient students as lacking, or as having language problems. Teachers could develop pedagogies to enhance those native language skills necessary for application to English-language settings. Otherwise, these educators could easily fall into what Macedo (in press) calls an entrapment pedagogy; that is, "a pedagogy that requires of students what it does not give them" (p. 6). An uncritical acceptance of the transitioning model could very well lead to such entrapment. Finally, I would urge educators to understand that, above all, the critical issue is the degree to which we hold the moral conviction that we must humanize transitioning linguistic minority students into the English-only mainstream by eliminating the hostility that often greets these students. This process would require what Macedo (in press) suggests,

> [an] anti-methods pedagogy that would reject the mechanization of intellectualism . . . [and] challenges teachers to work toward reappropriation of [the] endangered dignity [of both teacher and student] and toward reclaiming our humanity. The anti-methods pedagogy adheres to the eloquence of Antonio Machado's poem, "Caminante, no hay caminos. El camino se hace al andar" (Traveler, there are no roads. The road is created as we walk it [together]). (p. 8)

REFERENCES

Anyon, J. (1988). Social class and the hidden curriculum of work. In J. R. Gress (Ed.), *Curriculum: An introduction to the field*. Berkeley, CA: McCutchan, 366–389.

Au, K. H., & Mason, J. M. (1983). Cultural congruence in classroom participation structures: Achieving a balance of rights. *Discourse Processes, 6*, 145–168.

Avelar La Salle, R. (1991). The effect of metacognitive instruction on the transfer of expository comprehension skills: The interlingual and cross-lingual cases. Unpublished doctoral dissertation, Stanford University.

Bloom, G. M. (1991). The effects of speech style and skin color on bilingual teaching candidates' and bilingual teachers' attitudes toward Mexican American pupils. Unpublished doctoral dissertation, Stanford University.

Boykin, A. W. (1983). The academic performance of Afro-American children. In J. T. Spence (Ed.),. *Achievement and achievement motives: Psychological and sociological approaches*. San Francisco: W.H. Freeman, 322–369.

Carter T. P., & Chatfield, M. L. (1986). Effective bilingual schools: Implications for policy and practice. *American Journal of Education, 95*, 200–232.

Chall, J. (1983). *Stages of reading development*. New York: McGraw-Hill.

Chamot, A. U. (1983). How to plan to transfer curriculum from bilingual to mainstream instruction. *Focus*, (12), Rosslyn, VA: National Clearinghouse of Bilingual Education.

Clarke, M. A. (1988). The short circuit hypothesis of ESL reading—or when language competence interferes with reading performance. In P. L. Carrell, J. Devine, & D. E. Eskey (Eds.), *Interactive approaches to second language reading*. New York: Cambridge University Press, 114–124.

Cohen, E. G. (1986). *Designing groupwork: Strategies for the heterogeneous classroom*. New York: Teachers College Press.

Crawford, J. (1989). *Bilingual education: History, politics, theory and practice*. Trenton, NJ: Crane.

Cummins, J. (1989). *Empowering minority students*. Sacramento: California Association of Bilingual Education.

Diaz, S., Moll, L. C., and Mehan, H. (1986). Sociocultural resources in instruction: A context-specific approach. In *Beyond language: Social and cultural factors in schooling language minority students*. Los Angeles: California State University, Evaluation, Dissemination and Assessment Center, 187–230.

Edelsky, C., Altwerger, B., & Flores, B. (1991). *Whole language: What's the difference?* Portsmouth, NH: Heinemann Educational Books.

Erickson, F., & Mohatt, G. (1982). Cultural organization of participation structures in two classrooms of Indian students. In G. Spindler (Ed.), *Doing the ethnography of schooling: Educational anthropology in action*. New York: Holt, Rinehart and Winston, 133–174.

Escamilla, K. (1993). Promoting biliteracy: Issues in promoting English literacy in students acquiring English. In J. V. Tinajero and A. F. Ada (Eds.), *The power of two languages: Literacy and biliteracy for Spanish-speaking students*. New York: MacMillan/McGraw-Hill, 220–233.

Faltis, C. J. (1983). Transfer of beginning reading skills from Spanish to English among Spanish-speaking children in second grade bilingual classrooms. Unpublished doctoral dissertation, Stanford University.

Flores, B. M. (1982). Language interference or influence: Toward a theory for Hispanic bilingualism. Unpublished doctoral dissertation, University of Arizona at Tucson.

Flores, B., Cousin, P. T., & Diaz, E. (1991). Critiquing and transforming the deficit myths about learning, language and culture. *Language Arts, 68* (5): 369–379.

Freire, P. (1985). *The politics of education: Culture, power and liberation*. South Hadley, MA: Bergin & Garvey.

Freire, P. (1987). Letter to North-American teachers. In I. Shor (Ed.), *Freire for the classroom*. Portsmouth, NJ: Boynton/Cook, 211–214.

Freire, P., & Macedo, D. (1987). *Literacy: Reading the word and the world*. South Hadley, MA: Bergin & Garvey.

Garcia, E. (1988). Effective schooling for Hispanics. *Urban Education Review, 67* (2): 462–473.

Garcia, E. (1991). Effective instruction for language minority students: The teacher. *Boston University Journal of Education, 173* (2): 130–141.

Gee, J. P. (1989). Literacy, discourse, and linguistics: Introduction. *Journal of Education, 171* (1): 5–17.

Giroux, H. (1985). Introduction. In P. Freire, *The politics of education: Culture, power and liberation*. South Hadley, MA.: Bergin & Garvey, xi–xxv.

Heath, S. B. (1983). *Ways with words*. New York: Cambridge University Press.

Hernandez, J. S. (1991). Assisted performance in reading comprehension strategies with non-English proficient students. *The Journal of Educational Issues of Language Minority Students, 8*, 91–112.

Jones, B. F., Palincsar, A. S., Ogle, D. S., & Carr, E. G. (1987). *Strategic teaching and learning: Cognitive instruction in the content areas*. Alexandria, VA: Association for Supervision and Curriculum Development in cooperation with the Central Regional Educational Laboratory.

Lareau, A. (1990). *Home advantage: Social class and parental intervention in elementary education*. New York: Falmer Press.

Lucas, T., Henze, R., & Donato, R. (1990). Promoting the success of Latino language-minority students: An exploratory study of six high schools. *Harvard Educational Review, 60* (3): 315–340.

McDermott, R. P. (1977). Social relations as contexts for learning in school. *Harvard Education Review, 47* (2): 198–213.

Macedo, D. (in press). Preface. In P. McLaren & C. Lankshear (Eds.), *Conscientization and resistance*. New York: Routledge, 1–8.

Mehan, H. (1992). Understanding inequality in schools: The contribution of interpretive studies. *Sociology of Education, 65* (1): 1–20.

Menchaca, M., & Valencia, R. (1990). Anglo-Saxon ideologies in the 1920s-1930s: Their impact on the segregation of Mexican students in California. *Anthropology and Education Quarterly, 21*, 222–245.

Moll, L. C. (1988). Some key issues in teaching Latino students. *Language Arts, 65* (5): 465–472.

Moran, C. (1993). Content area instruction for students acquiring English. In J. V. Tinajero & A. F. Ada (Eds.), *The power of two languages: Literacy and biliteracy for Spanish-speaking students*. New York: MacMillan/McGraw-Hill, 264–275.

O'Malley, J., & Chamot, A. U. (1990). *Learning strategies in second language acquisition*. New York: Cambridge University Press.

Palincsar, A. S., & Brown, A. L. (1984). Reciprocal teaching of comprehension fostering and comprehension-monitoring activities. *Cognition and Instruction, 1* (23): 117–175.

Pérez, B., & Torres-Guzmán, M. E. (1992). *Learning in two worlds: An integrated Spanish/English biliteracy approach*. New York: Longman.

Philips, S. U. (1972). Participant structures and communication competence: Warm Springs children in community and classroom. In C. B. Cazden, V. P. John, & D. Hymes (Eds.),.*Functions of language in the classroom*. New York: Teachers College, Columbia University, 370–394.

Reyes, M. (1987). Comprehension of content area passages: A study of Spanish/English readers in the third and fourth grade. In S. R. Goldman & H. T. Trueba (Eds.), *Becoming literate in English as a second language*. Norwood, NJ: Ablex, 107–126.

Spener, D. (1988). Transitional bilingual education and the socialization of immigrants. *Harvard Education Review, 58* (2): 133–153.

Sue, S., & Padilla, A. (1986). Ethnic minority issues in the U.S.: Challenges for the educational system. In *Beyond language: Social and cultural factors in schooling language minority students*. Los Angeles: California State University, Evaluation, Dissemination and Assessment Center, 35–72.

Tinajero, J. V., & Huerta-Macias, A. (1993). Enhancing the skills of emergent writers acquiring English. In J. V. Tinajero & A. F. Ada (Eds.), *The power of two languages: Literacy and biliteracy for Spanish-speaking students*. New York: MacMillan/McGraw-Hill, 254–263.

Trueba, H. T. (1989). Sociocultural integration of minorities and minority school achievement. In *Raising silent voices: Educating the linguistic minorities for the 21st century*. New York: Newbury House.

U.S. Commission on Civil Rights (1973). *Teachers and students: Report V: Mexican-American study: Differences in teacher interaction with Mexican-American and Anglo students*. Washington, DC: U.S. Government Printing Office.

U.S. Department of Education (1991). *The condition of bilingual education in the nation: A report to the congress and the president*. Washington, DC: U.S. Government Printing Office.

Valencia, R. (1986, November 25). *Minority academic underachievement: Conceptual and theoretical considerations for understanding the achievement problems of Chicano students*. Paper presented to the Chicano Faculty Seminar, Stanford University.

Valencia, R. (1991). *Chicano school failure and success: Research and policy agendas for the 1990s*. New York: Falmer Press.

Walker, C. L. (1987). Hispanic achievement: Old views and new perspectives. In H. T. Trueba (Ed.), *Success or failure: Learning and the language minority student*. New York: Newbury House, 15–32.

Zamel, V. (1982). Writing: The process of discovering meaning. *TESOL Quarterly, 16* (2): 195–209.

Zhang, X. (1990). *Language transfer in the writing of Spanish speaking ESL learners: Toward a new concept*. Paper presented at the Fall Conference of the Three Rivers Association of Teachers of English to Speakers of Other Languages (ERIC Document Reproduction Service No. ED 329 129).

Part IV

Math and Science

INTRODUCTION

Until recently, concern about the education of students from non-English language backgrounds has focused on their English language development. But, as discussed in the last section, there has been a shift toward a broader perspective that encompasses content areas other than English. Younger students, who may require the full six years of elementary school to acquire academic facility in English, may be shortchanged of instruction in other subjects if the school's primary goal is to teach them English. Students who enter American schools at an older age without sufficient English fluency may be deprived of instruction in content areas that are necessary for high school graduation and college admission.

This section is devoted to an examination of two subjects that have generated the most concern. Mary Brenner outlines approaches to mathematics instruction for students from non-English language backgrounds. Alejandro Gallard and Deborah Tippins address parallel issues in the teaching of science.

Chapter 7 described a sociological approach to understanding language learning and use, an approach that stresses the importance of the social context of teaching and learning. Both chapters in this section take a social constructivist perspective on learning, a view that emphasizes how the social context shapes thinking and knowledge. The sociological approach claims that the power relations among groups in society affect what happens in the classroom. The social constructionist position goes one step further, asserting that social environment determines the configuration of knowledge.

The conception of knowledge embodied in the social constructivist perspective is not a fixed body of information "out there" residing in books and the minds of experts. Knowledge is rather defined as making sense of information in one's own head. Becoming knowledgeable means understanding and constructing ideas rather than acquiring information. As the philosophy of the Cheche Konnen science program for Haitian students (referred to in Chapter 9) states, the focus is not on what the teacher knows, but on what the student thinks.

The chapters in this section espouse new goals and methods for mathematics and science education for all students, including those whose native language is other than English. The new goals are in line with what Murphy (1991) identifies as a key feature of the latest wave of education reform: teaching for understanding. Both chapters stress meaningfulness; they define knowledge as understanding rather than memorizing and applying, and they define learning as creating rather than acquiring knowledge.

The pedagogical implication of these new goals is that students should be *doing* mathematics or science instead of *studying about* these subjects. The authors advocate having students imitate the practice of professional mathematicians and scientists in the classroom, as they view mathematics and science primarily as cultural practices rather than bodies of knowledge.

Although they agree on goals and methods, the two chapters in this section focus on different aspects, a dichotomy that parallels the different—inside vs. outside—perspectives taken in Chapters 6 and 7. Brenner's chapter concentrates on what happens in the classroom; Gallard and Tippins highlight the attitude and experience teachers and students bring to the classroom. Brenner presents the new standards for mathematics instruction in a framework that emphasizes communication. She illustrates the importance of communication by describing programs that incorporate the native culture and home experience of children into mathematics instruction. Gallard and Tippins present a vision of learning science as a sense-making activity, but they also focus on the larger picture, emphasizing the importance of taking a critical stance toward science instruction. A critical stance, they say, will both illuminate the reasons that many students from non-English language backgrounds do not progress well in science, and point the way to transforming science education for these students.

The new vision of mathematics and science education described in the two chapters raises several questions:

- How much of the poor performance of students from non-English language backgrounds (and American students in general) is due to the traditional approach to education now being criticized, and how much is due to inadequate and poor quality instruction in mathematics and science? When American fifth graders spend only 3.4 hours per week studying mathematics, compared to 7.6 hours for Japanese and 11.4 hours for Chinese students (Stigler & Baranes, 1988–1989), how can we expect them to know as much? When mathematics and science instruction for poor and minority children is not as good as for middle class children, how can we expect them to perform equally? By changing the objectives and teaching methods for mathematics and science, we will never know how students from different groups would perform if they were all offered excellent instruction in the traditional manner.

- There are, however, persuasive arguments for revamping mathematics and science education to focus on understanding rather than mechanical application. Math teachers in Japan focus on a few problems in depth, spending considerable time discussing and explaining as they teach (Stigler & Baranes, 1988–1989). But the scale of transformation advocated in Chapters 8 and 9, and by education reformers in general, will require the "thought re-education" of parents, teachers, and students. Parents may be easily persuaded that mathematics and science should make sense and that students should be able to relate what they learn to real-life situations, but they may need more convincing that there are multiple paths to solving a problem, that approximation is sometimes preferable to exact calculation, and that finding the "correct" answer or memorizing multiplication tables is not important.

  Teachers are being asked to play an unaccustomed role, as managers of learning experiences rather than disseminators of knowledge. Most evocations of the new vision of mathematics and science education, including the chapters in this section, focus on how enriching the experience will be for students, but give insufficient attention to describing what the teacher is expected to do and how—or if—the teacher's knowledge of mathematics and science will be conveyed to the students. Is it more important for a teacher to be skillful at classroom arrangement, adept at communication, and politically aware of social inequity than knowledgeable about subject matter?

Students, also, will have to be re-socialized away from the old cultural practice of school mathematics. Stigler and Baranes (1988–1989, p. 288) note that "despite our best efforts, students still see school mathematics as a formal body of knowledge that has nothing to do with the solution of problems in the real world." They illustrate this tendency by citing a study in which three-fourths of the students gave a numerical answer to this question: "There are 26 sheep and 10 goats on a ship. How old is the captain?" Re-socializing students to focus on understanding and meaningfulness will be difficult in an institutional environment that gives conflicting messages. According to one estimate (Faltis, 1992), American students are subjected to more than 50 standardized tests by the time they complete fifth grade.

- While it is certainly true that people learn best when they can relate new information to what they already know, implicit in the new vision of mathematics and science education is the notion that humans *cannot* learn unless their instruction incorporates their own culture, language, and home life. This notion contradicts the experience of those who have mastered ancient Greek, nuclear physics, computer programming, or other areas of study that bear little resemblance to everyday life. Do we know enough about the efficacy of relating information to the students' background to make a blanket recommendation? Perhaps this pedagogical approach is more important at the early stages of learning, or for children, and less crucial at more advanced levels of instruction or for adults.

- It is a paradox of social constructivism that the construction of knowledge is viewed as a social process, but the resulting understanding is very individualistic, with no guarantee of shared meanings. How can this view be reconciled with a traditional conception of science and mathematics as the codification of collective wisdom rather than idiosyncratic experience? The validity ascribed to the individualistic understanding of physical phenomena by social constructivism would seem to encourage a view of the world that is parochial at best and pseudo-scientific at worst. Educators decry the scientific illiteracy of the American public, but the new vision of mathematics and science education seems to espouse the same kind of reliance on personal experience that tells us that the sun, and not the earth, revolves. Isn't the time-honored purpose of education to expand one's knowledge beyond one's own experience?

- The new vision of mathematics and science education stresses understanding, communication, meaningfulness, and cultural embeddedness. What does this imply for students who have succeeded under the traditional curriculum—how have they done it, and will they be disadvantaged when the goals and methods change? How are we to understand the success of some students from non-English language backgrounds in mathematics and science, or claims that such subjects are more universal and less culture bound than literature or social studies? Does teaching for understanding account for the success of Japanese students on standardized exams? If Japanese and other Asian immigrant students have been schooled in a system that emphasizes understanding, what accounts for their success in traditional American mathematics and science classes, where understanding has been downplayed? The model of teaching for understanding in Japan includes teacher-directed instruction of large classes, while the new American vision emphasizes the role of peer and small student groups and de-emphasizes the role of the teacher as expert. How are we to understand these differences? Are both models designed to accomplish the same goal?

- Finally, the new vision of mathematics and science education assumes that the best way to learn is by doing, by imitating the practice of professional mathematicians and scientists. This has a logical appeal, but is it really the best approach to educating future scientists or scientifically literate citizens? Do we have any empirical examples of people who were educated in this new fashion? One assumption is that traditional education stifles creativity and interest, and gives students an unrealistic view of science and mathematics. Yet, scientists and mathematicians were educated in the traditional mode and, judging by patents and Nobel Prizes, American scientists are creative by any measure, managing to overcome the alleged impediments of their education.

The chapters in this section describe a new vision of mathematics and science education that challenges beliefs that have long undergirded instruction in these subjects. Instead of viewing mathematics and science as a hierarchy of formal and abstract skills to be transmitted from teacher to student, the new thinking is that basic skills are learned best when practiced through collaborative inquiry and argument. This model conceives of mathematics and science, like other domains of knowledge, as social and cultural constructions, a view that makes acceptable, and encourages, the inclusion of children's intuitive strategies for computing and solving numerical problems. It also legitimizes using children's cultural and linguistic backgrounds as a vehicle for learning.

Neither chapter delves too deeply into the complexities of the new vision. Several of the examples in Chapter 8 indicate that the emphasis on communication in the new standards for mathematics instruction may be more challenging to students from cultural backgrounds that do not encourage children to speak up or express their viewpoint in front of others. Neither chapter focuses on issues of the language of instruction in science and mathematics for students from non-English language backgrounds. And neither chapter details the steps needed to transform the educational system and the minds of educators to implement the new vision of mathematics and science education.

REFERENCES

Faltis, C. (1992). Talk given at conference "Educating Students from Immigrant Families: Meeting the Challenge in Secondary Schools," University of California, Santa Cruz, October 23–25.

Murphy, J. (1991). *Restructuring schools: Capturing and assessing the phenomena*. New York: Teachers College Press.

Stigler, J. W., & Baranes, R. (1988–1989). Culture and mathematics learning. *Review of Research in Education, 15*, 253–306.

✧ Chapter 8

A Communication Framework for Mathematics: Exemplary Instruction for Culturally and Linguistically Diverse Students

Mary E. Brenner

The sad truth is that in American schools there is little communication taking place in mathematics classrooms. Stodolsky's (1988) study of fifth grade classrooms found that students worked by themselves more often than they engaged in any other activity. Individual seatwork comprised 40 percent of students' class time. About 30 percent of the time students and teachers participated in recitations in which teachers posed close ended questions and students gave brief responses. Open ended discussion took up less than 1 percent of class time. The picture may be even bleaker for children who are culturally and linguistically different. The Study of Academic Instruction for Disadvantaged Students (Knapp et al., 1991) observed that fully half of each class period was spent on

233

individual work. Teacher lectures occurred in slightly more than half of the class days. Teacher-student discussions took place in only about one out of three class sessions, and these were mostly recitations of the sort described by Stodolsky.

Within the context of such classrooms, the available opportunities for communication are fewer for many students. Students with limited command of English may be less able to learn from formal teacher lectures and recitations than other students (Cummins, 1981) because they have not yet mastered formal discourse styles. Students from some cultures, particularly Native American students and African American students, find the stilted discussion style typical of mathematics recitations particularly shaming or meaningless (Heath, 1983; Philips, 1972). Other students believe their peers are more effective role models for mathematics than the teacher but they have little opportunity to interact with other students (Kagan, 1986; Lave, 1990).

It is particularly important to examine the forms of communication in mathematics for the language minority child in late elementary and junior high school. In addition to coping with cultural differences in communication style, children of this age are typically making the transition from dominant language instruction to English dominant classrooms. In both early and late bilingual transition programs the child begins to receive some instruction in English between grades 4 and 8. In a number of schools this transition occurs first in mathematics in the mistaken belief that mathematics is a universal language or entails minimal language use. As Cummins (1981) points out, the criteria for this transition typically rest upon a child's conversational skills in English. But academic discourse skills take years longer to develop, and mathematics instruction has its own particular forms of discourse that are now being systematically described (Durkin and Shire, 1991; Pimm, 1987). The difficulty of the transition to mathematics instruction in English may be the cause of the higher levels of test anxiety in mathematics that have been found for bilingual Latino children when compared to their peers who are still Spanish dominant or come from English speaking homes (Willig, Harnisch, Hill, & Maehr, 1983).

The late elementary and middle school years are critical to later mathematical achievement for all children because attitudes towards mathematics form in this age range and de facto tracking becomes a reality in many junior high schools. By fifth grade children have formed realistic self-concepts of mathematics ability that endure into high school (Newman, 1984). Generally positive attitudes towards mathematics by both females and minority students in the early elementary years decline significantly during the later elementary and junior high years (Anderson, Thorpe, & Clewell, 1989). In turn these negative attitudes lead to lower achievement for female students and a reduced likelihood of taking college preparatory mathematics for both females and minority students. Junior high also marks the turning point in the availability of mathematics classes and the tracking of students into different kinds of mathematics courses. While elementary schools have relatively equal amounts of time devoted to mathematics regardless of the composition of the student body, junior high schools serving predominantly minority students have fewer course offerings in mathematics (Oakes, 1990). Even within the same school, minority students tend to be tracked into lower level classes (Moses, Kamii, Swap, & Howard, 1989; MacCorquodale, 1988) as do female students. The effect is compounded for at least some groups of minority females such as Mexican American women who are the least likely group of all to take pre-algebra in junior high (MacCorquodale, 1988) when compared to Anglo males and females and Mexican American males in the same schools. Although the situation has been less systematically assessed for students with limited proficiency in English, it appears that mathematics instruction is also more limited for this group. In the elementary years this is often due to increased time spent on language instruction while at higher levels there are limitations in the number of bilingual mathematics teachers and materials in languages other than English.

The model of exemplary mathematics instruction proposed in this paper emphasizes effective communication as the intersection between the kinds of mathematics that we want students to learn and the ways in which we can reach culturally and linguistically diverse student populations. The paper begins with a brief overview of the mathematics reform movement and the role of communication within it. The rationale for emphasizing communication as a mathematical goal is further elaborated by drawing upon social constructivist theories of learning and anthropological studies of classrooms. An overview is then given of the Communication Framework for Mathematics. The details of the Framework are presented with examples of specific educational practices that have been used with diverse student populations in grades 4 to 8. The paper concludes with a consideration of how other aspects of the school context, including curriculum, instruction and institutional support, can enhance effective mathematics communication.

Background

The kind of instruction described by Stodolsky (1988) and Knapp et al. (1991) is based on transmissionist models of how students learn. In this model the teacher has mathematical knowledge which she dispenses to the students through lectures and modeling of mathematical procedures. The student's role is to then individually practice mathematical skills during seatwork and homework assignments. By the early 1980s many mathematics educators were convinced that traditional mathematics instruction was failing both the majority of students and the nation (National Council of Teachers of Mathematics, 1980; National Research Council, 1989). Although some students flourish under traditional instructional methods, most students do not. A report by the National Research Council states "Mathematics is the worst curricular villain in driving students to failure in school. When mathematics acts as a filter, it not only filters students out of careers, but frequently out of school itself" (1989, p. 7).

A number of problems follow from the low level of student achievement in mathematics (National Council of Teachers of Mathematics, 1989). Most students take only one year of high school mathematics. Consequently, not enough students are adequately prepared in mathematics to pursue technical professions, and women and minority students are particularly underrepresented in technical areas. Even jobs which do not traditionally require much skill in mathematics are becoming transformed as the United States moves from being an industrial society to an information society. Correspondingly, the American people need a higher level of mathematical literacy to deal with the new society and increasingly complex social problems. The mathematics reform movement arose in response to these problems and has advocated a complete rethinking of mathematics education as documented at both the national (National Council of Teachers of Mathematics 1980, 1989, 1991) and state level (e.g. California Department of Education, 1992).

In addition to prescribing more mathematics instruction and a revised set of mathematical topics at all levels of elementary and secondary school, the mathematics reform movement advocates a different vision of the mathematics learner. "Rather than being passive absorbers of knowledge, children actively create their own understanding of the world. In fact, by the time they come to school, they have already developed a rich body of knowledge about the world around them, including well-developed, informal systems of mathematics." (California Department of Education, 1992, pp. 32–33). The constructivist learner is explicitly believed to need active communication activities as part of the learning process. "Communication plays an important role in helping children construct links between their informal, intuitive notions and the abstract language and symbolism of mathematics" (National Council of Teachers of Mathematics, 1989, p. 26). In addition to helping children connect their old and new knowledge, the communication process enhances independent mathematical reasoning: "Emphasizing communication in a mathematics classroom helps shift the classroom from an environment in which students are totally dependent on the teacher to one in which students assume more responsibility for validating their own thinking" (National Council of Teachers of Mathematics, 1989, p. 79).

The emphasis upon communication derives from the recognition that learning proceeds most effectively within a social context. The social constructivist perspective has influenced current conceptualizations of mathematics learning through three distinct traditions. Vygotsky (1978) posited that learning takes place when the learner first collaborates with an adult or more competent peer to accomplish a task just beyond the learner's level of independent functioning, within the "zone of proximal development." What is accomplished in a social context is then internalized for individual mastery. Effective adult guidance of learning has been described as scaffolding or proleptic teaching in which the teacher is sensitive to the learner's current level of functioning and structures learning to take place within the zone of proximal development. Peer collaboration also can be effective in this perspective if there are joint goals and active dialogue about reasoning processes (Tudge, 1990).

Neo-Piagetian research provides a different perspective on the role of peers in the learning process. Rather than stressing the relative competencies of the peers, this line of research emphasizes that peers bring different pieces to the learning situation, some of which are complementary, some of which are conflicting. Sociocognitive conflict between peers of different levels of functioning can stimulate cognitive growth without the active peer tutoring implied in the Vygotskian model (Doise and Mugny, 1984). Growth can also occur when learners with different perspectives but equal competency "help each other incorporate new problem-attack and reasoning strategies into their repertoire" (Forman, 1989, p. 67). Cooperative collaboration of this sort enables students to accomplish tasks that may be beyond the competency of any individual participant.

The final socially based perspective views optimal mathematics learning as a process of enculturation (Bishop, 1991; Lampert, 1990; Schoenfeld, 1992). From this point of view, the learner enters into a community of practice with the ultimate goal of learning to think and act like a member of that community. Lampert (1990) compares school practices to descriptions of mathematical practice. School practices typically consist of learning a set of rules and skills and then applying them to various problems assigned by the teacher. In contrast, mathematical practice entails making conjectures and then devising mathematical arguments to support them. Developing mathematical practice in the classroom requires that different kinds of discourse occur, particularly an expansion in the student role during classroom discussions. The teacher's role changes as well to encompass doing mathematical discourse with students as well as acting as a guide to mathematical conventions and presenting a model of how to do mathematics.

While social constructivist theories of learning demonstrate the social interactional basis of learning, anthropological studies of schooling strongly suggest that forms of communication in classrooms need to be changed to enable all children to effectively participate. Work by Heath (1983), Jordan (1985), Au and Mason (1981) and Philips (1972) demonstrates the ways in which current styles of classroom organization have systematically blocked children from some cultural backgrounds from participating in classroom interactions. Philips (1972) introduced the idea of a participant structure, which she defined as the way in which interactions are organized. Participant structures vary along dimensions of how many students participate, who has the right to set the topic, who has the right to determine the speaker, who the audience is and so on. When the participant structures from home and from school differ substantially, students become reluctant to participate. In Philips' study, Native American students were uncomfortable in situations in which they had to speak alone in front of their peers and when the teacher designated whose turn it was to speak. Native Hawaiian children are also reluctant to participate in large group lessons. They are more apt to participate when the teacher shares control of small group discussion (Au and Mason, 1981) or when they are allowed to work with peers (Jordan, 1985). The educational changes inspired from this work have changed classroom participant structures to be more congruent with home participant structures, although they are not necessarily identical.

Heath's (1983) work with African American and working-class White students has shown how other incongruencies between home and school communication contribute to classroom problems. Teachers often use forms of questions which are totally alien or unanswerable to children of other cultural traditions. At home children learn to respond to certain kinds of questions, are systematically taught to ignore other kinds of questions and are simply not exposed to other types. Heath worked with teachers to help them to become aware of such communication differences and to build from the strengths children brought with them to school. At the same time materials were developed to explicitly teach children the differences between their natal forms of communication and school communication with a goal of gaining mastery over school forms of discourse.

Although most of the work on developing culturally compatible forms of communication in classrooms has focused on literacy training, many of these same instructional insights can be applied in mathematics classes. For instance, the work with Native Hawaiian children in the Kamehameha Early Education Program described above (Au and Mason, 1981; Jordan, 1985) has been applied by teachers in their mathematics instruction, resulting in clear improvement in mathematics achievement (Brenner, 1984, 1985). However, many teachers who readily change their language arts instruction are less likely to do so in mathematics until they change their beliefs about the nature of mathematical knowledge and what students should be doing in mathematics classrooms (e.g. Lampert, 1990; Wood, Cobb, & Yackel, 1991).

As outlined above, the emphasis upon communication in mathematics classrooms has support from current theories of learning and anthropological studies of classrooms. The nature of mathematical communication needs to be further elaborated in order to enable educators to implement pedagogies which support both mathematical learning and effective participation of students from diverse linguistic and cultural backgrounds. The next section of this paper describes the Communication Framework for Mathematics. The Framework provides a structure to examine the ways that classrooms should and can function effectively for diverse student populations.

Communication Framework: Overview

The Communication Framework for Mathematics attempts to systematically describe in detail the kinds of communication which are advocated in more general terms by the mathematics reform movement. Three of the six standards for instruction set by the National Council for Teachers of Mathematics (NCTM) (1991) directly deal with classroom discourse and the other three do so indirectly as shown in Figure 8.1.

Figure 8.1　NCTM Standards for Teaching Mathematics

Tasks
1. Worthwhile mathematical tasks

Discourse
2. Teacher orchestrates discourse
3. Active student participation
4. Multiple forms of discourse

Learning Environment
5. Teacher creates rich and challenging learning environment

Analysis of Teaching and Learning
6. Teacher monitors students' learning as basis of planning

Source: National Council of Teachers of Mathematics (1991). Paraphrased from pages 19–67.

Standard 2 emphasizes the teacher's role as orchestrator of diverse forms of discourse in the classroom. Particular emphasis is given to ways in which the teacher can enhance students' expression of their ideas orally, in writing and in the course of peer discussion. According to the Standards much of the teacher's discourse should focus on pursuing ideas raised by students and expanding upon them in formal mathematical terms. Standard 3 expands upon the ways in which students can more actively participate in classroom discourse. Students are expected to initiate problems and questions, to raise conjectures, to offer both examples and counterexamples, to convince themselves and others of the validity of their viewpoints and to use mathematical forms of argumentation. Standard 4 states that the discourse forms specified in the preceding standards can be realized in a variety of instructional formats and through various media including computers, stories, concrete models, writing and oral dramatizations. Students should be offered choices in addition to teacher-directed formats.

Although the other standards deal less directly with communication, effective discourse provides the environment in which these standards can be accomplished. Children are likely to find tasks more worth doing (Standard 1) when they are allowed to communicate their own approach to the tasks and when mathematics enhances their capacity to communicate about topics that interest them. Standard 6, which deals with assessing student progress, also depends upon effective communication. This standard specifies that the teacher should monitor ongoing student learning as the basis for planning. "Observing and listening to students during class can help teachers, on the spot, tailor their questions or tasks to provoke and extend students' thinking and understanding" (National Council of Teachers of Mathematics, 1991, p. 63). The standards also specify that assessment should go beyond paper and pencil methods to include monitoring student discussions, journal writing, and individual interviews. Standard 5 specifies parameters of the classroom environment which facilitate the various forms of communication outlined in the other standards.

Although the NCTM standards provide examples of classroom scenarios to demonstrate how the standards might look in practice, the Communication Framework proposed in this paper provides a systematic way of examining the communication skills required for different aspects of mathematical thinking and learning with reference to instructional techniques that have been used with linguistically and culturally different students. Thus, the more general communication goals can be linked to specific instructional arrangements which suit students with varying needs. Figure 8.2 shows the three major forms of mathematical communication.

Communication About Mathematics entails the need for individuals to describe problem solving processes and their own thoughts about these processes. Since the standards now indicate that much of the work which has been done in traditional classrooms as individual seatwork should now be accomplished through social interactions, students need to externalize processes that may not have even been consciously considered when working alone. This process of externalization may in itself contribute to high order reasoning as well as facilitating classroom communication. Communication In Mathematics means using the language and symbols of mathematical conventions. This is what traditionally has been seen as the real content of mathematics instruction. However, placing this kind of knowledge within a communication framework stresses the interconnectedness of mathematical concepts, in contrast to skills based approaches which see learning as mastery of discrete pieces. Communication With Mathematics refers to the uses of mathematics which empower students by enabling them to deal with meaningful problems. Mathematics can be used both as

Figure 8.2   Communication Framework for Mathematics

A. Communicate About Mathematics

    1. Reflection on cognitive processes
        Descriptive
        Metacognitive

    2. Communicate with others about cognition
        Give point of view
        Reconcile with others' views

B. Communicate In Mathematics

    1. Mathematical Register
        Special Vocabulary
        Particular Definitions of Everyday Vocabulary
        Modified Uses of Everyday Vocabulary
        Syntax, Phrasing
        Discourse

    2. Representations
        Physical Manipulatives
        Symbolic
        Verbal
        Diagrams, Graphs
        Geometric

C. Communicate With Mathematics

    1. Problem-Solving Tool
        Investigations
        Basis for meaningful action

    2. Alternative solutions
        Interpret arguments using mathematics
        Utilize mathematical problem solving in conjunction with
            other forms of analysis

an esoteric way of communicating intended to mystify and as an analytic tool for clarifying complex situations. All three kinds of mathematical communication are needed for developing useful mathematical understanding.

As will be shown, no single instructional arrangement can facilitate all forms of mathematical communication. Large group lessons allow the teacher to convey the information necessary for Communicating In Mathematics but children will have limited opportunity to develop their own skills at communicating their reasoning in this context. Likewise, peer based instruction or cooperative learning are not panaceas for the educational problems besetting many children in mathematics. When the actual content and structure of small group interactions are studied, it is found that a minor part of the student communication is about the content of mathematics or entails mathematical discourse (Wilkinson, Lindow and Chiang, 1985). Just as classroom recitations tend to emphasize drill and practice (Knapp et al., 1991), students replicate this within their small groups in certain forms of cooperative learning. In addition, small group participants are not given equal opportunities to participate, with gender and ethnicity being key dimensions along which participation varies (Cohen, 1984).

The Framework and Instructional Applications

Each of the three major categories of mathematical communication will be examined in detail with examples of instructional programs that have incorporated new forms of communication for language minority or culturally different students. As others have noted (Knapp et al., 1991; McKnight, 1991; Secada, 1991; Zucker, 1991) most research on educational innovation in mathematics has been done with relatively advantaged groups of students while classroom practice and research with less advantaged groups continues to stress mastery of basic skills. However, there are examples of exemplary practice and very recent research studies which show the feasibility of this emphasis upon communication skills and higher order mathematical thinking for students of all cultural, socioeconomic and linguistic backgrounds.

Communicating About Mathematics

Both teachers and students need to learn to talk about mathematics from their own point of view. This entails being able to reflect about one's own cognitive processes, both the steps one takes to solve a problem and the metacognitive considerations which guide the problem solving process. Although arithmetic has traditionally been viewed as the application of standard algorithms to computation, children spontaneously use a variety of strategies for even the simplest addition problems (Siegler, 1987). Even professional mathematicians (or particularly mathematicians!) do not always follow standard algorithms when solving problems, especially unfamiliar problems (Schoenfeld, 1985). Social constructivist theories of learning posit that mathematical knowledge and understanding develop through comparison of varying problem solving methods.

A necessary but even more difficult adjunct of describing one's problem solving processes is recognizing the metacognitive components. Effective problem solving includes setting goals, judging when those goals have been achieved, checking results and incorporating the general self-regulatory skills which enable one to do these things. Since learning when to use a certain procedure is probably more difficult than learning the procedure itself, recognition of metacognitive skills will enhance effective problem solving.

Equally important as recognizing one's own problem solving process is being able to communicate the process to others. In order to do this the learner must take a point of view thereby justifying and explaining what has been done and why. In addition, group work depends upon comparing this to what others have done and acknowledging differences. Within the new vision of mathematics learning presented by the NCTM standards, multiple solution routes are valued and students should be encouraged to present alternatives to the class. Mistakes also have a valued position within the Communication Framework. Certain apparent misconceptions may actually be what Moschkovich (1992) has labeled transitional conceptions, necessary and useful ideas that aid in the construction of the more standard ideas used within mathematics. Mistakes are also an opportunity for developing forms of mathematical argumentation. For this reason class discussion should focus on why ideas are correct, not whether they are correct or incorrect (Lampert, 1990).

For children from certain cultures or other educational traditions this process of externalizing cognitive processes may be more difficult or alien. Michaels and O'Connor (1990) present an example of a Haitian girl who seems unable to explain her reasoning about a balance scale task in the context of a classroom discussion when other children are doing so. The teacher thinks it might be a language problem because the girl's first language is Haitian Creole. However, an individual interview after the class revealed that the girl was perfectly capable of explaining her reasoning in English or Creole. She did not understand that the teacher's question required her to show this reasoning as part of the expected classroom discourse. A similar effect was found during a performance assessment study with Anglo and Latino students (Baxter, Shavelson, Herman, & Brown, in press). Even when matched for achievement test scores and classroom experience, the Latino children whose

home language was Spanish were less likely to explain their problem solving processes than Anglo children or Latino children whose
home language was English. Despite some training, the Latino students either did not understand what was expected or were less
willing to do it for their adult Anglo interviewers. These examples
demonstrate that as the content of classroom discourse changes,
some students will need the support of changed participant structures to develop the new communicative competence.

A recent classroom based experiment provides more information on what student discourse about cognitive processes looks like
when the class norms of communication change with support from
changed participant structures (Thornburg and Karp, 1992). This
experiment was based on the ideas of cognitive apprenticeship
(Collins, Brown, & Newman, 1989) and involved fourteen classrooms, five at the middle school grade levels. Seventy percent of the
children in these classrooms were language minority children, predominantly Spanish speaking. The teachers were taught to use a
variety of modeling and scaffolding strategies for teaching mathematical word problems with an emphasis upon verbalizing strategies for solving problems in the course of doing them. When the
teachers were bilingual, this was done first in the children's first
language and second language practice was phased in. The students practiced these skills in peer collaborative groups by taking
turns acting as the expert and novice with the expert using some of
the same strategies as the teacher. In addition to significantly
improving their achievement test scores after one year, the students changed the style of discourse they used. Classroom observations revealed that they gave more elaborate answers and used
more mathematical language during discussions with their peers,
particularly when teachers had modeled exploratory language use
in their own lessons. Two things are particularly notable about
these results. The first is that, apparently, regardless of the language of instruction, students first changed the way they talked
about mathematics in their first language and eventually over the
course of the year used more English although some kinds of talk
never shifted to English. The second is that students did not change
the way they responded to teacher questions, continuing to answer
briefly and unelaboratedly without demonstrating many of the
skills they utilized in peer discussions. This may be a result of the
instructional arrangement in which the students practiced the new
forms of discourse primarily with peers. In this study the children
clearly demonstrated new competency as evidenced in peer discussions and tests results, but these competencies need time and sup-

port to generalize to a second language or different participant structure.

A different variant on peer based learning has been incorporated by Project SOAR, a summer program for African American junior and senior high school students who are interested in attending Xavier University (Clewell, 1987). Part of this program is based on the pair problem solving methods of Whimbey and Lochhead (1982). One person of each pair acts as the problem solver and thinks aloud while working through a problem. The listener monitors the problem solver to make sure that each step of the process is vocalized and that taught problem solving procedures are followed. This approach to peer problem solving highlights the metacognitive component of problem solving by giving it an explicit role in peer communication. Project SOAR has had notable success with its participants including increased test scores showing improved analytical thinking skills as well as improved college completion rates in the sciences when compared to non-participants.

Teachers probably need to use a variety of strategies to enable children to build their communication skills about cognitive problem solving. Pairing children with the same first language may be preferable at the beginning as shown in the Thornburg and Karp study (1992). Richards (1991) has suggested the use of the Itakura method (Inagaki, 1981) which facilitates this process in large group discussion. Children are given several different positions on an issue and need to defend their adherence to one position over another. While all children need to choose a position, not all children need to publicly defend it. This way children with less assurance can participate without being put on the spot.

Since many programs emphasize communication among peers in discussions about problem solving, teachers may want to devise strategies for increasing teacher-student communication. Peyton (1990) has suggested methods of enabling language minority students to write dialogue journals to their teachers about school. This practice can be extended to mathematics as reported by Clarke, Stephens and Waywood (in press) for two different projects. In Project Impact students wrote to their mathematics teachers every two weeks to answer questions such as "what was the best thing to happen in math?" The project began with seventh grade students and has been extended down to fourth grade students. A number of instructional changes occurred as teachers learned about the student perceptions of their lessons. In the Vaucluse College Study, Clarke, Stephens, and Waywood (in press), observed female students at a private secondary school which served several distinct ethnic groups. These students wrote in a journal after every math class. Over time the students' views of math began to change from a very descriptive form to a more analytical look at mathematical meaning.

Communicating In Mathematics

There are characteristic words, grammatical structures and ways of talking within the mathematics community which constitute what Halliday (1978) called the mathematical register. Some of the vocabulary is unique to mathematics and clearly recognizable as such, words like coefficient, polynomial and hypotenuse. As shown in Figure 8.2, this constitutes the Special Vocabulary of mathematics. Words, such as square, power and set, which sound very much like everyday English but have a specifically defined meaning in mathematics (Spanos and Crandall, 1990) are referred to as Particular Definitions of Everyday Vocabulary. For the second language user these words may be particularly difficult because the differences between everyday usage and mathematical usage are not always apparent (Cuevas, Mann, & McClung, 1986). Everyday words are also used in mathematics with meanings akin to everyday usage but with more precise or restricted meanings, and are referred to as Modified Uses of Everyday Vocabulary in the Framework. These words also present difficulties because it is not easy to provide precise definitions, and their usage seems to be more consensual than many other words. Moschkovich (1992) gives the example of students attempting to use the word steeper in the context of describing lines on a graph. Although the students had been provided with a working definition of the word steeper at the beginning of a problem solving session, each pair of students had to negotiate its actual usage before being able to use it productively in further conversation.

Mathematics also has some syntactic structures which map important conceptual domains. For instance, Hargis and Knight (1977) note that mathematics has many comparative structures such as "more than/less than" and "as much as" because mathematics is the study of relationships. Word problems present difficulty to all students as well as language minority students because they have unique underlying schema that require mathematical skills beyond the computation involved and reading skills distinct from reading in other areas (De Corte and Verschaffel, 1985; Mayer, 1985).

All of the attributes of mathematical register mentioned above are embedded within the larger context of mathematical Discourse. While mathematical discourse is less clearly defined than other aspects of the mathematical register, Schoenfeld likens it to "sense-making through the dialectic of conjecture and argumentation" (1992, p. 363). Mathematical discourse is distinguished from regular discussions (Pimm, 1987) and from "school mathematics" (Thompson, 1985) as typically found in classrooms. While traditional school mathematics emphasizes correct answers and appeal to authority (e.g. textbook, teacher) for judging correctness, mathematical discourse focuses on the ways in which solutions are reached.

Helping children to deal with the mathematical register entails a number of instructional strategies. More care can be paid to specifying the mathematical meaning of terms as they appear in lessons, particularly those words which have multiple meanings. For the language minority child or child who speaks a nonstandard form of English, this at times may simply consist of translating specific terms from the home language into mathematical terms in standard English (Brenner, 1991; Cuevas, 1983). However, an emphasis on the semantic aspects of the mathematical register in the context of word problems may not be enough to help children gain competency in the mathematics register (Cuevas, Mann, & McClung, 1986) since issues of syntax and discourse are not addressed with this approach.

Word problems are expected to have a smaller part in the mathematics curriculum of the future (National Council of Teachers of Mathematics, 1989) because emphasis will be placed upon more complex problem solving. But word problems can be used to develop skills in the mathematical register through providing children with a starting point for discussing situations in which mathematics can be used. Lo, Wheatley, and Smith (1991) give some interesting examples of how a simple word problem about selling a plant evolved into a discussion of the possible different meanings of the problem depending upon the larger situation it was meant to represent. Cohen and Stover (1981) have shown that children can rewrite word problems to make them easier to solve through strategies such as simplifying the wording and adding diagrams. This procedure could be extended to have language minority and first language children work together to rewrite problems, thereby enhancing skills in the mathematical register. Children can also learn to write word problems or to write stories in which mathematics can be applied. My own experience doing this with Native Hawaiian children resulted in word problems which were more complex than any they would have encountered in their textbooks.

Richards (1991) reports that language minority children with a similar experience in writing problems but with no textbook experience at all scored at a mastery level on the section of a standardized test covering word problems. In contrast, none of their peers in a control class scored at this level.

Although the research literature does not at present offer any examples of mathematics classes for culturally different or language minority children which are taught exclusively as communities of practice with extensive mathematical discourse, Lampert's (1990) description of her own teaching practices and other examples listed in Schoenfeld (1992) provide examples of what this might look like.

The second major area of Communication In Mathematics is that of Representation, the various ways in which problems and solutions can be expressed in what would be considered mathematical form. Although school mathematics often treats the components of mathematics as discrete pieces and has reified this by separately teaching arithmetic, geometry, and algebra, mathematical knowledge in fact is a larger system of knowledge with multiple connections among the components. The various representation forms listed in Figure 8.2 are interconnected, and conceptual understanding in mathematics entails comprehension of the structures that tie together the different representations. Effective communication in mathematics thus depends upon effective translation between these various 'dialects' of mathematical language. Some of the most common forms of mathematical representation are physical manipulatives, symbolic representations, verbal statements, diagrams, graphs and geometric representations. Manipulatives may not seem like a dialect of mathematics but in fact some of the most common materials such as Diene's blocks and attribute blocks were designed to represent the structure of mathematics which underlies elementary arithmetic (Resnick & Ford, 1981).

Even as the use of a broader range of representations becomes accepted as good educational practice for promoting conceptual development in mathematics, the evidence mounts that students have difficulty in seeing the connections between the representations used. The use of base ten blocks to represent place value (Resnick & Omanson, 1986) and pattern blocks to represent fractions (Davis & Maher, 1990) do not necessarily improve computation or even connect to algorithms in many elementary students' minds. At the secondary level students who have successfully completed algebra courses may still fail to see the connections between the components of a linear equation and the graph which conveys the same information (Moschkovich, 1992; Schoenfeld, Smith &

Arcavi, in press). At times this problem may be exacerbated by classrooms that function along social constructivist lines with much peer discussion. As student-constructed procedures become more validated, it can be hard to insert the conventions of mathematics into the learning process. Resnick, Bill, Lesgold and Leer (1991) suggest one way of linking students' informal representations to formal ones. After small group discussions, the groups report back to the class at large. The teacher records the informal and sometimes idiosyncratic results in formal notation. As a result the formal notation becomes the lingua franca of the class as a whole.

The Algebra Project developed by Moses (Moses et al., 1989) has a standard topic development sequence which links both the mathematical register and various representations that might be utilized by students. This sequence was developed to help students, particularly minority students, make the transition from arithmetic to algebra with the goal of entering college preparatory mathematics at the beginning of high school. The sequence begins with physical events which embody a mathematical idea, for instance using the subway lines to represent number lines. After riding the subway, students then make a pictorial or other representation of this experience. The next step is to describe the mathematical concept in Intuitive Language, i.e., the student's own words. The students then learn to translate these to Regimented English which seems to correspond to the mathematical register. The final step is learning the symbolic representation. The program is now in use with students between sixth and eighth grades and has succeeded in placing many students into more advanced high school classes.

Communicating With Mathematics

While most students seem to acknowledge the importance of mathematics for understanding the world and for many kinds of jobs (National Center for Education Statistics, 1991), this does not necessarily mean that students find their classroom experiences in mathematics meaningful (Mitchell, 1992). A belief in the utility of mathematics is related to higher test achievement and many students claim that they are taking mathematics because it is preparation for attaining future goals such as attending college (Schoenfeld, 1989). But this future oriented view of the utility of mathematics may not be enough to sustain many students through years of a relatively difficult subject. The achievement of all students may be enhanced through more meaningful mathematical experiences beginning in the elementary school years. The final section of the Communication Framework looks at ways that students of the middle school years can communicate about aspects of their immediate world using mathematics.

A number of mathematics programs have incorporated exercises in which students have some opportunities to use mathematics as a tool. A typical example would be to have a classroom lesson which combines measurement and statistics by having students measure the height of each student in the class and then find out the mean, mode and median of the measurements. Similar classroom activities with a higher communication component enable students to investigate a topic of intrinsic interest using mathematics as the tool. In these investigations, the goal is to learn about some phenomenon rather than to practice arithmetic skills. Although Heath's (1983) work focused primarily on literacy, some of her examples show how children can do investigations of their communities which reveal differences between school and community usage of mathematics. One consumer mathematics class examined monetary transactions in a local store and then used these as the basis for writing word problems. The class extended their project to look at miscommunications during financial transactions and kept track of these through journals. Heath claims that such investigations enable children to make sense of the differences between their home and school lives and also familiarize the teachers with the community of the students.

The Finding Out/Descubrimiento integrated science and mathematics program for children in grades 2–5 is based on the principle that children of any cultural group are naturally interested in understanding the physical world (DeAvila, Duncan, & Navarette, 1987). Learning is enhanced when school provides children with the skills that enable them to explore and understand the world because they gain a sense of mastery over their environment. This program is designed for children with different levels of language and literacy skills as well as science and mathematics background. The hands-on activities provide several instances of each scientific and mathematical concept so students have multiple exposure to them and an opportunity to keep developing the depth of their understanding. Materials are in both Spanish and English and the tasks have pictograph directions as well. The students receive training in social skills to facilitate the cooperative group work required on each activity. Children who participate in the program acquire enhanced language and problem solving skills as well as improved achievement test scores.

While the examples given above enable students to use mathematics to learn more about the world, Mellin-Olsen (1987) argues that for mathematics to be meaningful to young people who are currently disenfranchised by the school system, it must become the basis for action in the world. He gives examples of how activities that young people do in the world such as sewing symmetrical patterns or constructing club houses can become part of the classroom lesson. Mathematics can also be used to address conditions of life outside of school such as the wage structure of local employers or potentially dangerous traffic patterns around the school. The analysis of everyday situations then becomes the data supporting a report to the city council asking for more traffic lights or the basis of a request for more youth services at local clubs. Mellin-Olsen stresses how the end product of the mathematical activities should be more than a poster or report that stays within the classroom.

The examples given above about the utility of mathematics for communication about the world need to be supplemented with a perspective which makes people discriminating users and consumers of mathematics. Koblitz (1984) and Schoenfeld (1991) give multiple examples of ways in which mathematics has been used to make a point through mystification or misdirection. Poor use of statistics, misleading graphs, and multiple equations which have no mathematical validity are all too common in both the popular and academic media. The analysis of such examples from the daily newspaper can supplement other kinds of classroom activities and provide the basis for very directed classroom discussions. The students can learn to use valid mathematical analysis to interpret the arguments put forward by others through critiquing and re-analyzing faulty arguments.

Equally important for student empowerment is recognition that a mathematical analysis alone does not always provide the best solution to a problem. For instance it is possible to do a mathematical analysis of how many items people should be allowed to buy in the express line at the supermarket. This would entail quantifying the relevant variables and then gathering data on how long it takes the cashier to ring up different numbers of items, whether the total number of items should fit in one bag and how long it takes people to pay for the items. However, the real utility of the express line might be to give people the impression that they are preceded by people with only a few items and this sense of 'few' depends upon local definitions of relative quantity. There are also cultural constraints about which problems are best addressed mathematically. Many Native American children are familiar with traditional games of chance (Cheek, 1984) and these games provide a good context for analyzing concepts of probability. For children in communities with certain religious traditions, games of chance are considered gambling and are not a good context for analyzing probability.

One very recent mathematics curriculum explicitly incorporates other forms of reasoning into student problem solving activities. The Mathematics of the Environment curriculum (Mitchell, Baab, Campbell-LaVoie, & Prion, 1992) asks students to find solutions to environmental problems of specific nations using real data about human population, food and energy. Students are taught to use logic chains to identify problems and evaluate potential solutions to those problems. Within this context there are clearly multiple possible solutions to a problem such as an imbalance between population growth and food production. One mathematically satisfying solution to this problem (satisfying in the sense of being supported by clear data and a parsimonious solution process) is to reduce population growth. However, the cultural norms of a country may preclude this solution and a more difficult solution involving increased food production or importing of food must be assessed.

Contexts for Improving Mathematics Communication

The Communication Framework for Mathematics provides a set of ideas for improving mathematics learning through increased interactional opportunities in the classroom. To move from traditional instructional methods to a communications rich format takes time and effort on the part of both teachers and students. There are concomitant changes in other aspects of mathematics education that can facilitate the success of instructional innovations aimed at increasing mathematical discourse. The final section of this chapter addresses contextual issues in the areas of curriculum, other instructional concerns and institutional support.

Curricular Contexts

Implicit within the Communication Framework for Mathematics is a new conception of the mathematics curriculum. In order for students to communicate across different forms of mathematical representations and about more meaningful situations, students will need a wider range of mathematical tools at their disposal. Traditionally the presecondary mathematics curriculum has focused on computational skills, and this continues to be the case for so-called disadvantaged students in particular (Knapp et al., 1991). How-

Figure 8.3 NCTM Curriculum Standards
Grades 5 to 8

Processes

- Problem Solving
- Communication
- Reasoning
- Connecting topics and concepts

Content

- Number/Operations/Computation
- Patterns and functions
- Algebra
- Statistics
- Probability
- Geometry
- Measurement

Source: National Council of Teachers of Mathematics, *Curriculum and Evaluation Standards for School Mathematics (1989)*. Adapted from pp. 65–119.

ever, the research base for mathematics education indicates that the traditional emphasis on mastery of basic skills prior to teaching conceptual or higher level thinking in mathematics has been ineffective and insufficient for American students (Romberg & Carpenter, 1986; Schoenfeld, 1992). The mathematics reform movement as embodied in such documents as the National Council of Teachers of Mathematics Curriculum Standards (1989) and the California State Framework for Mathematics (California State Department of Education, 1992) emphasizes that *all* students should have access to a full range of mathematical topics which include an emphasis on more advanced mathematical processes including problem solving, reasoning, estimation and communication. Figure 8.3 lists the processes and topic areas recommended for middle grade students. Mathematical achievement for diverse student populations depends upon access to a higher level mathematics curriculum, one which is now denied to many students from culturally and linguistically different backgrounds (Oakes, 1990).

Instructional Contexts

The communication framework for mathematics assumes that children from any given culture can become effective communicators in a variety of different mathematical contexts. However, the educational community docs not yet know how to make this happen equally well for all children. There are three unresolved issues that need to be considered when observing or designing exemplary mathematics programs for diverse student populations: matching instructional group arrangements to student needs, the language of instruction, and the role of technology.

The many examples given about educational projects that have incorporated different aspects of mathematical communication should have made clear that there are many different instructional arrangements in which mathematical communication can be fostered—pair problem solving, cooperative groups, large group discussion, individual student journals and regular written assignments. Teachers face the issue of deciding when to use which kind of structure for which students. The success of recently introduced small group instructional techniques has at times been taken to imply that many children can learn only in such contexts, and post hoc cultural explanations have been developed to support this point of view. Several recent articles on Native American groups, the Navajo (McCarty, Wallace, Lynch, & Benally, 1991) and the Yup'ik Eskimo (Lipka, 1991), provide examples of successful large group lessons. In both cases the authors emphasize that whole group instruction was facilitated because the teachers share certain social values with their students and because the material was culturally relevant to the students. The examples given by these authors are important, although they are not about mathematics instruction, because there are times when the class as a whole is the best forum for developing mathematical ideas. As Magidson (1992) points out, it is not possible for a teacher in a normal sized class to effectively monitor every student's (or group of students') construction of mathematical knowledge. In addition, the diversity of ideas that seems essential to social constructivist theories of learning is more apt to be obvious when the class as a whole pools its knowledge. More study of the participant structures of large group lessons is needed in order to find culturally appropriate ways of engaging students in whole class instruction in ways that avoid the pitfalls of the traditional recitation.

The emphasis given here to communication in mathematics classrooms raises the issue of what language should be used for mathematics learning for students in the United States who have limited proficiency in English. A recent literature review (Secada, 1992) summarizes the extant literature as follows: "Hence the research on bilingual education indicates that LEP students are likely to be better off receiving instruction in their native language. But we are only beginning to learn about the processes by which the use of the native language might translate into better mathematics achievement" (page 644). The Communication Framework for Mathematics puts the emphasis upon styles of discourse as the essence of communication rather than language more narrowly construed as vocabulary and syntax. Certainly, the forms of communication described in the Framework can be done in any language and practice in discourse styles probably transfers across languages. At the same time it should be recognized that the forms of discourse described here may be particularly alien for a child entering the American school system from another school system. American children are likely to have experience with inquiry methods of learning, group work and the expression of individual opinions in other subjects such as social studies (Stodolsky, Salk, & Glaessner, 1991) or science. When given a choice, many students seem to prefer practicing the new discourse styles in their native language (Thornburg and Karp, 1992) before trying them in a second language.

Many claims have been made for how technology can enhance communication in the mathematics classroom. For instance the video-based series *The Adventures of Jasper Woodbury* is said to promote complex problem solving skills in a context where the effects of different reading skill levels of students and prior experiences are mitigated through the visual presentation of engaging stories (The Cognition and Technology Group, 1990). The computer has also been seen as a tool which promotes active discussion in mathematics classrooms in ways that differ from pencil and paper tasks (Hoyles, Sutherland, & Healy, 1991). A number of reasons are given for how the computer does this. It may facilitate student talk by providing an external focus for conversation. Or perhaps it forces more collaboration through the need to make joint decisions before taking a unitary action on the computer.

Unfortunately, to date there is little information on how innovative technology can be used with culturally and linguistically diverse student populations. DeVillar and Faltis (1991) provide a critique of the claims made for innovative instruction with technology. They point out that the increased talk reported by many authors has not been adequately described in terms of either its content or distribution among different participants in the classroom. DeVillar and Faltis claim that social integration and cooperation are necessary within the heterogeneous classroom before computers have the desired benefits for communication and content learning. González-Edfelt's (1990) research provides some empirical evidence about how the computer supports communication goals. She found that while using problem solving software, student talk was indeed extensive and often in forms, such as explanations, which are known to promote learning in mathematics. Spanish-speaking students with limited proficiency in English were most likely to participate verbally when they were matched with partners who also spoke Spanish and they could use Spanish at least part of the time. However, pairs constituted of an English monolingual student and a student with very limited proficiency in English resulted in very passive behavior on the part of the latter students. These students apparently benefitted little from having the computer as a tool in this context.

At present, expensive technology is not equally available to all students and may be creating what some authors have called "a virtual epidemic of inequality" (Cole, Griffin, & The Laboratory for Comparative Human Cognition, 1987, p. 54). In addition, the uses made of computers seem to differ by gender, class and ethnicity, with more advantaged groups using computers for purposes that more closely match the goals implicit in the Communication Framework for Mathematics. Even within the research literature, the emphasis continues to be on how computers can remediate basic skills deficits for such disparate groups as Chapter 1 students, bilingual students and special education students (Swan, Guerrero, Mitrani, & Schoener, 1990).

Institutional Contexts

Most of the examples given here about how communication can be fostered in mathematics have been focused on classroom level dynamics. However, the environment of the school or school district may be critically important for the long term success of changes in instructional methods. Heath's (1983) work stands out as exemplary in documenting how classrooms can be altered to fit the cultures of the participants while enhancing communication across cultures. Heath also bluntly reports on how the innovations developed by individual teachers disappeared as the school district instituted more criterion referenced testing and more of a top down emphasis on skills based teaching.

The Algebra Project (Moses et al., 1989) in contrast provides an example of how an entire school cooperated to support the students' preparation for high school algebra. The curricular changes were initiated in eighth grade classrooms but eventually the new curricular emphasis was extended to all grade levels, sixth through eighth, for students of all achievement levels. Thus, expectations were raised for all students in the schools. The school community was expanded to include parents as an integral part of the changes. A study of high schools that are particularly effective with Latino language-minority students (Lucas, Henze, & Donato, 1990) presents a similar picture of the comprehensive effort that facilitates mathematics as well as other academic achievement. Throughout the curriculum more emphasis was given to the students' cultures and the Spanish language. Even many Anglo teachers had learned Spanish and Spanish was allowed in most school contexts. Expectations for mathematics achievement were raised by providing advanced mathematics courses in Spanish as well as by reducing the number of remedial mathematics courses. Teachers had become familiar with mathematics instruction in Mexico and were able to help students learn new material using the skills they had been taught in Mexican schools. As in the Algebra Project, parents were involved in the school changes.

Summary and Conclusions

The Communication Framework for Mathematics has been presented as a tool for facilitating analysis of communication in mathematics classrooms. In this chapter it has been used to examine how instructional innovations advocated by the mathematics reform movement can meet the needs of linguistically and culturally different students when learning mathematics. Although the research base is still somewhat limited, an effort was made to demonstrate that a variety of teaching-learning arrangements can increase student involvement with corresponding gains in achievement. Several aspects of the suggested reforms hold particular promise for linguistically and culturally different students. A much wider range of instructional methods are favored including peer collaboration, open-ended problem solving, and open-ended large group discussion, which will enable teachers to accommodate the participant structures that are comfortable for more students. The constructivist model of the learner is acknowledged and gives rise to recommendations for more active learning modes which will engage a wider range of students. The recognition that students need to connect new knowledge to prior knowledge will encourage teachers to use meaningful problems, including those based on real situations from the lives of students.

At the same time, many of the communication skills required by the mathematics reform movement will pose a challenge, or perhaps even a barrier to many students, particularly linguistic minorities. A wider range of discourse styles will be expected of students and it is not clear whether bilingual programs or ESL teaching methods will prepare students for all of them. Writing will be a much larger part of the mathematics curriculum, once again providing a hurdle to second language speakers, as well as many native speakers of English. To some degree traditional mathematics instruction fits prescriptions of what has come to be called sheltered English instruction (Snow, 1990): predictable lesson structures, extensive review, language-independent presentation of materials (e.g. symbolic computation), explicit teacher modeling and frequent comprehension checks. These are less likely to be features of mathematics instruction in innovative classrooms. Thus teachers and students alike will need to come to grips with a high level of language demand, a task which many mathematics teachers, as well as students, are ill-equipped to do.

As the mathematics reform movement gains momentum, researchers and practitioners alike need to consciously consider the implications of educational innovations for all students. Since some of the stated goals of the reform movement are to incorporate currently under-represented groups in more advanced mathematics training and to raise the general level of mathematical literacy in American society, the needs of students of linguistically and culturally diverse populations must be incorporated into all aspects of educational change from planning to implementation to assessment.

REFERENCES

Anderson, B. T., Thorpe, M. E., & Clewell, B. (1989, March). *Theory and research in learning and instruction: Implications for instructing minority and female students in mathematics and science during the middle school years.* Paper presented at the meeting of the American Educational Research Association, San Francisco, CA.

Au, K. H., & Mason, J. M. (1981). Social organizational factors in learning to read: the balance of rights hypothesis. *Reading Research Quarterly, 17*, 115–152.

Baxter, G., Shavelson, R. J., Herman, S. J., & Brown, K. A. (in press). Mathematics performance assessment: Technical quality and diverse student impact. *Journal for Research in Mathematics Education.*

Bishop, A. J. (1991). *Mathematical enculturation: A cultural perspective on mathematics education*. Dordrecht, The Netherlands: Kluwer Academic Publishers.

Brenner, M. E. (1984). *Standardized arithmetic testing at KEEP (1975, 1977)* (Working paper). Honolulu: Center for the Development of Early Education.

Brenner, M.E. (1985). *Arithmetic achievement at Ka Na'i Pono, 1984. Results from standardized testing* (Tech. Rep. No. 126). Honolulu: Center for the Development of Early Education.

Brenner, M.E. (1991, April). *Context and language in beginning math skills*. Presented at the meeting of the American Educational Research Association, Chicago, IL.

California State Department of Education. (1992). *Mathematics framework for California public schools: Kindergarten through grade twelve*. Sacramento, CA: Author.

Cheek, H. N. (1984). A suggested research map for Native American mathematics education. *Journal of American Indian Education, 23*, 1–9.

Clarke, D., Stephens, W. M., & Waywood, A. (in press). Communication and the learning of mathematics. In T. A. Romberg (Ed.), *Mathematics assessment and evaluation: Imperatives for mathematics educators*. Albany, NY: The State University of New York.

Clewell, B. C. (1987). What works and why: Research and theoretical bases of intervention programs in math and science for minority and female middle school students. In A. B. Champagne & L. E. Hornig (Eds.), *Students and science learning*. Washington, DC: American Association for the Advancement of Science, 95–135.

Cognition and Technology Group at Vanderbilt. (1990). Anchored instruction and its relationship to situated cognition. *Educational Researcher, 19*, 2–10.

Cohen, E. G. (1984). Talking and working together: Status interaction and learning. In P. Peterson, L. Wilkinson, & M. Hallinan (Eds.), *The social context of instruction: Group organization and group process*. New York: Academic, 171–187.

Cohen, S. A., & Stover, G. (1981). Effects of teaching sixth-grade students to modify format variables of math word problems. *Reading Research Quarterly, 16*, 175–200.

Cole, M., Griffin, P., & Laboratory of Comparative Human Cognition. (1987). *Contextual factors in education: Improving science and mathematics education for minorities and women*. Madison, WI: Wisconsin Center for Education Research.

Collins, A., Brown, J. S., & Newman, S. (1989). Cognitive apprenticeship: Teaching the craft of reading, writing and mathematics. In L. B. Resnick (Ed.), *Knowing, learning, and instruction: Essays in honor of Robert Glaser*. Hillsdale, NJ: Lawrence Erlbaum, 453–494.

Cuevas, G. J. (1983). Language proficiency and the development of mathematics concepts in Hispanic primary school students. In T. H. Escobedo (Ed.), *Early childhood bilingual education: A Hispanic perspective*. New York: Teachers College Press, 148–163.

Cuevas, G. J., Mann, P. H., & McClung, R. M . (1986, April). *The effects of a language process approach program on the mathematics achievement of first, third and fifth graders*. Paper presented at the meeting of the American Educational Research Association, San Francisco, CA.

Cummins, J. (1981). The role of primary language development in promoting educational success for language minority students. In California State Department of Education (Ed.), *Schooling and language minority students: A theoretical framework*. Los Angeles: Evaluation, Dissemination and Assessment Center, California State University, Los Angeles, 3–49.

Davis, R. B., & Maher, C. A. (1990). What do we do when we "do mathematics"? In R. B. Davis, C. A. Maher, & N. Noddings (Eds.), *Constructivist views on the teaching and learning of mathematics. Journal for Research in Mathematics Education* (Monograph 4), 65–78.

De Avila, E. A., Duncan, S. E., & Navarrete, C. J. (1987). *Cooperative learning: Integrating language and content-area instruction*. (Teacher resource guide series.) Washington, DC: National Clearinghouse for Bilingual Education.

De Corte, E. , & Verschaffel, L. (1985). Beginning first graders' initial representation of arithmetic word problems. *The Journal of Mathematical Behavior, 4*, 3–21.

DeVillar, R. A., & Faltis, C. J. (1991). *Computers and cultural diversity: Restructuring for school success*. Albany, NY: State University of New York Press.

Doise, W., & Mugny, G. (1984). *The social development of the intellect*. Oxford: Pergamon Press.

Durkin, K., & Shire, B. (1991). *Language in mathematical education*. Bristol, PA: Open University Press.

Forman, E. (1989). The role of peer interaction in the social construction of mathematical knowledge. *International Journal of Educational Research, 13*, 55–70.

González-Edfelt, N. (1990). Oral interaction and collaboration at the computer: Learning English as a second language with the help of your peers. In C. J. Faltis & R. A. DeVillar (Eds.), *Language minority students and computers*. New York: Haworth Press, 53–90.

Halliday, M. A. K. (1978). *Language as social semiotic*. London: Edward Arnold.

Hargis, C., & Knight, L. (1977). Math language ability: Its relationship to reading and math. *Language Arts, 54,* 423–428.

Heath, S. B. (1983). *Ways with words*. Cambridge: Cambridge University Press.

Hoyles, C., Sutherland, R., & Healy, L. (1991). Children talking in computer environments: New insights into the role of discussion in mathematics learning. In K. Durkin & B. Shire (Eds.), *Language in mathematical education*. Bristol, PA: Open University Press, 162–176.

Inagaki, K. (1981). Facilitation of knowledge integration through classroom discussion. *The Quarterly Newsletter of the Laboratory of Comparative Human Cognition, 3* , 26–28.

Jordan, C. (1985). Translating culture: From ethnographic information to educational program. *Anthropology and Education Quarterly, 16,* 105–123.

Kagan, S. (1986). Cooperative learning and sociocultural factors in schooling. In Bilingual Education Office (Ed.), *Beyond language: Social and cultural factors in schooling language minority students*. Los Angeles: Evaluation, Dissemination and Assessment Center, State University of California, Los Angeles, 231–298.

Knapp, M., Adelman, N. E., Needels, M. C., Zucker, A. A., McCollum, H., Turnbull, B. J., Marder, C., & Shields, P. M. (1991). *What is taught, and how, to the children of poverty: Interim report from a two-year investigation*. Washington, DC: United States Department of Education.

Koblitz, N. (1984). Mathematics as propaganda. In D. M Campbell & J. C. Higgins (Eds.), *Mathematics: People, problems, results, volume III*. Belmont, CA: Wadsworth International, 248–254.

Lampert, M. (1990). When the problem is not the question and the solution is not the answer: Mathematical knowing and teaching. *American Educational Research Journal, 27,* 29–64.

Lave, J. (1990). The culture of acquisition and the practice of understanding. In J. W. Stigler, R. A. Shweder, & G. Herdt (Eds.), *Cultural psychology: Essays in comparative human development*. New York: Cambridge University Press, 309–327.

Lipka, J. (1991). Toward a culturally based pedagogy: A case study of one Yup'ik Eskimo teacher. *Anthropology and Education Quarterly, 22,* 203–223.

Lo, J-J. , Wheatley, G. H., & Smith, A. C. (1991, April). *Learning to talk mathematics*. Paper presented at the meeting of the American Educational Research Association, Chicago, IL.

Lucas, T., Henze, R., & Donato, R. (1990). Promoting the success of Latino language-minority students: An exploratory study of six high schools. *Harvard Educational Review, 60,* 315–340.

MacCorquodale, P. (1988). Mexican-American women and mathematics: Participation, aspirations, and achievement. In R. R. Cocking & J. P. Mestres (Eds.), *Linguistic and cultural influences on learning mathematics*. Hillsdale, NJ: Erlbaum, 137–160.

Magidson, S. (1992, April). *From the laboratory to the classroom: A technology-intensive curriculum for functions and graphs*. Paper presented at the meeting of the American Educational Research Association, San Francisco, CA.

Mayer, R. E. (1985) Implications of cognitive psychology for instruction in mathematical problem solving. In E. A. Silver (Ed.), *Teaching and learning mathematical problem solving*. Hillsdale, NJ: Erlbaum, 123–138.

McCarty, T. L., Wallace, S., Lynch, R. H., & Benally, A. (1991). Classroom inquiry and Navajo learning styles: A call for reassessment. *Anthropology and Education Quarterly, 22,* 42–59.

McKnight, C. (1991). Mathematics education, the disadvantaged, and large-scale investigations: Assessment for stability versus assessment for change. In M. S. Knapp & P. M. Shields (Eds.), *Better schooling for the children of poverty: Alternatives to conventional wisdom*. Berkeley: McCutchan, 169–188.

Mellin-Olsen, S. (1987). *The politics of mathematics education*. Dordrecht, The Netherlands: D. Reidel Publishing Company.

Michaels, S., & O'Connor, M. C. (1990). *Literacy as reasoning within multiple discourses: Implications for policy and educational reform*. Presented at the Council of Chief State School Officers 1990 Summer Institute.

Mitchell, M. (1992, April). *Situational interest: Its multifaceted structure in the secondary mathematics classroom*. Paper presented at the meeting of the American Educational Research Association, San Francisco, CA.

Mitchell, M., Baab, B., Campbell-LaVoie, F., & Prion, S. (1992). *An innovative approach to mathematics: Mathematics of the environment*. San Francisco: School of Education, University of San Francisco.

Moschkovich, J. (1992). *Making sense of linear equations and graphs: An analysis of students' conceptions and language use*. Unpublished doctoral dissertation, University of California, Berkeley.

Moses, R., Kamii, M., Swap, S. M., & Howard, J. (1989). The Algebra Project: Organizing in the spirit of Ella. *Harvard Educational Review, 59*, 423–443.

National Center for Education Statistics. (1991). *The state of mathematics achievement: NAEP's 1990 assessment of the nation and the trial assessment of the states*. Washington, DC: United States Department of Education.

National Council of Teachers of Mathematics. (1980). *An agenda for action: Recommendations for school mathematics of the 1980s*. Reston, VA: Author.

National Council of Teachers of Mathematics. (1989). *Curriculum and evaluation standards for school mathematics*. Reston, VA: Author.

National Council of Teachers of Mathematics. (1991). *Professional standards for teaching mathematics*. Reston, VA: Author.

National Research Council. (1989). *Everybody counts: A report to the nation on the future of mathematics education*. Washington, DC: National Academy Press.

Newman, R. S. (1984). Children's achievement and self-evaluations in mathematics: A longitudinal study. *Journal of Educational Psychology, 76* , 857–873.

Oakes, J. (1990). *Multiplying inequalities: The effects of race, social class and tracking on opportunities to learn mathematics and science*. Santa Monica, CA: Rand Corporation.

Peyton, J. K. (1990). Dialogue journal writing: Effective student-teacher communication. In A. M. Padilla, H. H. Fairchild, & C. M. Valadez (Eds.), *Bilingual education: Issues and strategies*. Beverly Hills, CA: Sage, 184–194.

Philips, S. U. (1972). Participant structures and communicative competence: Warm Springs children in community and classroom. In C. B.

Cazden, V. P. John, & D. Hymes (Eds.), *Functions of language in the classroom*. New York: Teachers College Press, 370–394.

Pimm, D. (1987). *Speaking mathematically: Communication in mathematics classrooms*. New York: Routledge.

Resnick, L. B., Bill, V. L., Lesgold, S. B., & Leer, M. N. (1991). Thinking in arithmetic class. In B. Means, C. Chelemer, & M. S. Knapp (Eds), *Teaching advanced skills to at-risk students*. San Francisco, CA: Jossey-Bass Publishers, 27–53.

Resnick, L., & Ford, W. W. (1981). *The psychology of mathematics for instruction*. Hillsdale, NJ: Erlbaum.

Resnick, L. B., & Omanson, S. F. (1986). Learning to understand arithmetic. In R. Glaser (Ed.), *Advances in instructional psychology Vol. 3*. Hillsdale, NJ: Erlbaum, 41–95,

Richards, J. J. (1991). Commentary on "Using Children's Mathematical Knowledge." In B. Means, C. Chelemer, & M. S. Knapp (Eds.), *Teaching advanced skills to at-risk students: Views from research and practice*. San Francisco: Jossey-Bass, 102–111.

Romberg, T. A., & Carpenter, T. P. (1986). Research on teaching and learning mathematics: Two disciplines of scientific inquiry. In M. Wittrock (Ed.), *Handbook of research on teaching*, 3rd ed. New York: Macmillan, 850–873.

Schoenfeld, A. S. (1985). *Mathematical problem solving*. New York: Academic Press.

Schoenfeld, A. S. (1989). Explorations of students' mathematical beliefs and behavior. *Journal for Research in Mathematics Education, 20*, 338–355.

Schoenfeld, A. S. (1991). On mathematics as sensemaking: An informal attack on the unfortunate divorce of formal and informal mathematics. In J. F. Voss, D. N. Perkins, & J. W. Segal (Eds.), *Informal reasoning and education*. Hillsdale, NJ: L. Erlbaum, 311–343.

Schoenfeld, A. S. (1992). Learning to think mathematically. In D. Grouws (Ed.), *Handbook for research on mathematics teaching and learning*. New York: Macmillan, 334–370.

Schoenfeld, A. S., Smith J. P., & Arcavi, A. (in press). Learning: The microgenetic analysis of one student's evolving understanding of a complete subject matter domain. In R. Glaser (Ed.), *Advances in instructional psychology, Vol. 4*. Hillsdale, NJ: Erlbaum.

Secada, W. G. (1991). Selected conceptual and methodological issues for studying the mathematics education of the disadvantaged. In M. S. Knapp & P. M. Shields (Eds.), *Better schooling for the children of poverty: Alternatives to conventional wisdom*. Berkeley: McCutchan, 149–168.

Secada, W. G. (1992). Race, ethnicity, social class, language and achievement in mathematics. In D. Grouws (Ed.), *Handbook for research on mathematics teaching and learning*. New York: Macmillan, 623–660.

Siegler, R. S. (1987). The perils of averaging across strategies: An example from children's arithmetic. *Journal of Experimental Psychology: General, 116*, 250–264.

Snow, M. A. (1990). Instructional methodology in immersion foreign language education. In A. M. Padilla, H. H. Fairchild, & C. M. Valadez (Eds.), *Foreign language education: Issues and strategies*. Newbury Park, CA: Sage, 156–171.

Spanos, G., & Crandall, J. (1990). Language and problem solving: Some examples from math and science. In A. M. Padilla, H. H. Fairchild, & C. M. Valadez (Eds.), *Bilingual education: Issues and strategies*. Newbury Park, CA: Sage, 157–170.

Stodolsky, S. S. (1988). *The subject matters*. Chicago: University of Chicago.

Stodolsky, S. S., Salk, S., & Glaessner, B. (1991). Student views about learning math and social studies. *American Educational Research Journal, 28*, 89–116.

Swan, K., Guerrero, F., Mitrani, M., & Schoener, J. (1990). Honing in on the target: Who among the educationally disadvantaged benefits most from what CBI? *Journal of Research on Computing in Education, 23*, 381–403.

Thompson, A. (1985). Teachers' conceptions of mathematics and the teaching of problem solving. In E. A. Silver (Ed.), *Teaching and learning mathematical problem solving: Multiple research perspectives*. Hillsdale, NJ: Erlbaum, 281–294.

Thornburg, D. G., & Karp, K. S. (1992, April). *Resituating mathematics and science instruction for language different students*. Poster presented at the meeting of the American Educational Association, San Francisco, CA.

Tudge, J. (1990). Vygotsky, the zone of proximal development and peer collaboration: Implications for classroom practice. In L. C. Moll (Ed.), *Vygotsky and education: Instructional implications and applications of sociohistorical psychology*. Cambridge: Cambridge University Press, 155–172.

Vygotsky, L. S. (1978). *Mind in society*. Cambridge: Harvard University Press.

Whimbey, A., & Lochhead, J. (1982). *Problem solving and comprehension*. 3rd ed. Philadelphia, PA: The Franklin Institute Press.

Wilkinson, L. C., Lindow, J., & Chiang, C. (1985). Sex differences and sex segregation in students' small-group communication. In L. C. Wilkinson & C. B. Marrett (Eds.), *Gender influences in classroom interaction*. Orlando, FL : Academic Press, 185–207.

Willig, A. C., Harnisch, D. L., Hill, K. T., & Maehr, M. L. (1983). Sociocultural and educational correlates of success-failure attributions and evaluation anxiety in the school setting for Black, Hispanic and Anglo children. *American Educational Research Journal, 20*, 385–410.

Wood, T., Cobb, P., and Yackel, E. (1991). Change in teaching mathematics: A case study. *American Educational Research Journal, 28*, 587–616.

Zucker, A. A. (1991). Review of research on effective curriculum and instruction in mathematics. In M. S. Knapp & P. M. Shields (Eds.), *Better schooling for the children of poverty: Alternatives to conventional wisdom*. Berkeley, CA: McCutchan, 189–208.

✧ Chapter 9

Language Diversity and Science Learning: The Need for A Critical System of Meaning

Alejandro J. Gallard and Deborah J. Tippins

Juan,[1] like many limited English proficient adolescents, is a bright and articulate student. Yet, Juan refused to participate in his science class at Audubon Middle School[2] in a rural part of Florida. The following vignette is an example of his behavior, and sadly enough illustrates the experiences of many other Juans or Juanitas.

Upon entering the science classroom, one notices that Juan has tilted his desk and has rested the back support on the wall. He doesn't say anything, and doesn't disturb anyone. His only activity is that every now and then, he decides to draw[3] in his spiral binder.

During an interview,[4] Juan is asked to describe the use of a lever. He accurately describes a lever as a tool to help one do work. When asked to explain what he meant, he said: "You can use it to lift things or open things." Juan explained that he used levers while working in the fields after school, to open box lids. He also went on to explain that a lever makes work easier depending on where, and how, you hold the lever. "The closer you hold it to the end the harder it is for you to open the box. If you hold the handle far away from the box lid the easier it is to open."

Juan seems to understand some aspects of the notion of force and work. At least he knows enough to grip the handle of a lever in a spot that makes his work easier and not harder. Furthermore, his knowledge about science was not derived from a text, a list of English science vocabulary words, or even his classroom, but directly from out-of-school experiences.

Actually, Juan knows more science than his classroom teacher allows him to demonstrate, even though he may not realize it. For example, the following is a portion of a conversation between Juan and one researcher:

> **R:** Let's talk about force and travelling in a straight line. What happens when a bat hits a ball?
>
> **J:** Man that's easy. The bat when it hits the ball is a really strong force and this makes the ball travel in a straight line.
>
> **R:** O.K. you've hit the ball, and it is traveling in a straight line and then slowly but surely it starts toward the ground. Why?
>
> **J:** That's because gravity is a force and it becomes stronger than the bat.

At this time the researcher who was interviewing him asked: "Juan, why don't you participate in school? You are a bright person and you understand science. Why do you sit around and do nothing?"

> **J:** I don't have anyone to talk to.
>
> **R:** What do you mean you do not have anyone to talk to?
>
> **J:** There are no other Mexicans in class.

His answer was surprising. While it was true that he was one of two Mexican students in a class of 35, where only one other person was White and the rest Black, there had never been any signs of racial or ethnic tension. Quite to the contrary, Juan seemed to get along well with everyone and when asked if this was true he said, "Yes." It was not until we started looking at how the teacher taught science, that we recognized other factors hindering all students' participation, and in particular Juan's participation in science. The teaching style of the teacher was such that Juan could not communicate what he knew. His knowledge, or understanding of scientific phenomena, was not what the science teacher was interested in. Ms. Smith[5] taught via the textbook and workbook. Unfortunately, the learning environment established by Ms. Smith served to preclude her students' ways of understanding science phenomena. This limited opportunities for students to bring their out-of-school experiences to the classroom. As such, we believe that the problem was not a lack of Mexican students, but, rather the absence of an open communication environment, a learning environment where what students know is recognized as viable and tenable by the teacher and by peers. Furthermore, we believe that another problem was the teacher's view of knowledge as something that was contained in textbooks and workbooks.

Although meaningful science learning for all students was constrained by the lack of a facilitative learning environment and a non-contextual view of knowledge, this was particularly the case for Juan, because he spoke more than one language. For example, during the interviews, Juan used the language in which he could best express himself to frame answers to questions. This is not surprising, for questions and answers are always framed by context; although a researcher would start an interview in English, Juan frequently chose to answer in English or Spanish. Juan used English or Spanish as languages that could best convey his experiences or the sense he made of the world. Unfortunately, his science classroom environment was very limiting, in that only English was spoken by the teacher and students; students were not expected or encouraged to share their knowledge, but to simply reconfirm words present in their textbooks and workbooks. In essence Juan did not have an opportunity to join in dialogue directed toward what he knew about science phenomena. Nor did the classroom teacher facilitate the construction of new knowledge by creating opportunities for Juan to experience dissonance needed to facilitate conceptual change.

This is not a surprising outcome in a reductionist world, where one seeks truth and the belief that knowledge is somehow waiting to be discovered prevails. This outcome would indeed be a surprise if it were to take place in a constructivist setting because the only knowledge that can exist is what the knower/learner brings to the setting. "The world we live in can be understood also as the world of our experience, the world as we see, hear, and feel it.

This world does not consist of 'objective facts' or 'things in themselves' but of such invariants and constancies as we are able to compute on the basis of our individual experience" (von Glasersfeld, 1987, p. 315). The idea of creating knowledge, or understandings of your surrounding world, is the framework for constructivism. One constructs knowledge through new experiences or experiences that serve to perturbate existing experience.

Learning Science: A Critical Perspective

Constructivism is a theory of learning which deals with an individual's sense-making of the world. It is post-epistemological in that it posits a relationship between knowledge and the "real world" in which we can no longer separate the knower from the known, or the teacher from the learner and other components of the learning environment. Consequently, instructional practices are no longer viewed as objective or neutral, and issues of science teaching and learning are inextricably connected with language, meaning and context. From a constructivist point of view, learning is the process of making sense in terms of what is already known (von Glasersfeld, 1989). It is an active process in which learners construct knowledge in a way that makes personal sense and it is a subjective process, in which learners draw on their own backgrounds to make sense of new information. Because it is mediated by a socio-cultural milieu, it can also be considered to be a social process of making sense.

When a "critical" system of meaning is applied to constructivism, science learning takes on new significance: understanding oneself, one's relation to society and the construction of self-concept and world view are of paramount importance. By using the word "critical" we take the position that learning does not take place in an economic and social vacuum. Accordingly, not all self-concepts are equal, nor are all students treated or viewed equally. For example, even though Juan had a wealth of experiences they could only be realized if the educational environment was conducive to cherishing that which Juan has learned through experience. Unfortunately, it is our perception that the experiences of a migrant worker, who can sometimes explain himself in English and other times in Spanish, too frequently are of little value in a world in which how to talk, act, and indeed, how to look, is predisposed—a world where students are required to "fit" the school, rather than having the school fit the needs of the student.

As science educators who use critical constructivism as a referent for our actions, we see the world as being socially constructed and students and teachers as people who seek to understand what constitutes reality for themselves in the home, school and science classroom. Thus, who a student is, what he or she knows, how he or she is able to convey meaning and assumptions about knowledge and the process of learning are issues of utmost importance. As we are able to step back and develop insight into different ways of knowing and different forms of knowledge, we come to understand how implicit rules guide our generation of knowledge about science teaching and learning. These rules are constructed through linguistic codes, cultural signs, embedded power, and are influenced by particular world views, values, and definitions of intelligence.

For example, returning to Ms. Smith's room we find a situation in which it is easy to underscore how instruction is based in the English language, and is text-driven. There is nothing inappropriate in using the English language, textbooks, or workbooks for instructional purposes. Too often it is these surface characteristics that start and end pedagogical debates about teaching and learning. More importantly, the issue is that there is a culture of pedagogy that prevails in all classrooms, and this culture supersedes students' needs in a teaching-learning situation. In this case, the use of textbooks, workbooks, and instruction solely in English represents a view of the teaching-learning world that prescribes legitimate classroom functions and roles for both the teacher and student.

It did not matter to Ms. Smith what the student knew, only what he did not know. This is a rather simple way of representing a very complex issue that is embraced by even more complex economic, political, social and technological issues. From our critical constructivist perspective, if what the student knows is central to the teaching-learning task, in that his or her knowledge is viewed as a legitimate form of multiple knowledges, then by necessity the role of the teacher is to facilitate learning, and that of the student to construct new meaning. The assumption inherent in situations where the teacher is facilitating and the student constructing new meanings, is that the classroom must become a place of prestige for the cultural, economic, linguistic and social experiences of all students.

Critical constructivist science educators recognize that science teaching is deeply rooted in our personality and experience as a learner. It is not a constant and predictable activity, as it occurs in a world of uncertainty. Nor is it a neutral process, considering the complex relationships between the teacher and the learner, power and knowledge and other components of the learning environment.

Grant and Secada (1987) have described the bridge metaphor which has frequently been used to illustrate traditional approaches to educating diverse learners, particularly those with second languages. Engineers would not purposefully build a bridge on unstable, shifting ground. Thus, the bridge metaphor is no longer a useful way of thinking about science teaching and learning when we consider the uncertain, unpredictable and value laden nature of all we do and come to know as teachers and learners. Nor is it a useful metaphor if we dispel the myth that a student's native language is a liability rather than an asset with respect to science teaching and learning.

Many of the questions that we are now asking about science teaching need to be grounded in a "critical system of meaning." The application of critical theory to constructivism leads science educators to rethink and redefine the kinds of questions that one asks about learning. Accordingly, two questions that are central to limited English proficient (LEP) students' learning of science are:

- What does learning science mean?

- How can we engage students and teachers in meaningful science learning?

When critical constructivism is used as a referent for science teaching, the focus on learning science should be a sense-making activity. In other words, learning science should not be based solely on "hands-on" experiences, but rather on experiences that facilitate a student's construction of new knowledge. Students must be able to use their experiences, which include language and culture, as they interpret science phenomena. Science classrooms must be places where intellect is protected and cultivated and interpretive ability is encouraged. When learning science is viewed as a process of making sense that is culture dependent, language then becomes an important part in the creation of the world as we know it. Therefore, students must have opportunities to make sense of science phenomena in their own language, through diverse multi-sensory events.

Myths about Practice

From a critical constructivist perspective, the issue of exemplary practice and science teaching and learning, as it relates to linguistically diverse students, is somewhat paradoxical. On the one hand, programs such as Cheche Konnen seem to be grounded in the ideas of critical constructivism, critical theory, and Grundy's (1989) notion of a curriculum with emancipatory interests. On the other hand, English as a Second Language (ESL) programs seem to espouse a reductionist view of the world where what students know, and can represent in their language, is only as important as what they can speak, read and write in English. In most schools, learning English is even further reduced to preparing language minority students to take standardized tests which ask them to think in terms of linear causation and quantification; promoting students to the next grade; and studying a discipline's vocabulary in English in order to provide a better understanding of the content involved. Thus, it is not surprising that while many language minority students may find science boring or meaningless, in the absence of alternative models, they come to accept the prevailing definitions of knowledge.

Such curricular events can be interpreted in terms of cultural myths, an example of which is the notion of "exemplary practice." Britzman (1991, p. 8) explained that some myths serve as a framework to repress certain notions of pedagogy while others can be facilitative to generating alternative images of teaching and learning. The myth of exemplary practice, for example, characterizes science teaching as identified with a norm, toward which all science teachers should clearly be moving. This parallels a cognitive approach to second language learning where linguistic norms are defined by the competence of native speakers. In contrast, a sociocultural approach to learning replaces "notions like language proficiency . . . with notions like communicative effectiveness and social appropriateness" (Snow, 1992, p. 17).

Alternative Conceptions of the Curriculum

How one defines a curriculum, as well as curricular pedagogical interests, is very important because it serves to frame the assumptions made about knowledge, teaching, learning, students and teachers. For example, we see curriculum as embedded in culture and defined as the sum of all activities in a classroom. These activities would include prior experiences that both teachers and students bring with them to the classroom, the beliefs and attitudes of both teachers and students, textbooks and all of the political, social and technical activities that influence teaching and learning. Those who view the world in a more objectivist manner would perceive curriculum as a set of printed documents which contain knowledge or truth. Erik, a middle school science teacher involved in action research, initially conceptualized the curriculum as a "rock." However, after opportunities for learning to think reflectively, he began to view curriculum as "the sand on the beach" which changes as the students change. Such an alternative conception of curriculum is one which enables students to use multiple languages in ways which enhance and challenge their abilities to frame issues or confirm and disconfirm scientific evidence.

Alternative conceptions of curriculum such as Erik's "sand on the beach" metaphor are illustrated in Rivera and Zehler's (1990) report on a project that reviewed the following programs: (a) Partners for Valued Youth: Dropout Prevention Strategies for At-Risk Language Minority Students; (b) AIM for the Best: Assessment and Intervention Model for the Bilingual Exceptional Student; (c) Community Knowledge and Classroom Practice: Combining Resources for Literacy Instruction; and (d) Cheche Konnen: Collaborative Scientific Inquiry in Language Minority Classrooms. There were three themes the authors found to be common in all four programs, and they were very consistent with critical constructivism: (1) self-reflection about practice, beliefs and attitudes, (2) teachers and students mutually learning, and (3) the belief that there are many forms of knowledge that are legitimate. It would seem that underlying these three themes are non-traditional beliefs about curriculum, beliefs which reflect interests designed to provide students with opportunities to arrive at scientific meaning in ways that parallel the ways in which scientists arrive at similar meanings (i.e., by facilitating social negotiation, inclusion of the insights of their community members, and experimenting with one's own ideas by searching for meanings and not truths).

These three themes are very consistent with Grundy's notion of emancipatory curriculum as opposed to technical or practical interests:

> "While the other two interests are concerned with control and understanding respectively, the emancipatory interest is concerned with empowerment, that is, the ability of individuals and groups to take control of their own lives in autonomous and responsible ways. The emancipatory cognitive interest could be defined as follows: A fundamental interest in emancipation and empowerment to engage in autonomous action arising out of authentic, critical insights into the social construction of human society." (Grundy, 1989, p. 19)

Our observation of science classrooms has led us to believe that much time is spent by students in preparation for replicating what is in textbooks or verification of cookbook laboratory experiments, rather than engaging in activities that promote understanding through opportunities to challenge personal theories, develop new ones, and explore further. Especially for students who do not speak the dominant language, much time is spent in memorization of abstract science vocabulary that is supposed to somehow reflect or capture understanding of a particular phenomenon (e.g. photosynthesis, environment, force, or energy).

These words are representative of deep and complex science processes and phenomena. If students can write about them by using words that convey meaning to the reader, then the assumption is that they can understand them. At the risk of repeating ourselves, scientists do not just invent words that are immediately, and without question embraced by the scientific community. The ideas behind these words must go through a process of hypothesis development, collegial exchange of ideas, and a series of challenges. Much time is spent in trying to make sense of the phenomena in question. Students also need to develop their own ideas, share them with their peers, challenge each other and arrive at their own answers about science phenomena. This can be done by carefully planning for a very perturbating classroom environment, which has opportunities for students to think reflectively, a classroom environment in which the teacher refrains from saying "yes that is correct," or "yes, but . . . " to one in which new and difficult questions are constantly posed to students.

A curriculum developed along the line of emancipatory interests is not a license for students to do what they want to do. It is an opportunity for students to do what is necessary, through reflection and action (Grundy, 1989), to construct meaning for the task at hand. Nor does this type of curriculum imply that science teachers can just turn students loose and fold their arms as students go about constructing knowledge—quite the contrary. When emancipatory interests are at the heart of the curriculum, learning becomes the responsibility of the learner. Accordingly, the teacher needs to facilitate learning in very complex and challenging ways. From an emancipatory and a constructivist perspective, many of the traditional beliefs about knowledge, the role of the teacher and student, and power relations are looked at in very critical ways. Teachers who have been taught to believe that they are the fountain of unchallengeable knowledge, and that students should fill their glasses at this well, can feel threatened by a curriculum with emancipatory interests. The following is an example of a teacher who met this challenge and was willing to let go of some of her traditional ideas about teaching and learning.

Building the Curriculum from the Students' World

The setting is a grade seven classroom in a rural combination middle and high school in the northern part of Florida. The classroom teacher was Ms. Jones,[6] a second year teacher who had majored in social studies, but was now teaching science. In the class period that was being observed, all of the students' first language was Spanish and they were the daughters and sons of Mexican or Central American migrant workers. Many of these students were already working in the fields. They had many years of exposure to botany as a result of working in the fields and having listened to hours of their parents' and friends' conversations about agriculture.

Ms. Jones spoke Spanish with a fair degree of fluency. However, she was concerned because she was not certified to teach science and felt that her background in science was weak. Her questions and requests for help indicated that she was interested in what tips, tricks or techniques we could share with her about teaching science.

In one of our interaction group sessions[7] we asked Ms. Jones if she would consider teaching a botany unit. Her response was that she did not know enough about botany to teach it. However, if we were to help and call in university teaching "experts" in botany she would give it a try. At this time we suggested to her that her students were experts and perhaps they needed an opportunity to share experiences they had accumulated about agriculture.

Ms. Jones consulted with her students and within a two-week period they were designing experiments in the school's greenhouse. Furthermore, Ms. Jones decided that students could carry out the design and implementation of the experiments in either English or Spanish.

It was during a classroom observation period that we became impressed with how Ms. Jones planned and implemented this science unit. Students were working in cooperative groups and were engaged in discussions about the plants they were growing. They were measuring, drawing and recording their observations in science logbooks.

While students were working in their groups, Ms. Jones would move about the room and participate in the various groups. The exchange between teacher and students was interesting in several ways. For example, she did not insist that students use any descriptive vocabulary about plants, other than words that were a familiar part of students' everyday language. A second example was that whenever students would engage in so-called off-task conversations she would participate, as well.

This vignette provides an example of a teacher meeting the challenge to change her practice with respect to science teaching. It is also indicative of how a teacher's beliefs and interests can drive practice. When Ms. Jones considered using her students as content experts, she reconceptualized learning in a way that facilitated students' drawing on their own experiences. Knowledge was not only integrated across different subject areas, but was directly related to the needs established through students' interests in agriculture. Ms. Jones' previous experiences had led her to believe that experts are those who write textbooks or work as scientists—certainly not students. Thus, knowledge for her was not what students knew, but what the experts had published, and what the students had to "learn" in terms of mandated curriculum. This is a critical distinction because, as long as Ms. Jones viewed knowledge in this way she could not facilitate learning that centered on what students knew, nor could she recognize the importance of negotiation as a process of making sense of specific experiences.

The consequences of Ms. Jones' beliefs about knowledge also affected her professionally. She had a fear of teaching science, primarily because of her inadequate science background, but also due to her lack of teaching experience. Her solution was not unlike that of many novice science teachers: she searched for an outside person who could bring to her classroom neat and colorful ideas about teaching science and she attempted to surround herself with content experts, or people who had what she believed to be legitimate scientific knowledge. Her beliefs about knowledge parallel those of prospective teachers in science "methods" courses who accumulate reams of science activities to use with people they have never met, (so that they can be more successful teachers). Along these same lines, how many workshops, inservices or professional development hours have been spent collecting science teaching activities from people who have never (a) been inside a participating teacher's school, or (b) have never talked with one of the school's students about their beliefs concerning science and learning?

Nevertheless, when Ms. Jones did respond to the idea of students as experts, she provided an atmosphere that facilitated learning. She promoted learning by not only encouraging students to demonstrate what they knew, but also encouraging them to communicate this knowledge in the language with which they were most comfortable. Her actions were also sensitive because they took into consideration the complexity of the whole situation, which included encouraging the use of the language the students understood best, and use of commensurate experiences. In this sense, Ms. Jones went beyond the idea of a curriculum built from the experience of students. She embraced a vision of the student as learner whose cultural identity influences the way in which scientific knowledge is constructed, selected and organized. Ms. Jones' actions were similar to those of a risk-taker, because she was willing to share her authority with the students, empowering them to become responsible for their own learning. Ms. Jones' openness to changing so quickly was unique, indeed, rare. However, change may be less risky when there is a variety of support being offered in the context of a learning community which values learning to think reflectively.

Ms. Jones' vision of meaningful science learning embraces the idea that students, through their own experiences, make sense of science phenomena prior to any emphasis on vocabulary development. Because students do need to communicate in standard, or culturally acceptable ways it is important that Ms. Jones constrains students' experiences by using their current level of understanding as a base for further learning. We do not advocate that students do or say whatever they like, simply that they should be able to say or do anything as they are learning. However, students should be provided many opportunities to share with their peers what they have learned; it is at these times that students will have to develop the vocabulary to communicate with others.

Deconstructing Tacit Assumptions Embedded in Science Programs for Linguistically Different Students

We have alluded to the importance of "hands-on" experiences and the construction of meaning. It is our belief that linguistically different students need more than meaningful "hands-on" experiences—they need experiences that provide them with opportunities to construct new meanings. This idea coincides with the concepts underlying a hands-on, minds-on emancipatory curriculum. With this in mind, we reviewed three different programs that center on the teaching and learning of science with respect to limited English proficient students: Cognitive Academic Language Learning

Approach (CALLA), Cheche Konnen, and Finding Out/Descubrimiento (FO/D).

As we examined these programs, and pertinent literature, we tried to uncover the tacit assumptions embedded within the understanding of language, science learning and teaching. We had three framing questions that were applied to each program:

- Are these programs based on a Cartesian-Newtonian view of the world, or do they reflect a world view consistent with constructivist beliefs?

- Do these programs emphasize the development of certain skills that are needed to acquire knowledge that is somehow "out there" with a life of its own, or do they emphasize a view of knowledge as a personal and social construction?

- Are the interests of these programs technical in nature, or do they reflect more practical and emancipatory interests?

When we looked at English as a Second Language (ESL) programs such as Cognitive Academic Language Learning Approach (CALLA), we were struck by the apparent dismissal of what students know and can express in their native tongue, by emphasizing what they do not know in English. The emphasis is clearly on the development of vocabulary and presumes the existence of a linguistic norm. Though there is talk about the importance of hands-on activities, the underlying objective is to learn the language of science in the English language, and not to construct new meanings. The CALLA system, with its emphasis on isolated strategies, is a reductionist approach in which learning is defined as the mastery of bits of knowledge in the English language. This approach signifies a transmission model of teaching in which the teacher's role is that of disseminator of knowledge and study skills.

In the CALLA program (Chamot & O'Malley, 1987, 1989) there is reference to the term academic language skills. We cannot be certain of the beliefs underpinning the development of the CALLA program; however, it does seem that curriculum is viewed as being a fixed entity which contains knowledge or truths represented by certain science words. What gives us this impression is the push for learning science vocabulary so that students can participate in science classes in meaningful ways. We disagree with this vision of science learning because it places the emphasis on learning science through the mastery of science vocabulary. Quite frankly, the learning of science vocabulary as the means for understanding science is precisely the approach that has prevailed in mainstream classes for decades, with dismal results. By dismal results, we mean that the outcome for students is rote memorization, and a denial of the wonders of science.

Cheche Konnen (Warren, Rosebery, & Conant, 1992) seems to emphasize more of an emancipatory curriculum. There is great value placed on experiences in which students and teachers can construct new meanings rather than search for truths. Knowledge is not viewed as something to be found "out there," nor is science English vocabulary essential to classroom participation. In Cheche Konnen the vision of science teaching and learning is one in which "creativity and construction, rather than discovery, predominate . . . science is projective rather than objective; scientists build stories about a possible world, they do not discover truth that already exists 'out there'" (Rosebery, Warren, Conant & Hudicourt-Barnes, 1992). Another key component of the Cheche Konnen program is that the teacher is seen as a facilitator and a learner, and not as the center of all intellectual attention. "What the students think—rather than what the text states or teacher thinks—is at the center of the activity." Does this program support an environment in which science learning can take place? Yes, we believe that not only does learning take place, but the tools to becoming scientifically literate are cultivated in this approach.

With regard to the Finding Out/Descubrimiento (FO/D) program, we felt that knowledge was defined in a non-objectivist manner. The interests behind this program appear to be practical[8] in nature. An interesting aspect of this program is the idea that students develop knowledge in, and out of the classroom. However, rather than using the word knowledge the term "repertoire" is used as a synonym for knowledge.

Where this program reflects some aspects of technical interest[9] is in the manner in which the role of the teacher is conceptualized, especially in a cooperative learning setting. The teacher is viewed as a "fountain" of knowledge which students need to "tap" if meaningful learning is to take place. This raises questions about the epistemological underpinnings as reflected in a particular view of knowledge, or what is referred to as repertoire. On the one hand, there is an emphasis placed on the knowledge that students bring to the classroom, strongly suggesting that there are many types of knowledge. On the other hand, there is a strong suggestion that some of the student's repertoire is of little value in society. Accordingly, it is the teacher's role to facilitate the "pouring in" of appropriate knowledge, or at least to act as a reservoir of appropriate knowledge. This apparent contradiction in beliefs is somewhat confusing and creates a tension which raises many questions in our minds.[10]

Breaking the Bonds of Orthodox Science Teaching and Learning

The role of language, culture and power in the transformation of inservice and preservice science teacher education programs takes on new meaning when the ideas of critical constructivism and emancipation are used as referents for making sense. For many years, instructional efforts have concentrated on showing practicing and prospective teachers new "methods" or "tricks" that supposedly enhance learning. We believe that a major reason that a "methods" approach has not adequately prepared teachers for diversity is that it presupposes one body of knowledge and classrooms that exist in a politically and socially neutral world. Our beliefs about learning and teaching stand in stark contrast: science is not a body of knowledge that is politically and socially neutral and ahistorical; science classrooms are not simply places where neutral instruction takes place. Rather, they are "contested cultural sites" (Giroux, 1989) where certain ways of speaking and particular forms of knowledge are legitimate, others are not.

Science is what each individual has interpreted about the world. "Knowledge is produced in the classroom through the interaction of student experience with information derived from the disciplines of science. . . . No student walks through the school doors without a wealth of information, likes and dislikes and untapped abilities." Educators must begin "with the search for this student experience in the construction of teaching moments" (Kincheloe, Steinberg and Tippins, 1992, pp. 63, 230). Thus, each student walks into the classroom with a science curriculum that is based on his or her own constructions through experience. As such, teacher education and inservice programs must promote the idea that science teaching methods come from the classroom environment and that no two classroom environments are exactly the same.

Prevailing practices in many teacher education programs reflect traditional approaches to science teaching, where prospective teachers are guided by a politically neutral "world view" through which they are taught not to examine instructional goals and strategies within a broader social and political context. Larke

(1990), for example, reported some of the following findings after administering an adapted version of the Cultural Diversity Awareness Inventory to 51 prospective elementary teachers: 54.1 percent of the prospective teachers indicated they were uncomfortable with people who spoke non-standard English; 49 percent felt that a student's spoken language should be corrected by modeling and nearly 80 percent of the respondents supported ESL programs for non-English speaking students. As this study suggests, students enter our teacher education programs with well entrenched beliefs about the role of culture and language in (science) teaching and learning. This is not surprising, when one considers that most prospective teachers have spent the past twelve years as students internalizing beliefs learned at home or in their community, and reinforced at school. Banks (1992) points out that teachers and students who are socialized within the mainstream culture "rarely have an opportunity to identify, question and challenge their cultural assumptions, beliefs, values and perspectives." At the same time, language minority teachers and students "are usually forced to examine, confront and question their cultural assumptions when they enter school."

Teachers As Researchers Collaborating for Inquiry

Action research is a powerful process through which teachers can confront the complex issues associated with language minority students' learning of science. Action research involves the identification of problems, investigation of these problems, and sharing of findings by those most intimately connected to the lives of students-the teachers themselves. When prospective and practicing teachers become empowered as researchers in their own classrooms, they are able to generate questions and analyze school and classroom events in terms of cultural differences. Ultimately, as Cochran-Smith and Lytle (1992) have suggested, as teachers engage in action research they begin to "construct local meanings of cultural diversity and to create courses of action appropriate to particular contexts." When teachers, as researchers, critically approach issues of language and diversity, they begin to rethink their beliefs and assumptions about culture, learning, language and power. As they uncover the tacit assumptions underlying the purposes and structures of schooling, hidden aspects of their own practice become visible. This process of "becoming critical" can lead to change which enhances the quality of science instruction for language minority and all students.

Critical theory is concerned with extending a teacher's consciousness of himself or herself as a social being, and thus promotes self-reflection. As a science teacher gains such a consciousness, he or she begins to understand science teaching and learning in terms of how political opinions, religious beliefs, gender role, racial self-concept or educational perspectives have been influenced by the dominant culture. If teacher education programs begin to use a critical constructivist perspective as a referent for analyzing science education, teaching and learning will be viewed in a new and different way—as a manifestation of larger social processes.

Implications for Change:
Reforming Science Teacher Education

There are certain conditions we believe are necessary for reforming our science teacher education programs, with respect to preparing teachers for language diversity. From the sociocultural perspective employed in this paper, a science curriculum cannot be meaningfully separated from the teacher, the learner and other aspects of the learning environment. Reform of curriculum and science teacher education programs must necessarily involve the actions of teachers and learners (Tippins, Tobin, & Hook, 1992). Reflection is an important component of reform. Teacher education programs must include opportunities for learners to develop an understanding of how beliefs with respect to language minority students develop. Science educators should focus their research efforts on the abilities, experiences and understandings that language minority students bring with them to the science classroom.

We began this chapter by asking two questions that are central to the learning of science for not only LEP students, but all students: (1) what does learning science mean? and (2) how can we engage students and teachers in meaningful science learning? We are not so naive as to suggest that easy answers to these questions exist. We can begin to understand the meaning of learning science, however, as we embrace the notion that "no scientific investigation, no exploration of the physical universe was undertaken in isolation from the larger attempt to understand the relationship between the components of the universe" (Kincheloe, Steinberg, and Tippins, 1992, p. 222). In much the same way, meaningful science learning cannot take place in isolation from all aspects of the learning environment, including a student's first language. If we are to engage students and teachers in meaningful learning we must include the voices and understandings of those who do not speak English as a first language. While there are no monolithic solutions, we believe that if critical theory is applied to constructivism as a basis for analyzing and reconceptualizing science teacher education programs, a powerful pedagogical symbiosis can occur.

NOTES

1. Pseudonym.

2. Pseudonym.

3. Juan would spend his time drawing caricatures of Latino(as), and automobiles. What Juan was doing in his spiral binder was ascertained after a series of observations and an interview in which one of the authors asked him to explain what he was drawing in his binder.

4. All interviews took place in either the English or Spanish languages and the determination of a language depended on the language initiated by the student. Indeed, at times both English and Spanish were used together in the same sentence by both the interviewer and student. We do not feel that the language(s) of the interview is important, but that the student could communicate in a language that best served his needs, and was understood.

5. Pseudonym.

6. Pseudonym.

7. For the purpose of this chapter, interaction group sessions are those in which there is an assembly of science teachers who are helping each other improve their practice through reflection. It can also be thought of as a support group.

8. Using Grundy's (1989) definition "The practical interest is a fundamental interest in understanding the environment through interaction based upon a consensual interpretation of meaning." (p. 14)

9. Grundy (1989) defines technical interest as "a fundamental interest in controlling the environment through rule-following action based upon empirically grounded laws." (p. 12)

10. Our source of consternation comes from DeAvila, E., Duncan, S., and Navarrete, C., (1987) in their publication Cooperative learning: Integrating language and content-area instruction, particularly the paragraph entitled The teacher as facilitator. The last four sentences provide the fol-

lowing description of the role of a teacher: "The cooperative learning teacher is also a manager, chiefly responsible for the smooth running of the classroom. The teacher is the final arbiter. The teacher is the child's access to knowledge. Without the teacher there is little, if any, learning that is meaningful in a modern society" (p. 7). This description of the role of the teacher is contrary to earlier claims about knowledge, teaching and learning. For us this raises questions as to how they view knowledge, teaching, and learning.

REFERENCES

Banks, J. (1992). Multicultural education: For freedom's sake. *Educational Leadership, 49* (4): 32–36.

Britzman, D. P. (1991). *Practice makes practice*. Albany: State University of New York Press.

Chamot, A. W., & O'Malley, J. M. (1987). The cognitive academic language learning approach: A bridge to the mainstream. *TESOL Quarterly, 21* (2): 227–249.

Chamot, A. W., & O'Malley, J. M. (1989). The cognitive academic language learning approach. In P. Rigg & V. C. Allen (Eds.), *When they don't all speak English*. Urbana: National Council of Teachers of English, 108–125.

Cochran-Smith, M., & Lytle, S. (1992). Interrogating cultural diversity: Inquiry and action. *Journal of Teacher Education, 43* (2): 104–115.

Giroux, H. (1989). Educational reform and teacher empowerment. In H. Holtz et al.(Eds.), *Education and the American dream*. Granby, MA: Bergin and Garvey.

Grant, C., & Secada, W. (1987). Preparing teachers for diversity. In W. R. Houston (Ed.), *Handbook of research on teacher education*. New York: Macmillan Publishing Company, 402–422.

Grundy, S. (1989). *Curriculum: Product or praxis*. Philadelphia, PA· The Falmer Press.

Kincheloe, J. L., Steinberg, S., and Tippins, D. J., (1992). *The stigma of genius: Einstein and beyond modern education*. Durango, CO: Hollowbrook Press.

Larke, P. (1990). Cultural diversity awareness inventory: Assessing the sensitivity of preservice teachers. *Action in Teacher Education, 12* (3): 23–30.

Rivera, C., & Zehler, A. (1990). *Collaboration in teaching and learning: Findings from the Innovative Approaches Research Project.* Arlington, VA: Development Associates, Inc.

Rosebery, A., Warren, B., Conant, F., & Hudicourt-Barnes, J. (1992). Cheche Konnen: Scientific sense-making in bilingual education. *Hands-on Math and Science Learning, 15* (1): 1,16.

Snow, C. (1992). Perspectives on second-language development: Implications for bilingual education. *Educational Researcher, 21* (2): 16–19.

Tippins, D., Tobin, K., & Hook, K. (April, 1992). Ethical decisions at the heart of teaching: Making sense from a constructivist perspective. Paper presented at the annual meeting of the American Educational Research Association, San Francisco.

von Glasersfeld, E. (1987). *The construction of knowledge. Contributions to conceptual semantics.* Seaside, CA: Intersystems Publications.

von Glasersfeld, E. (1989). Cognition, construction of knowledge, and teaching. *Synthese, 80* (1): 121–140.

Warren, B., Rosebery, A., & Conant, F. (1992). Appropriating scientific discourse: Findings from language minority classrooms. *The Journal of the Learning Sciences, 1*(2), 61–94.

CONCLUSION

The past decade has witnessed widespread dissatisfaction with the
state of American education, leading to calls for reform. Some advocate a return to traditional schooling, but with better educated
teachers, more motivated students, and a more disciplined atmosphere. Others blame the traditional system for the failure of large
numbers of students, and urge a rethinking of the entire enterprise.
As Part I of this book makes clear, this controversy is taking place
in the context of swift demographic change; students come to school
with increasingly different educational, social, economic, cultural,
and linguistic backgrounds.

How should schools handle this diversity? Again, some advocate that schools revive their traditional role of Americanizing
immigrants and ethnic minorities to prepare them to enter the
mainstream of American society. Others argue that the mainstream is changing as the United States becomes more ethnically
diverse, and that curriculum and instruction ought to reflect that
reality. As the major agent of socialization for young people, schools
become the arena in which questions of national character are
played out.

Critics of the traditional system also point to the new role of
the United States as a participant in a global economy. If interna-

289

tional competitiveness is cited as the primary justification for education reform, then our schools need to prepare students not only for mainstream American society but also for dealing with countries outside the United States.

A major message of this book is that schools must change radically for students from non-English backgrounds to succeed. Some would refute that assertion, charging instead that poor teaching, poor schools, and poor motivation are to blame for low academic achievement among these students, not the system itself. Whichever claim is true, the controversy raises much deeper questions about education for all students. What is the vision of education underlying these two views? What does it mean to be an educated person in today's world?

Many of the chapters in this book talk about moving from one vision of education to another:

- From an emphasis on innate ability, determined by genetics or social circumstance, to a belief in the capability of all students to learn. This represents a shift from a nature to a nurture philosophy, and places responsibility for creating motivating educational environments on the schools. In this new vision, schools would operate in a non-stratified manner, and hold much higher standards for all students.

- From a concept of knowledge as a body of information, and education as skill acquisition, to a view of knowledge as social construction and cultural practice. In this new vision, education is seen as learning to learn, and becoming an educated person, rather than as mastering material.

- From a view of the optimal learning environment as orderly and individually based, to a variety of learning environments, including collaborating with others.

- From a teacher-directed classroom to one in which student initiative and input plays a major role in curricular choices.

- From a view of knowledge as abstract to one that is grounded in experience, from textbook instruction and standardized testing to instruction that presents information in context, incorporates students' background, and assesses learning authentically.

- From a monocultural focus to a multicultural one.

This shift challenges deeply held assumptions and values. Oakes (1992, p.19) comments about the difficulty of changing one element—such as tracking—in an internally consistent system that supports societal beliefs. "Tracking reformers must face the inveterate American values for competition and individualism over cooperation and the common good that further bolster and legitimize tracking—norms implying that 'good' education is a scarce commodity available only to a few." But Oakes asks "whether sorting students to prepare them for a differentiated work force with unequal economic rewards is what schools should do." It has become common to regard schooling as a path to individual success, but Oakes points out that the original intent of public education was "to promote community interests by preparing children for participation in democratic governance." Social norms are never static; they cycle slowly between opposite poles. Instead of altering the fundamental character of American society, the new vision of education described above may be seen as resurrecting older values of community and common good and redressing the exclusive emphasis on individualism and competition.

The challenge in a diverse nation is to reach a common vision of the common good. For their part, educators must comprehend the profound cultural and personal impact of education; schools can either affirm or undermine students' cultural and linguistic identity. The potential for personal harm and cultural disruption is great when, as is the case, children of myriad cultural and linguistic backgrounds are taught almost exclusively by teachers from European American backgrounds. Such teachers can become enlightened participants in designing a vision of the common good; they cannot define it themselves.

On the other hand, parents from both minority and majority groups cannot expect schools to mirror their own group's values and priorities. As educational philosopher Kenneth Strike (1991, p.207) says, "Schools should not be vehicles for enforcing parental conceptions of a good life on children." Rather, education should provide the context that allows students to explore various conceptions of a good life as a means of developing good citizenship in a participatory democracy. If schools, communities, and the nation are to work toward a common vision of a meaningful sense of community, then every participant must be willing to learn and compromise.

What are the implications of this social ferment for the education of students from non-English language backgrounds? Whether their background is considered a problem or a challenge, an obstacle or a resource, depends on the goal of education. Is it to socialize children into "traditional" American culture? Brumberg (1986) concludes from his study of Jewish immigrants in New York schools at the turn of the century that schools were largely successful in this mission because of the certainty of their cause.

But this surety of purpose is gone forever. Along with research demonstrating the crucial importance of language and culture in learning is the nagging doubt about stripping children of their heritage and their connection to family and community. At a time when 30 to 70 percent of the world's languages are threatened with extinction (Chung, 1992), should educators be extinguishing the ones that appear in their classrooms, or allowing them to flourish?

If a goal of education is to develop competence in the dominant language and culture of the country where you reside, and, in addition, to become conversant with another language and culture, then English language- and other language-background children are each halfway there. Competence in two languages is not only a recommendation of education reformers and a traditional mark of a highly educated person, it is a reality for much of the world's population and a necessity in the global marketplace. Adopting this as a goal for all students would go a long way toward fostering the success of those whose language has long been seen as a liability rather than an asset.

REFERENCES

Brumberg, S. F. (1986). *Going to America, going to school: The Jewish immigrant public school encounter in turn-of-the-century New York City*. New York: Praeger.

Chung, S. (1992, October 9). Speech given at the investiture of the chancellor of the University of California, Santa Cruz.

Oakes, J. (1992). Can tracking research inform practice? Technical, normative, and political considerations. *Educational Researcher, 21* (4): 12–21.

Strike, K. A. (1991). Liberal justice: Aspirations and limitations. In D. Verstegen, & J. Ward (Eds.), *Spheres of justice in education: The 1990 American Finance Association Yearbook*. New York: Harper Business, 195–219.

LIST OF CONTRIBUTORS

Lilia I. Bartolomé is currently Assistant Professor of Education at the Harvard Graduate School of Education in Language and Literacy. She teaches courses in bilingualism and literacy and multicultural education. Her research interests include oral and written language acquisition patterns of Latino and other linguistic minority students and cross-cultural literacy practices in home and school contexts.

Mary E. Brenner is an educational anthropologist who conducts research about the mathematics learning of children in different cultures. Her dissertation research looked at the impact of the local cultures on school instruction in Liberia, particularly in mathematics classrooms. She then worked at the Kamehameha Schools Early Education Division (formerly the Center for the Development of Early Education) for three years. During that time her research focused on the way children use mathematics in nonschool settings. She also worked with teachers to develop the elementary mathematics curriculum. From Kamehameha she went to the University of California, Berkeley, where she taught in the Graduate Group for Science and Mathematics Education (SESAME) and continued her research in Liberia. Brenner is now an Assistant Professor in the Graduate School of Education at the University of California, Santa

Barbara, where she is examining the impact of innovative mathematics programs on Latino students.

Alejandro Jose Gallard is currently an Assistant Professor of Science Education at Florida State University. In his present position he serves as the coordinator for undergraduate studies, student teaching, and Latin American collaboratives. Prior to coming to Florida State University, Dr. Gallard taught at all educational levels including bilingual elementary classrooms. His research is classroom-based and focuses on the teaching and learning of science and limited English proficient students. He has worked extensively in Latin America researching the fit between educational policy development, such as national science curricula, and the teaching and learning of science. Dr. Gallard has also, in Latin America, played a key role in developing science teacher education programs at the tertiary level and participated in national educational reformation efforts.

Patricia Gándara is a member of the faculty of the Division of Education at the University of California at Davis. Her recent research has focused on school organization and reform as they affect limited English and immigrant students, and on educationally ambitious Chicano and Chicana students. She has also conducted extensive research on year-round schooling and academically at-risk students. Professor Gándara teaches in the areas of educational psychology and education policy.

Barry McLaughlin is Professor in the Program in Experimental Psychology at the University of California, Santa Cruz. His research interests include second-language acquisition in adults and children. He has published *Second-Language Acquisition in Childhood. Volume 1: Preschool Children* (Lawrence Erlbaum Associates, 1984), *Second-Language Acquisition in Childhood. Volume 2: School-Age Children* (Lawrence Erlbaum Associates, 1985), and *Theories of Second-Language Learning* (Arnold Publishers, 1987). He has served as consultant on bilingual matters for the California State Department of Education and has published numerous articles on second-language learning and bilingualism. He is currently Director of the Bilingual Research Group at the University of California, Santa Cruz, and Co-Director of The National Center for Research on Cultural Diversity and Second Language Learning, funded by the U.S. Department of Education.

Beverly McLeod is currently the coordinator for the Student Diversity Study, from which the material for this book emerged.

She is a social psychologist with a background in anthropology and teaching English as a Second Language. With a particular interest in cross-cultural and language issues, she has conducted research on second language learning, foreign student adjustment, and the long-term accommodation of professional-level Chinese immigrants to the United States.

Hugh Mehan is Professor of Sociology and Director of the Teacher Education Program at the University of California, San Diego, appointments which link his commitments to research and practice. He has studied classroom organization, educational testing, tracking and untracking, computer use in schools, and the construction of identities such as the "competent student," the "learning disabled student," the "mentally ill patient," and the "genius." He has worked closely with K–12 educators so that they can make informed decisions to insure that equitable educational opportunities are available to all children. He has authored three books (*The Reality of Ethnomethodology, Learning Lessons*, and *Handicapping the Handicapped*) and edited four more. His more than sixty articles have appeared in *Language in Society, Harvard Educational Review, Anthropology and Education Quarterly, Ethos, Discourse and Society,* and *The Sociology of Education.*

Christine E. Sleeter is Professor of Teacher Education at the University of Wisconsin-Parkside, where she is also Director of the Ethnic Studies Center. She teaches both graduate and undergraduate courses in multicultural education and consults nationally in this area. She has published numerous articles about multicultural education in various journals, including *Harvard Educational Review, Journal of Education, Phi Delta Kappan, Journal of Teacher Education,* and *Teachers College Record.* Her most recent books include *Empowerment through Multicultural Education* (SUNY Press, 1991), *Keepers of the American Dream* (Falmer Press 1992), *Turning on Learning* (with Carl Grant, Merrill, 1989), and *Making Choices for Multicultural Education* (with Carl Grant, Merrill, 1988).

Roland G. Tharp is Professor of Education and Psychology at the University of California, Santa Cruz. He is perhaps best known for his work in cultural compatibility of service delivery for children, particularly as the leader of the Kamehameha Early Education Program (KEEP) for over 20 years. He is author of the books *Rousing Minds to Life, Self-Directed Behavior, Perspectives in Cross-Cultural Psychology, Behavior Modification in the Natural Environ-*

ment, and hundreds of articles, reports, and reviews. An award-winning filmmaker, he is also a widely published author of fiction and poetry. He has worked with Native American groups for more than thirty years, including the Maya, the Navajo, the Zuni, and the Hawaiians. He has been consulted frequently by First Nation projects in Canada, especially educational programs in British Columbia. His theoretical work is central to The National Center for Research on Cultural Diversity and Second Language Learning (USA), in which he is a Principal Investigator. He is the 1993 recipient of the Grawemeyer Award, the preeminent international award for achievement in education.

Deborah Tippins is an Assistant Professor of Science Education at the University of Georgia. She is currently serving as the Director of Research for the National Science Teachers Association. Her research focuses on sociocultural and ethical dimensions of science teaching and learning. She has published in journals such as *Teaching and Teacher Education, The International Journal of Science Education, The Journal of Teacher Education, The Elementary School Journal, The Journal of Moral Education*, and *The Journal of Education in Teaching.* She recently coauthored *The Stigma of Genius: Einstein and Beyond Modern Education*, a critical analysis of Albert Einstein's perspectives on education. Most recently, she conducted The Northern Arizona University Title VII CACTUS Institute (Collaborating Across Cultures to Understand Sciences) for Native American Teachers and Teachers of Native American Students.

AUTHOR INDEX

297

SUBJECT INDEX